Better Homes and Gardens ®

ENCYCLOPEDIA
of
COOKING

Volume 6

A favorite home-baked dessert features Apple Dumplings. Each juicy apple, tucked inside a flaky pastry shell, is basted with hot maple syrup during baking. (See *Dumplings* for recipe.)

On the cover: Peach-Pecan Mold features "peaches and cream" in a show-off dessert. Pecans add crunch to ice cream mold ringed with peach slices. Serve with peach sauce atop.

BETTER HOMES AND GARDENS BOOKS
NEW YORK • DES MOINES

©Meredith Corporation, 1971. All Rights Reserved.
Printed in the United States of America.
First Edition. Second Printing, 1971.
Library of Congress Catalog Card Number: 73-129265
SBN 696-02006-8

CUPCAKE—A small, individual cake baked in a muffin pan, a paper bake cup supported by a muffin pan, or a small custard cup. Batters for shortened cakes, sponge cakes, and chiffon cakes may be baked as cupcakes. If recipe instructions are not given for cupcakes, use the same baking temperature as recommended for baking the cake in layers, but decrease baking time slightly. If overbaked, the cake texture is dry and top is crusty.

Paper bake cups offer the advantage of serving the cake in the baking cup. If using muffin pans or custard cups, grease well for shortened cake batters. No preliminary treatment is needed, however, with paper bake cups. These are especially good for sponge and chiffon cake batters.

Depending upon the amount of leavening in the cake, paper bake cups or muffin pans are filled about ½ to ⅔ full. If filled too full, the cake overflows the cup as it bakes, forming a crusty rim. If not enough batter is used, the cupcake appears small and sunken when done.

After baking, cupcakes should be cooled on a wire cooling rack before they are frosted. Allow cupcakes baked in muffin pans or custard cups to cool in the pan about five minutes before removing. Using a sharp knife, cut around each cake, loosening the sides from the pan. Invert pan to remove the cupcakes.

Cupcakes may or may not require frosting. Some may be sprinkled with confectioners' sugar or a cinnamon-sugar mixture, while others may have a baked-in topping or filling which takes the place of the frosting. If a frosting is desired, however, the process is quite simple when the cakes are baked in paper bake cups. Dip the top of the cupcake in the frosting and twirl to frost. Cupcakes not baked in paper bake cups may be frosted on sides as well as on top, if desired. This helps to keep the cakes moist. Whole or chopped nuts, flaked coconut, semisweet chocolate pieces, decorative candies, or decorator icing can be used for added trim on the cupcakes.

Cupcakes offer a convenient method for serving cake. They are easily transported, providing an ideal dessert for boxed lunches, picnics, and barbecues. Baked in individual serving portions, they can be pre-pared ahead and stored in the freezer. Shortly before serving time, simply remove the number of cupcakes needed.

Cupcakes are an excellent refreshment for children's parties. Eaten out-of-hand, they are managed easily and cleanup time is minimal. The cakes can be decorated to correspond with the theme of the party. Peppermint candy sticks, animal crackers, decorator alphabet letters, gumdrops, or birthday candles inserted in the top of each cake add special appeal. (See also *Cake*.)

Cranberry Cupcakes

    ½ cup shortening
    1 cup brown sugar
    2 eggs
 1½ cups sifted all-purpose flour
    1 teaspoon ground cinnamon
    1 teaspoon ground nutmeg
    ½ teaspoon salt
    ½ teaspoon baking soda
    ½ cup dairy sour cream
    ½ cup canned jellied cranberry
        sauce
    ½ cup chopped walnuts

        • • •

        Fluffy Butter Frosting
        Canned jellied cranberry sauce

In mixing bowl thoroughly cream together shortening and brown sugar. Add eggs and beat well. Sift together flour, cinnamon, nutmeg, salt, and baking soda. Add to creamed mixture alternately with sour cream and ½ cup cranberry sauce; beat smooth. Add nuts.

Fill paper bake cups in muffin pans half full. Bake at 350° for 20 to 25 minutes. Cool. Frost with Fluffy Butter Frosting. Using hors d'oeuvre cutters, make cutouts from additional canned jellied cranberry sauce. Just before serving, top each cake with a cranberry cutout. Makes about 2 dozen cupcakes.

Fluffy Butter Frosting: In mixing bowl combine ½ cup butter or margarine, softened; 1 egg yolk; 2 tablespoons buttermilk *or* milk; ½ teaspoon vanilla; and 3 cups sifted confectioners' sugar. Blend together. Beat at medium speed on electric mixer for 3 minutes.

If frosting is soft, beat in additional sifted confectioners' sugar to make of spreading consistency. Frosts 24 cupcakes.

Cheese-Filled Chocolate Cupcakes

    1 package 2-layer-size chocolate
        cake mix
    1 8-ounce package cream cheese,
        softened
    ⅓ cup sugar
    1 egg
    1 6-ounce package semisweet
        chocolate pieces (1 cup)

Mix cake according to package directions. Fill paper bake cups in muffin pans two-thirds full. Cream the cheese with the sugar; beat in egg and dash salt. Stir in chocolate pieces.

Drop one rounded teaspoon cheese mixture into each cupcake. Bake according to package directions for cupcakes. Makes 30 cupcakes.

Peanut Butter Cupcakes

Cream ½ cup chunk-style peanut butter and ⅓ cup shortening. Gradually add 1½ cups brown sugar, beating till light. Add 1 teaspoon vanilla and 2 eggs, one at a time, beating till fluffy. Sift together 2 cups sifted all-purpose flour, 2 teaspoons baking powder, and ½ teaspoon salt; add alternately with 1 cup milk, beating after each addition.

Fill paper bake cups in muffin pans half full. Bake at 375° for 15 to 20 minutes. Cool; frost with peanut butter. Makes 24 cupcakes.

Everyday Cupcakes

    ½ cup shortening
    1¾ cups sifted all-purpose flour
    1 cup sugar
    2½ teaspoons baking powder
    ½ teaspoon salt
    1 egg
    ¾ cup milk
    1 teaspoon vanilla

Place shortening in mixing bowl. Sift in dry ingredients. Add egg and *half* the milk; mix till flour is moistened. Beat 2 minutes at low speed on electric mixer. Add remaining milk and vanilla; beat 1 minute longer. Fill paper bake cups in muffin pans half full. Bake at 375° till done, about 20 minutes. Cool; frost with desired frosting. Makes 18 cupcakes.

Frost cupcakes in a hurry. Dip top of each cake into fluffy-type frosting. Twirl cupcake slightly, then turn right side up.

CURD—The semisolid mass which results from the coagulation of milk protein. A curd is formed when milk sours or when an acid or enzyme is added. The curd, used in cheese, separates from the whey.

CURDLE—To cause the formation of a curd. The curdling of milk is the first step in the making of cheese. In cooking, curdling is undesirable and occurs when milk or sour cream is heated to too high a temperature. Curdling occurs frequently when acid foods are combined with milk, as in the preparation of tomato soup. To prevent curdling, slowly add the acid food to the milk, stirring constantly.

CURED—To preserve food by one of many special processes. Meat and fish may be cured by soaking them in a brine solution, or by salting, drying, or smoking. Cheese is often cured by injecting or spraying with a mold culture. Curing imparts a characteristic flavor and texture to a food, depending upon the curing ingredients and whether the cure is light or heavy.

Festive cupcakes

Fresh-baked Cranberry Cupcakes sport cran- →
berry cutouts nestled in fluffy frosting. Cranberry also is used in the spicy batter.

Curly endive adds variety to tossed salads. Slightly bitter, the tightly curled leaves vary from rich green to yellowish white.

CURLY ENDIVE—A leafy, green vegetable which grows in a bunchy head and is eaten as a salad green. A heavy rib supports the narrow, ragged-edged leaves which are tightly curled. The outer leaves appear darker green, while the inside leaves are bleached. Although higher in vitamins, the darker leaves have a more bitter flavor than the lighter ones. (See also *Endive*.)

CURRANT—1. A small, seedless, raisinlike fruit made from a specific variety of grape which has been dried. 2. A small, round, red berry which grows on a bush of the same name. Although these two fruits carry the same name, they are not related.

Dried grape currants: They were first commercially important in Greece in the sixteenth century. A popular ingredient in cooking, they were exported to France and other European countries. The French called the fruit *raisins de Corinthe* since most of them were imported from Corinth, Greece. The name was eventually shortened and they became known as currants.

Today, the Mediterranean countries are still the major producers of dried currants. However, some are produced also in the United States. They are made from the Black Corinth grape grown in California. In addition to dried black currants, another variety known as white Zante (named after the Greek island which exports them) is available on the market.

Dried currants are quite high in carbohydrates; one-half cup of the fruit provides 208 calories. They also contain calcium, phosphorus, and iron.

This raisinlike fruit has a relatively long storage life and is most often found in the supermarket packaged in boxes. Refrigeration of this fruit is required only after the box has been opened at which time it should be stored in a tightly covered container to maintain freshness.

Used alone or in combination with raisins and/or other fruits, dried currants are usually added to cakes, cookies, and breads. They are more tart and have a more concentrated flavor than do raisins.

Fresh berry currants: The first written reference to the fresh or red berries known as currants dates back to the fifteenth century where they were mentioned as a garden-fruit plant. These berries were probably called currants because they resembled the dried fruit of the same name.

Cultivated best in cool climates, they were first grown in northern Europe. They accompanied the early settlers to America and although they are still produced in the colder regions of the United States, their cultivation is restricted. This restriction is a conservation measure since the currant bush is a carrier of a fungus which destroys the white pine. However, some disease-resistant varieties of currants have been developed, making their cultivation more acceptable. In addition to the cultivated crop, a few wild currant bushes are often found throughout the country.

Fresh currants, much lower in calories than dried currants, contain about 34 calories per half cup. They also contribute vitamin C, phosphorus, and iron.

Three different varieties of fresh currants are grown—red, white, and black. The peak growing season for fresh currants is from June through August. At other times the fruit is available only in the local markets. In selecting fresh currants, look for firm, ripe berries with a good color and attached stems. If purchased for jellymaking, avoid overripe fruit as it does not jell as well as fruit which is slightly underripe.

Fresh currants should be sorted after purchasing and stored in the refrigerator in a covered container. Avoid keeping berries over one or two days as they may soften and become overripe. When ready to use, wash fruit and remove stems.

Fresh currants may be served alone although they usually require sugar as they are quite tart—much more so than dried currants. White currants, the least tart variety, can be served fresh in salads. The most popular use of the red and black varieties is in jellymaking. A famous French jam, *bar-le-duc,* is made by suspending the whole berries in a clear jelly. *Bar-le-duc* is available in specialty shops. Black currants are used also in the making of *cassis,* an alcoholic beverage. (See also *Fruit.*)

Currant-Raisin Sauce

⅓ **cup raisins**
½ **cup water**
⅓ **cup currant jelly**
½ **teaspoon grated orange peel**
½ **cup orange juice**
2 **tablespoons brown sugar**
1 **tablespoon cornstarch**
Dash ground allspice
Dash salt

Combine raisins, water, jelly, orange peel, and orange juice in saucepan; bring to boiling. Combine brown sugar, cornstarch, allspice, and salt; stir into orange mixture. Cook, stirring constantly, till thickened and clear. Serve warm sauce over cooked ham slice.

Currant Glaze

In saucepan melt ½ cup currant jelly, stirring till jelly is smooth. Add 1 tablespoon vinegar, ½ teaspoon dry mustard, ¼ teaspoon ground cinnamon, and dash ground cloves; blend together thoroughly. Brush ham with fruit glaze occasionally during last 30 minutes of heating time and just before serving.

A traditional dessert for the festive holidays is steamed Black Currant Pudding. Currants, raisins, mixed candied fruits, and almonds add a seasonal note to this moist and delicately spiced dessert. Serve warm with light and fluffy hard sauce.

Black Currant Pudding

A holiday dessert that can be made ahead—

½ pound beef suet, ground
(2¾ cups)
2 cups fine dry bread crumbs
1 cup sifted all-purpose flour
1 cup sugar
1 cup finely chopped blanched
almonds
1 cup dried currants
⅔ cup mixed candied fruits and
peels
⅔ cup golden raisins
½ cup dark raisins
½ teaspoon ground nutmeg
½ teaspoon ground cinnamon
½ teaspoon ground allspice
½ teaspoon salt

. . .

¾ cup milk
4 slightly beaten eggs
½ cup brandy *or* rum
1½ teaspoons grated lemon peel
¼ cup lemon juice

. . .

Hard Sauce

In large bowl combine suet, crumbs, flour, sugar, chopped almonds, currants, mixed fruits, raisins, nutmeg, cinnamon, allspice, and salt; mix well. In second bowl combine milk, eggs, brandy *or* rum, lemon peel, and lemon juice; stir into fruit mixture. Mix thoroughly.

Turn into well-greased 7½-cup ovenproof bowl or mold; cover tightly. Place on rack in deep kettle or Dutch oven. Pour boiling water in kettle to 1-inch depth; cover kettle. Gently boil water, steaming pudding for 5 hours. (Add more boiling water, if necessary.)

When finished cooking, remove mold from kettle. Cool about 30 minutes in mold. Unmold pudding; let stand until completely cooled. Wrap in foil; refrigerate till ready to use.

To reheat pudding, place foil-wrapped pudding on rack in deep kettle or Dutch oven. Use same steaming method given above; steam pudding for 1 to 1½ hours.

Serve pudding warm with *Hard Sauce:* In mixing bowl thoroughly cream together 1 cup butter or margarine, softened, and 4 cups sifted confectioners' sugar. Add 2 teaspoons vanilla; mix well. Makes 12 to 16 servings.

Currant-Orange Chicken

Tart and peppy fruit sauce adds elegance—

½ cup currant jelly
¼ cup frozen orange juice
concentrate, thawed
2 teaspoons cornstarch
1 teaspoon dry mustard
Dash bottled hot pepper sauce

. . .

½ cup all-purpose flour
1 teaspoon salt
1 2½- to 3-pound ready-to-cook
broiler-fryer chicken, cut up
Shortening

. . .

1 cup chopped celery
¼ cup chopped onion
¼ cup butter or margarine
2 tablespoons frozen orange juice
concentrate, thawed
½ teaspoon salt
1⅓ cups uncooked packaged
precooked rice

In saucepan combine jelly, ¼ cup orange juice concentrate, and ⅓ cup water; cook and stir till jelly melts and mixture is smooth.

Blend cornstarch, dry mustard, and bottled hot pepper sauce with 1 tablespoon cold water; stir into jelly mixture. Cook, stirring constantly, till thickened and clear; set aside.

Combine flour and 1 teaspoon salt in paper bag. Add 2 or 3 pieces of chicken at a time; shake to coat. In skillet brown chicken in hot shortening over medium heat, turning occasionally. Drain off excess fat. Pour currant-orange sauce over chicken in skillet. Cover; simmer over very low heat till tender, about 45 minutes; baste occasionally with sauce.

Serve chicken with Orange Rice: Cook celery and onion in butter or margarine till tender but not brown. Stir in 2 tablespoons orange juice concentrate, 1¼ cups water, and ½ teaspoon salt; bring to boiling. Add uncooked rice; continue cooking according to directions on rice package. Makes 4 servings.

CURRY—Food cooked in a liquid seasoned with curry powder or served in a sauce seasoned with curry powder. Meat, fish, poultry, eggs, vegetables, and fruits may

Curried Ham Rolls add glamour and an intriguing blend of flavors to a late-evening supper. Rice mix adds convenience to this main dish; prepare ahead, then heat just before serving.

be curried. Most readily identified with the cooking of India and countries of the Far East, curry varies from country to country, both in method of preparation and in manner and customs of serving.

A main dish curry is served with steamed rice and assorted accompaniments. A limited number of accompaniments, usually only fresh, grated coconut and a hot mango chutney, are served with an authentic Indian curry. The Americanized version offers additional accompaniments such as nuts, green onions, raisins, kumquats, and peppers. They are served in bowls and sprinkled atop the curry in layers. (See also *Indian Cookery*.)

CURRY POWDER—A ground blend of spices used as a seasoning to impart the characteristic flavor of Indian curry cookery. Sometimes, 16 or more spices are used in making curry powder. Depending upon the manufacturer, each blend differs slightly; however, cumin, coriander, fenugreek, turmeric, and red pepper are found in varying amounts in every curry powder. Additional spices sometimes used include caraway seed, cinnamon, allspice, cardamom, cloves, fennel, ginger, yellow mustard, mace, and black or white pepper.

Curry powder is one of the world's oldest seasonings. Popular in India and the Far East, curry has been used as a seasoning for almost fifteen hundred years. However, Indian curries are most frequently made with a spice blend which is ground daily in the home. Thus, each blend varies somewhat, depending upon how it is used.

The "hotness" of the curry blend differs within the Indian culture. A milder spicing is preferred in the North while in Southern India, the hotter the spice, the better. Red peppers, which are primarily responsible for the hotness of curry, were unknown in ancient curries. These pungent peppers, which originated in the Western Hemisphere, did not become a part of the spice blend until after the discovery of America. Today, red peppers are considered an essential ingredient in all curries.

The popularity of using a highly spiced curry powder in India and in tropical countries is based in part on the effect it has on the body temperature. Eating "hot" dishes promotes perspiration, which in turn, helps keep the body cool. Also, most spices needed for a good curry blend are readily available in tropical climates.

Although the Indian housewife usually makes her own curry blend, commercial curry powders are sold in the bazaars. In the United States mild-flavored commercial blends are used almost exclusively.

As with all spices, curry powder is more flavorful and aromatic when fresh. Avoid long storage and always store in a tightly covered container in a cool, dry place.

Curry powder adds flavor to meats, fish, poultry, vegetables, salads, salad dressings, sauces, and soups. Used sparingly, it enhances the natural flavor of food. For an Indian-type curried dish in which the spice blend dominates the food, a larger amount of seasoning is needed. (See *Spice, Indian Cookery* for additional information.)

Curry cooking tips

A more flavorful curry dish results if the curry powder is moistened or cooked in a little fat before using. Long, slow cooking generally improves the flavor also.

Enhance curry flavor in sauce or salad dressing by chilling mixture several hours.

Curried Ham Rolls

As pictured on preceding page—

    1 6-ounce package curried rice
        mix
    ¾ cup golden raisins
    2 hard-cooked eggs, chopped
    1 tablespoon snipped parsley
    3 tablespoons butter or margarine
    2 tablespoons cornstarch
    1 teaspoon curry powder
    ¼ teaspoon salt
    2¼ cups milk
    12 square slices boiled ham

Cook rice mix according to package directions. Add raisins, chopped eggs, and parsley; mix well. In saucepan melt butter; blend in cornstarch, curry powder, and salt. Add milk; cook and stir till thick and bubbly. Add *half* of the curry sauce to rice mixture; mix well. Place rice in 10x6x1¾-inch baking dish.

With spatula make 5 crosswise indentations in rice starting about 1½ inches from ends of casserole. Put 2 ham slices together; curve to form roll. Insert one side of roll into end of casserole; tuck second side into first indentation. Repeat with 2 more ham slices, tucking first side of roll into same indentation with previously made roll and second side into next indentation. Continue forming rolls with remaining ham. Pour remaining sauce atop. Bake at 350° for 30 to 35 minutes. Serves 6.

Curried Beef Cubes

Cut 2 pounds beef chuck in ¾-inch cubes. Coat beef cubes with ⅓ cup all-purpose flour. In skillet brown meat in ⅓ cup hot shortening. Add 1 large onion, sliced; cook just till onion is tender but not brown.

Combine two 8-ounce cans tomato sauce; 1½ cups water; 1 clove garlic, minced; 1 teaspoon salt; and ¼ teaspoon pepper. Pour mixture over meat. Cover and cook slowly over low heat till meat is tender, about 1½ hours. Stir in 2 to 3 teaspoons curry powder.

Add one 9-ounce package frozen cut green beans to meat mixture. Cook till tender, about 15 minutes, separating beans with a fork as they heat. Serve meat mixture over hot cooked rice or noodles. Makes 6 to 8 servings.

Chicken Curry

Another time serve curry in rice ring—

1 tablespoon butter or margarine
1 cup finely chopped peeled apple
1 cup sliced celery
½ cup chopped onion
1 clove garlic, minced
2 tablespoons cornstarch
2 to 3 teaspoons curry powder
¾ teaspoon salt
¾ cup cold chicken broth
2 cups milk
2 cups diced cooked chicken
1 3-ounce can sliced mushrooms,
    drained (½ cup)
    Hot cooked rice
    Curry accompaniments

In saucepan melt butter; add apple, celery, onion, and garlic. Cook till onion is tender. Combine cornstarch, curry, salt, and cold chicken broth. Stir into onion mixture; add milk. Cook and stir till thick and bubbly. Stir in chicken and mushrooms. Heat through.

Serve over hot cooked rice; pass curry accompaniments—raisins, shredded coconut, chopped peanuts, and chutney. Serves 5 or 6.

Curried Lamb

2 pounds lean lamb, cut in 1-inch
    cubes
3 tablespoons all-purpose flour
2 tablespoons butter or margarine
1 cup chopped onion
1 clove garlic, minced
1 to 1½ tablespoons curry powder
1½ teaspoons salt
1 teaspoon grated fresh gingerroot
    or ½ teaspoon ground ginger
2 tomatoes, peeled and chopped
¼ cup water
    Hot cooked rice
    Grated raw carrot
    Curry accompaniments

Coat lamb with flour. Brown meat in butter; remove from skillet. Add onion and garlic to skillet; cook till tender. Return meat to skillet. Stir in curry powder, salt, gingerroot, tomatoes, and water. Cover; simmer, stirring occasionally, till lamb is tender, 45 to 60 minutes. Toss rice with grated carrot; serve with lamb. Pass accompaniments—whole preserved kumquats, mango chutney, sliced green onions, golden raisins, shredded coconut, and shelled peanuts. Makes 6 to 8 servings.

Exotic and colorful Chicken Curry offers a new idea for a dinner party. Serve over rice and pass assorted accompaniments—raisins, shredded coconut, peanuts, and chutney.

Curry Salad

For best flavor, prepare dressing ahead and chill several hours or overnight—

    ½ teaspoon beef-flavored gravy
          base
    ¼ cup hot water
    1 cup mayonnaise or salad
          dressing
    1 clove garlic, minced
    1 tablespoon curry powder
    ¼ teaspoon Worcestershire sauce
    6 to 8 drops bottled hot pepper
          sauce

    •   •   •

    6 cups torn mixed salad greens
    4 cups torn fresh spinach
    1 16-ounce can artichoke hearts,
          chilled, drained, and halved
    ¼ cup sliced radishes

To make dressing, dissolve beef-flavored gravy base in hot water; blend into mayonnaise or salad dressing. Stir in garlic, curry powder, Worcestershire sauce, and bottled hot pepper sauce; mix well. Chill thoroughly.

In large bowl combine torn mixed salad greens, torn fresh spinach, halved artichoke hearts, and sliced radishes. Just before serving, toss lettuce mixture lightly with chilled salad dressing. Makes 10 servings.

CUSK—An edible saltwater fish belonging to the cod family. Found in North Atlantic waters from Greenland south to Cape Cod, cusk is characterized by a long black fin extending from just behind the head to the tail. A medium-sized fish, cusks average from 5 to 10 pounds in weight and from 1½ to 2½ feet in length.

Although cusk is most often marketed in fillets, it is sometimes available salted and smoked. Fresh cusk is prepared in the same way as cod or haddock.

Far-East flavor

For a touch of India, serve zesty Curry Salad featuring artichoke hearts, fresh spinach, sliced radishes, and mixed salad greens.

CUSTARD—An egg and milk mixture in which the egg acts as a thickening agent during cooking. If sweetened and flavored, the mixture is served as a dessert. If unsweetened, it is used as a main dish with meat, cheese, or vegetables added.

A dessert-type custard, known as soft or stirred custard, is cooked and stirred over low heat in a heavy saucepan or in the top of a double boiler over hot water. Stirred custard has much the same consistency as heavy cream. If baked in the oven without stirring, it is known as baked custard. The finished product holds its shape when unmolded. Main-dish custards made in a pastry shell generally are baked in the oven and can be cut for serving.

Usual proportions for dessert-type custards are one or one and one-half eggs plus two tablespoons sugar for each cup of milk. For a firmer custard, use more eggs. Likewise, increase the amount of sugar for a sweeter product. Custard is sometimes unmolded and used to make fancy cutouts for garnishing. This type of custard must be quite firm; thus, a greater number of eggs are needed.

Custard substitutions

Basic substitutions are possible in a standard custard which result in a product of about the same consistency. However, the color and flavor may vary slightly.

If several eggs are used, use one of the following substitutions for *one of the eggs:*

  two egg yolks
  two egg whites
  one tablespoon all-purpose flour

Custard is an excellent way of adding to the diet important nutrients which are found in milk and eggs. Due to its soft texture, often it is included in special diets.

Custard should always be refrigerated after baking if it is to be held for any length of time before serving.

To make custard add sugar and salt to slightly beaten eggs and stir in scalded milk, which has been cooled.

For soft custard, cook and stir over low heat in a heavy saucepan or in the top of a double boiler over simmering, but not boiling water. When done, the mixture coats a metal spoon. Immediately remove from heat and place pan in cold water. When slightly cooled, stir in the flavoring.

Custards lend themselves to many variations. Soft custard may be served warm or chilled as a sauce over fruit, cake, or pudding. Popular in England, soft custard accompanies many desserts just as cream often tops off American desserts. Floating island dessert is made by spooning soft meringue atop soft custard.

For baked custard, pour the mixture into individual custard cups or into one large baking dish. Place the cups or baking dish in a shallow baking pan on the oven rack. Add hot water to the baking pan to a depth of one inch and bake at a moderate oven temperature. The custard is done when a knife inserted halfway between the center and outside edge of the custard comes out clean. After cooking, remove from the hot water to stop the cooking.

Baked custard, delicious either warm or chilled, is commonly served with a dash of ground nutmeg or a dollop of tart, red jelly. Variations include the addition of instant coffee powder, unsweetened cocoa powder, shredded coconut, or caramelized sugar. Baked in a pie shell, custard is a holiday favorite when pumpkin is added.

Overcooking custard results in an undesirable product. For a stirred custard, the mixture takes on a curdled appearance due to over-coagulation of egg protein. Although this change cannot be reversed, the appearance is improved somewhat by beating the mixture with a rotary beater. When a baked custard is overcooked, tiny bubbles appear around the edge of the dish, and there is a separation of liquid from solid when the custard is cut.

Main-dish custards, which are unsweetened, add variety to the menu. A custard mixture poured over layers of bread and cheese and baked in a baking dish is known as a strata; in addition, meat is sometimes added. A favorite French dish, Quiche Lorraine, is made with crisp-cooked crumbled bacon and cheese in a custard mixture, baked in a pastry shell.

Toasted Coconut Pie

      3 beaten eggs
  1½ cups sugar
      ½ cup butter or margarine, melted
      4 teaspoons lemon juice
      1 teaspoon vanilla
      1 3½-ounce can flaked coconut
          (1⅓ cups)
          Plain Pastry for 1-crust 9-inch
          pie (See *Pastry*)

          • • •

          Whipped cream
          Toasted coconut

Thoroughly combine eggs, sugar, butter, lemon juice, and vanilla; stir in flaked coconut.

Line 9-inch pie plate with pastry. Pour coconut-custard filling into pastry-lined pie plate. Bake at 350° till knife inserted halfway between center and edge comes out clean, about 40 to 45 minutes. Cool. Garnish with whipped cream and toasted coconut.

Caramel Custard Pie

      1 14½-ounce can evaporated
          milk (1⅔ cups)
      2 eggs
      1 cup brown sugar
      3 tablespoons all-purpose flour
      2 tablespoons butter or margarine
          Plain Pastry for 1-crust 9-inch
          pie (See *Pastry*)

Combine evaporated milk, eggs, and ⅓ cup water; beat till well mixed. Set aside. Combine brown sugar and flour; cut in butter till mixture resembles coarse crumbs. Add milk mixture to brown sugar mixture; beat well.

Line 9-inch pie plate with pastry. Pour in custard filling. Bake at 400° till knife inserted halfway between center and edge comes out clean, about 30 minutes. Cool. If desired, garnish with whipped cream.

Custard with extra flavor

←Coconut adds chewiness to creamy custard in Toasted Coconut Pie. Garnish with toasted coconut atop whipped cream wreath.

Custardy Rhubarb Pie

A scrumptious summertime dessert—

  1½ cups sugar
      ¼ cup all-purpose flour
      ¼ teaspoon ground nutmeg
      3 slightly beaten eggs
      1 pound rhubarb, cut in 1-inch
          slices (4 cups)

          • • •

          Plain Pastry for 9-inch lattice-
          top pie (See *Pastry*)
      2 tablespoons butter or margarine

Combine sugar, flour, and nutmeg; beat into eggs. Stir in sliced rhubarb. Line 9-inch pie plate with pastry. Fill with rhubarb mixture. Dot butter or margarine atop filling. Top with lattice crust; flute edge. Bake at 400° for 50 to 60 minutes. Cool.

Trifle Delight

Custard mix offers a quick variation of a favorite English dessert—

  2¼ cups milk
      1 2¾-ounce package no-bake
          vanilla custard mix

          • • •

      1 20½-ounce can pineapple tidbits,
          drained
      1 16-ounce can pitted dark sweet
          cherries, drained and halved
      ½ cup cream sherry

          • • •

      6 shortcake dessert cups *or* 6 slices
          pound cake

In small saucepan stir milk into vanilla custard mix; cook, stirring constantly, over high heat till mixture is boiling. Remove custard from heat; chill in the refrigerator.

In bowl combine drained pineapple tidbits, drained and halved cherries, and cream sherry. Chill fruit mixture 3 to 4 hours.

Drain chilled fruit mixture, reserving ¼ cup of the cream sherry. Beat custard smooth with rotary beater. Add reserved ¼ cup sherry; mix well. To serve, spoon chilled fruit onto shortcake dessert cups *or* pound cake slices; top with custard sauce. Makes 6 servings.

Delicately flavored Baked Custard makes an attractive dessert topped with tart jelly. Or, serve warm in cups with dash of nutmeg.

Baked Caramel Custard

2 cups milk
3 slightly beaten egg yolks
2 slightly beaten eggs
½ cup sugar
½ teaspoon vanilla
. . .
½ cup sugar

Scald milk over low heat; cool slightly. In bowl combine slightly beaten egg yolks, whole eggs, and ½ cup sugar; slowly stir in milk. Stir in vanilla; set mixture aside.

In heavy skillet stir ½ cup sugar over low heat till melted. When golden brown, remove from heat. Pour melted sugar into 1-quart casserole. Rotate casserole to coat sides with sugar syrup. Pour custard into casserole.

Set casserole in shallow baking pan on oven rack; pour hot water around casserole to depth of 1 inch. Bake at 325° till knife inserted halfway between center and edge comes out clean, about 1¼ hours. Chill. To serve, unmold onto serving platter. Makes 6 servings.

Baked Custard

3 slightly beaten eggs
¼ cup sugar
¼ teaspoon salt
2 cups milk, scalded and slightly cooled
½ teaspoon vanilla
. . .
Tart jelly (optional)
Ground nutmeg (optional)

Combine eggs, sugar, and salt; slowly stir in milk and vanilla. Pour into six 5-ounce custard cups*. Set cups in shallow baking pan on oven rack. Pour hot water into pan to depth of 1 inch. Bake at 325° till knife inserted halfway between center and edge comes out clean, about 40 to 45 minutes. Serve warm; or, chill, unmold, and top with tart jelly or sprinkle with nutmeg. Makes 6 servings.

*For one large custard, bake the custard in a 1-quart casserole for about 60 minutes.

Caramel Custard Cups

Melt 12 vanilla caramels in ¼ cup milk over low heat, stirring constantly. Divide caramel sauce among six 5-ounce custard cups.

Prepare Baked Custard (see above); pour over sauce. Bake, following recipe directions. Serve warm, or chill and unmold. Serves 6.

Orange-Pumpkin Pudding

3 slightly beaten eggs
1 cup canned pumpkin
½ cup sugar
½ teaspoon ground cinnamon
¼ teaspoon ground allspice
¼ teaspoon grated orange peel
1 14½-ounce can evaporated milk (1⅔ cups)

Combine first 6 ingredients; slowly stir in evaporated milk. Pour into six 5-ounce custard cups. Place in shallow baking pan; pour hot water around cups to depth of 1 inch. Bake at 325° till knife inserted halfway between center and edge comes out clean, about 50 minutes. Chill. Garnish with whipped cream and a sprinkle of ground cinnamon, if desired. Serves 6.

Cherry Bread Pudding

    2 cups milk
    3 slightly beaten eggs
    2 cups 1-inch day-old bread cubes
  ½ cup sugar
  ¼ teaspoon ground cinnamon
    1 teaspoon vanilla
    1 20-ounce can pitted tart red
        cherries (water pack)
  ½ cup sugar
    1 tablespoon cornstarch
       Few drops red food coloring
    2 to 3 drops almond extract
  ¼ cup flaked coconut, toasted

Combine milk and eggs; pour over bread cubes in mixing bowl. Stir in ½ cup sugar, cinnamon, vanilla, and ¼ teaspoon salt. Drain cherries, reserving syrup. Add *1 cup* of the drained cherries to bread mixture; toss lightly.

Spread mixture in greased 10x6x1¾-inch baking dish. Place dish in shallow baking pan on oven rack. Pour hot water around dish to depth of 1 inch. Bake at 350° till knife inserted halfway between center and edge comes out clean, about 40 to 45 minutes.

Meanwhile, add water to reserved cherry juice to make 1 cup. Combine ½ cup sugar and cornstarch in medium saucepan. Stir in cherry juice; cook and stir till thick and bubbly. Stir in remaining cherries, red food coloring, and almond extract; simmer 2 minutes longer.

To serve, sprinkle pudding with toasted coconut. Pass cherry sauce. Serves 8 or 9.

Pineapple-Cheese Parfaits

    1 2¾-ounce package no-bake
        vanilla custard mix
    2 cups milk
    2 3-ounce packages cream cheese,
        softened
  ½ teaspoon vanilla
    1 21-ounce can pineapple pie
        filling, chilled

Prepare custard according to package directions using the milk. Remove from heat. Gradually stir hot mixture into cheese; mix well. Stir in vanilla. Chill. To serve, spoon alternate layers of custard mixture and pie filling into parfait glasses. Makes 6 to 8 servings.

Zuppa Inglese

    6 egg yolks
  ½ cup cold water
 1½ cups granulated sugar
  ½ teaspoon vanilla
  ½ teaspoon orange *or* lemon
       extract
 1½ cups sifted cake flour
  ¼ teaspoon salt
    6 egg whites
  ¾ teaspoon cream of tartar
  ½ cup rum
    1 cup strawberry preserves

       • • •

      Custard Filling
 1½ cups whipping cream
    1 teaspoon vanilla
    3 tablespoons confectioners'
        sugar
      Candied cherries

Beat egg yolks till thick and lemon-colored; add water. Beat till very thick, about 5 minutes. Gradually beat in granulated sugar, then ½ teaspoon vanilla and orange extract.

Sift flour with salt; fold into egg-yolk mixture a little at a time. Beat egg whites with cream of tartar till stiff peaks form. Carefully fold egg whites into cake mixture. Bake in *ungreased* 10-inch tube pan at 325° about 1 hour. Invert pan to cool.

When thoroughly cooled, remove from pan. Using wooden picks as a marking guide, split cake into 3 layers. Divide rum and sprinkle atop each layer. Place bottom layer on cake plate; spread with *half* of the preserves, then with *1 cup* of the Custard Filling.

Top with second layer. Spread with remaining preserves and Custard Filling. Top with remaining layer. Whip cream with 1 teaspoon vanilla and confectioners' sugar; frost entire cake. Garnish with candied cherries. Chill dessert thoroughly, about 3 to 4 hours.

Custard Filling: In saucepan combine ⅓ cup granulated sugar, 1 tablespoon all-purpose flour, 1 tablespoon cornstarch, and ¼ teaspoon salt. Gradually stir in 1½ cups milk. Cook and stir till thick and bubbly; cook and stir 2 to 3 minutes more. Stir a little of the hot mixture into 1 slightly beaten egg yolk; return to hot mixture. Bring just to boiling; stir constantly. Stir in 1 tablespoon butter or margarine, and 1 teaspoon vanilla. Cool.

Custard Pie

    4 slightly beaten eggs
    ½ cup sugar
    ½ teaspoon vanilla
    2½ cups milk, scalded and
        slightly cooled
      Plain Pastry for 1-crust 9-inch
        pie (See *Pastry*)

Blend first 3 ingredients and ¼ teaspoon salt. Slowly stir in milk. Line 9-inch pie plate with pastry. Pour filling into pastry-lined pie plate. Sprinkle with nutmeg, if desired.

Bake at 350° till knife inserted halfway between center and edge comes out clean, about 35 to 40 minutes. Serve cool or well chilled.

Slipped Custard Pie

Prepare filling for Custard Pie (above). Place buttered 8-inch pie plate in shallow baking pan. Fill pie plate with custard (pour extra into custard cups and bake with pie filling).

Fill pan with hot water. Bake at 350° till knife inserted halfway between center and edge comes out clean, 35 to 40 minutes. Cool. Run spatula around edge. Shake to loosen. Hold custard just above far rim of *baked* 9-inch pastry shell; gently slip into shell. Chill.

To avoid spills, place pastry-lined pie plate on oven rack. Pour in custard mixture, filling the pie plate just to fluted edge.

Potato-Cheese Custard

    2 cups raw, diced, peeled potato
        •   •   •
    2 cups milk
    1 5-ounce jar process cheese spread
        with bacon
    1 teaspoon instant minced onion
        •   •   •
    2 beaten eggs
    1 tablespoon snipped parsley
    ½ teaspoon salt
    ½ teaspoon dry mustard
      Dash pepper
      Bacon, crisp-cooked and
        crumbled

In saucepan add water to potatoes to cover; bring to boiling. Remove from heat; drain. Arrange potatoes in 10x6x1¾-inch baking dish.

In saucepan heat together milk, cheese spread, and instant minced onion, stirring occasionally till cheese melts. Meanwhile, in mixing bowl combine eggs, parsley, salt, dry mustard, and pepper. Gradually stir hot milk mixture into egg mixture; pour over potatoes.

Bake at 325° till knife inserted halfway between center and edge comes out clean, about 35 to 40 minutes. Top with crisp-cooked, crumbled bacon. Let casserole stand 5 minutes before serving. Makes 6 servings.

When custard-type pie or casserole mixture is done, knife inserted halfway between center and edge will come out clean.

Corn-Custard Casserole

    1 10½-ounce can condensed cream
        of celery soup
    2 tablespoons all-purpose flour
    1 tablespoon prepared mustard
      Dash salt
    1 12-ounce can whole kernel corn,
        undrained
    1 6-ounce can evaporated
        milk (⅔ cup)
    2 tablespoons chopped green
        pepper
    2 tablespoons chopped onion
    2 tablespoons chopped canned
        pimiento
    2 slightly beaten eggs
    1 teaspoon Worcestershire sauce

Blend cream of celery soup, flour, prepared mustard, and salt. Stir in undrained corn, evaporated milk, green pepper, onion, pimiento, beaten eggs, and Worcestershire sauce.

Turn mixture into 10x6x1¾-inch baking dish. Bake at 350° till knife inserted halfway between center and edge comes out clean, about 30 to 40 minutes. Makes 6 servings.

Herbed Spinach Bake

    1 10-ounce package frozen chopped
        spinach
            • • •
    1 cup cooked long-grain rice
    4 ounces sharp process American
        cheese, shredded (1 cup)
    2 slightly beaten eggs
    ⅓ cup milk
    2 tablespoons butter or margarine,
        softened
    2 tablespoons chopped onion
    1 teaspoon salt
    ½ teaspoon Worcestershire sauce
    ¼ teaspoon dried rosemary leaves,
        crushed, *or* dried thyme leaves,
        crushed

Cook spinach according to package directions; drain. Stir in remaining ingredients. Pour mixture into 10x6x1¾-inch baking dish. Bake at 350° till knife inserted halfway between center and edge comes out clean, 20 to 25 minutes. Cut in squares to serve. Serves 6.

Swiss and Crab Pie

      Plain Pastry for 1-crust 9-inch
        pie (See *Pastry*)
    4 ounces natural Swiss cheese,
        shredded (1 cup)
    1 7½-ounce can crab meat, drained,
        flaked, and cartilage removed
    2 green onions with tops, sliced
    3 beaten eggs
    1 cup light cream
    ½ teaspoon salt
    ½ teaspoon grated lemon peel
    ¼ teaspoon dry mustard
      Dash ground mace
    ¼ cup sliced almonds

Line 9-inch pie plate with pastry. Sprinkle cheese over bottom of unbaked shell. Top with crab; sprinkle with onions. Combine remaining ingredients except almonds. Pour mixture over crab. Sprinkle with almonds. Bake at 325° till knife inserted halfway between center and edge comes out clean, about 45 minutes. Remove from oven; let stand 10 minutes. Serves 6.

Onion Pie

    1 cup finely crushed saltine
        crackers (28 crackers)
    ¼ cup butter or margarine, melted
            • • •
    2 cups thinly sliced onion,
        separated into rings (2 medium)
    2 tablespoons butter or margarine
    ¾ cup milk
    2 slightly beaten eggs
    ¼ cup shredded sharp process
        American cheese
      Dash paprika

Mix crumbs with ¼ cup melted butter. Press onto bottom and sides of 8-inch pie plate.

Cook onion in 2 tablespoons butter till tender but not brown; place in crumb shell. Combine milk, eggs, ¾ teaspoon salt, and dash pepper; pour over onions. Sprinkle pie with cheese and paprika. Bake at 350° till knife inserted halfway between center and edge comes out clean, about 30 minutes. Garnish with additional cooked onion rings and parsley, if desired. Serve hot. Makes 4 to 6 main dish servings, or 10 to 12 appetizers.

Snow Pudding

    ¾ cup sugar
    ¼ teaspoon salt
    1 envelope unflavored gelatin
        (1 tablespoon)
    ½ cup cold water
            • • •
    ¾ cup cold water
    1 teaspoon grated lemon peel
    ¼ cup lemon juice
    2 egg whites
            • • •
    3 egg yolks *or* 1 whole egg plus
        2 egg yolks
    3 tablespoons sugar
      Dash salt
    1½ cups milk, scalded and slightly
        cooled
    1 teaspoon vanilla
      Tart red jelly

In small saucepan combine ¾ cup sugar, ¼ teaspoon salt, and unflavored gelatin. Add the ½ cup cold water. Cook over low heat, stirring constantly, till gelatin dissolves.

Remove from heat; stir in ¾ cup cold water, lemon peel, and lemon juice. Chill till partially set. Turn into large mixing bowl. Add egg whites. Beat with electric or rotary beater till mixture begins to hold its shape.

Turn pudding mixture into eight 5-ounce custard cups. Chill till pudding is firm.

To make sauce, beat 3 egg yolks *or* 1 whole egg plus 2 egg yolks in top of double boiler. Add 3 tablespoons sugar and dash salt.

Gradually stir in slightly cooled milk. Cook and stir over hot, *not boiling*, water till mixture coats a metal spoon. Remove from heat; cool at once by placing pan in bowl of cold water and stirring a minute or two. Stir in vanilla; chill custard sauce.

Just before serving, unmold snow puddings into serving dish. Ladle some custard sauce over puddings; dot with tart, red jelly. Pass remaining custard sauce. Makes 8 servings.

Golden custard sauce

Drizzle creamy custard sauce atop airy puffs of Snow Pudding. Tart, red jelly adds the crowning touch to this delicate dessert.

CUSTARD APPLE—The name given to several fruits of various tropical and subtropical shrubs or small trees. The fruit most commonly termed custard apple has a dark brown surface marked with depressions, giving it a quilted appearance. The pulp is reddish yellow with a very soft texture—thus, the name. It has a sweet flavor, yet is very bland, which contributes to its popularity in hot climates. Other fruits closely related to custard apple include cherimoya, sweetsop, and soursop.

CUT IN—To mix solid shortening or butter with dry ingredients using a pastry blender or two knives. Ingredients should be evenly and finely divided.

CUTLERY—Sharp-edged cutting utensils or tools, such as knives and kitchen shears, used for slicing, peeling, chopping, coring, boning, or trimming in the preparation of food. (See *Kitchen Shears, Knife* for additional information.)

CUTLET—1. A thin slice of meat, especially veal, mutton, or pork cut from the leg and cooked by broiling or frying. Formerly, a cutlet was cut from the rib section of the animal. 2. A flat croquette made of minced meat or fish, shaped to resemble a meat cutlet. (See also *Veal*.)

Veal Parmigiano

Melt 3 tablespoons butter or margarine in 10x6x1¾-inch baking dish. Combine ½ cup cornflake crumbs, ¼ cup grated Parmesan cheese, ½ teaspoon salt, and dash pepper.

Cut 1 pound veal cutlets, about ¼ inch thick, into 4 serving-size pieces. Dip in 1 slightly beaten egg, then in cornflake crumb mixture. Place cutlets in baking dish. Bake at 400° for 20 minutes. Turn cutlets; bake till tender, about 15 to 20 minutes longer.

Meanwhile, in saucepan combine one 8-ounce can tomato sauce; ½ teaspoon dried oregano leaves, crushed; ½ teaspoon sugar; and dash onion salt. Heat mixture to boiling, stirring frequently. Pour tomato sauce mixture over cooked cutlets. Arrange 4 ounces sliced mozzarella cheese atop meat. Return casserole to oven to melt cheese. Makes 4 servings.

Fondue Veal Strips

   1½ pounds veal cutlets
   ¼ cup all-purpose flour
   2 beaten eggs
   ½ cup fine dry bread crumbs
      Salad oil
      Horseradish Sauce
      Mustard Sauce

Pound veal to ⅛-inch thickness. Cut in 3x1-inch strips. Coat strips with mixture of flour and ¼ teaspoon salt, then dip in egg. Roll in bread crumbs. Loosely thread each strip accordion-fashion on bamboo skewer.

Pour salad oil into metal fondue cooker to ½ capacity. Heat to 425° on range (do not let oil smoke). Add 1 teaspoon salt to hot oil. Place cooker over fondue burner. Let each guest fry veal strips in hot oil till browned. Dip in assorted sauces. Makes 4 servings.

Horseradish Sauce: Whip one 8-ounce package softened cream cheese with 2 to 3 tablespoons prepared horseradish till fluffy. Chill.

Mustard Sauce: Combine 1 cup dairy sour cream, ¼ cup milk, 3 tablespoons dry onion soup mix, and 2 tablespoons prepared mustard. Heat and stir, but do not boil. Serve hot.

Veal Bertrand

   6 veal cutlets (about 2 pounds)
   ⅔ cup dry sherry
   1 6-ounce can whole mushrooms, drained
   ¼ cup snipped parsley
      Dash garlic powder
   6 tablespoons butter or margarine
   3 slices process Swiss cheese

Pound veal cutlets to ¼-inch thickness. Combine sherry, drained mushrooms, parsley, and garlic powder. Pour over veal. Marinate 30 minutes, turning several times.

Melt butter in skillet. Drain meat, reserving marinade. Quickly cook *half* of the meat in hot butter, about 3 minutes on each side. Remove from skillet; repeat with remaining meat. Return cooked meat to skillet; add reserved marinade. Bring to boiling; reduce heat. Arrange cheese slices over meat. Cover; heat just till cheese melts. Remove to warm platter; spoon sauce atop meat. Makes 6 servings.

The cutting board is a most versatile piece of kitchen equipment. Choose a size appropriate for the amount of cutting to be done.

The recipe which follows illustrates the "croquette" definition of the word "cutlet." The patty shape gives interesting and appealing menu variation for this breaded meat mixture.

Polish Cutlets

    ¼ cup milk
    ¼ cup butter or margarine,
        melted
    1 cup soft bread crumbs
        (about 1½ slices)
    ½ teaspoon lemon juice
    ½ teaspoon salt
    ½ teaspoon paprika
        Dash pepper
 1½ pounds ground veal
        • • •
    1 beaten egg
    2 tablespoons water
    ½ cup fine dry bread crumbs
    2 tablespoons shortening
        Gravy

Combine milk, butter, soft bread crumbs, lemon juice, salt, paprika, and pepper; add veal and mix well. Form meat mixture into 6 patties, ¾ inch thick. Combine egg with water; dip patties into egg mixture, then dip into dry bread crumbs. In skillet brown patties on both sides in hot shortening. Simmer, covered, till meat is done, about 15 to 20 minutes.

To prepare *Gravy:* Remove patties to warm platter. Pour off pan drippings, reserving 1 tablespoon. To reserved drippings in skillet, blend in 1 tablespoon all-purpose flour, ¼ teaspoon ground nutmeg, ¼ teaspoon salt, and dash pepper. Add 1 cup milk all at once. Cook, stirring constantly, till mixture thickens and bubbles. Stir in 1 teaspoon lemon juice. Serve with patties. Makes 6 servings.

CUTTING BOARD—A smooth, hardwood board used for slicing, cutting, mincing, or chopping foods. Cutting board sizes vary greatly. Small ones are used for a small amount of food preparation; larger boards, either portable or built into the counter, are suitable for larger quantities.

With some exacting care, cutting boards can provide long, sanitary service. The application of several coatings of hot salad oil improves sanitation by sealing the wood pores. After using a board, wash and dry it. As an additional health precaution and as prevention against warped wood, don't allow the board to rest in the sink while other food preparation goes on.

CUTTLEFISH—A 10-armed saltwater mollusk similar to squid or octopus. It differs from them by having a calcified internal shell called the cuttlebone.

This seafood is common to Grecian, Indian, Italian, Japanese, and Spanish diets. The meat is edible only after being made sufficiently tender by beating. It is then cooked like octopus. (See *Octopus, Squid* for additional information.)

CYDER—The British spelling for the alcoholic beverage, cider. (See also *Cider.*)

CYMLING SQUASH—Another name for pattypan squash, a summer variety identified by its shape—scalloped, flat, and dishlike. (See also *Pattypan Squash.*)

D

DAB – 1. A very small portion of food, for example, a small dollop of jam used to garnish a cookie. 2. The name of a flatfish related to the flounder family. These fish are found off the North American and European coasts of the North Atlantic Ocean as well as in the Pacific Ocean. Dabs are lean fish with a distinctive flavor and a delicate texture. The flesh tastes slightly sweet but is not oily. A comparatively thick layer of flesh on either side of the backbone is delightfully free from bones. Dabs can be panfried like other types of panfish. (See also *Flounder*.)

DACE – A small, silvery fish of both European and North American fresh waters. Dace belong to the carp family.

Dace flesh is tough but completely edible. These fish are usually fried in the same way as are smelts. (See *Carp, Smelt* for additional information.)

DAFFODIL CAKE – A light and delicate foam-type cake that was originally a combination of angel food (made with egg whites) and sponge cake (made with egg yolks). Daffodil cake takes it name from the attractive intermingling of white and yellow colors throughout the cake. A quick, easy way to produce the same effect in a delicious cake is given here in the cake mix-base recipe Easy Daffodil Cake.

Easy Daffodil Cake

A subtle merger of yellow and white captures that springtime feeling—

> 1 package angel cake mix
> 1 teaspoon water
> ¼ teaspoon yellow food coloring
>   • • •
> 2 egg whites
> 1 cup sugar
> 2 tablespoons lemon juice
> ¼ teaspoon cream of tartar
>   Dash salt
> 1 cup miniature marshmallows
> ½ teaspoon grated lemon peel

Prepare angel cake mix according to package directions; divide batter in half. Combine water and yellow food coloring; fold into *half* the batter. Spoon colored and plain cake batters alternately into *ungreased* 10-inch tube pan. Bake as directed on package. Invert cake in pan; cool the cake thoroughly.

Meanwhile, prepare lemon frosting by combining egg whites, sugar, lemon juice, cream of tartar, and salt in top of double boiler. Beat mixture for 1 minute with electric or rotary beater. Cook over boiling water, beating till stiff peaks form. Carefully fold in miniature marshmallows and lemon peel.

When cake is cool, remove from pan. Frost sides and top with lemon frosting.

DAIKON *(dī' kan)* — A large white radish, available throughout the year, which is eaten raw by the Chinese, Japanese, and the Koreans. This heavy, root vegetable may grow to be three feet long, six inches thick, and weigh up to fifty pounds. Imported from Hawaii or Japan, it can be found in the Western states in one of three forms: oblong, spherical, or cylindrical. The small oblong radish, generally four inches long and three inches thick, is the favorite of the Chinese. The Japanese favor the larger and longer spherical and cylindrical varieties of daikon.

The Oriental radish has a somewhat more spongy texture than the Western radish, but the flavor is similar. The vivid, green radish foliage is sought after as a special green vegetable by cultivating the daikon seedlings. A long, slender white taproot is tied around bunches of twenty or more plants and sold in markets.

To non-Oriental cooks, daikon is best known in preserved versions of vegetables pickled in soy sauce, seaweed derivatives, and other flavorings. Well chilled, thinly sliced, pickled daikon is an essential item for those serving Oriental menus. The root is often carved into a variety of shapes, such as roses or fishnets, for garnishes. Shredded, raw daikon may be used as a bed for Nipponese raw fish or as a Suki-yaki condiment. It may also be mixed in with warm soy sauce dip. Pickled daikon can be paired with American hamburgers and hot dogs for an unusual accompaniment. (See *Japanese Cookery, Radish* for additional information.)

DAIQUIRI *(dī' karē, dak' uh rē)* — A tart cocktail made of white rum, lime juice, and sugar shaken with finely shaven ice. The cocktail, named after a mining town in southeastern Cuba where American troops landed after the Spanish-American War, is popular as a summer drink.

The ingredients, white rum (preferred because of delicate flavor), lime juice, and sugar, are poured over finely shaven ice and shaken or blended just until the drink is thoroughly chilled—too much shaking or blending will cause the ice to dissolve and dilute the cocktail. To produce an even foamier daiquiri, add a dash of egg white to the mixing glass just before shaking. Make two or three small fresh cocktails in a shaker at a time for maximum flavor. The classic daiquiri is sometimes strained to remove small ice particles which cause dilution. Pour the iced drink into a chilled cocktail glass. You may add a lime slice or wedge and serve along with a short straw. The cocktail is to be sipped slowly.

A frozen daiquiri is prepared the same way, but the mixture is combined with crushed ice in an electric blender and blended until it looks like snow. Interesting daiquiri variations can be prepared by adding fresh or frozen orange juice or chopped peaches to the standard mixture before blending. (See also *Cocktail.*)

Daiquiri

Combine ½ jigger lime juice, 1 jigger (1½ ounces) light rum, powdered sugar to taste, 1 teaspoon Triple Sec (optional), and crushed ice in a shaker. Shake well and strain into a stemmed cocktail glass. Makes 1 cocktail.

DAIRY SOUR CREAM — A commercial dairy product sold in American markets and produced by a culture of lactic acid bacteria acting upon sweet light cream.

Pasteurization and homogenization processes assure even fat distribution before the addition of the lactic acid bacteria to the cream. The cream, then, is subjected to proper temperatures for a measured length of time and then chilled to stop the bacteria action. The cream is packaged as commercial dairy sour cream and is uniform in texture at all times.

When dairy sour cream is exposed to high cooking temperatures, curdling may occur. In certain cases, holding it at a low temperature for a longer length of time may also produce the same reaction. To avoid this keep the temperature low and usually add the dairy sour cream near the end of the cooking time when using in most cooked dishes. The curdling, however, only affects the appearance and not the flavor. Smooth, thick dairy sour cream is used in dips, soups, main dishes, desserts, and cakes. (See also *Sour Cream.*)

DAMPF NOODLE—A yeast dumpling served with stewed fruit, jam, or a sauce. These German dumplings, or *dampfnudeln,* are shaped from dough which has been enriched with sugar, eggs, and butter.

The small, round biscuitlike balls are placed in a baking dish and allowed to rise. They are parboiled (boiled for a short time; not cooked completely) in milk, then steamed and browned in the oven.

These dumplings can be arranged on a heated platter or individual serving dishes with a sauce spooned over them. Sauce suggestions include hot vanilla sauce, caramel, or dried fruit sauce.

DAMSON PLUMS *(dam' zen)*—A small bluish purple plum eaten fresh or used in preserves. The plums were cultivated more than 2000 years ago in Damascus, Syria, where the plum's name originated. Today they are cultivated in tree orchards and also grow wild. The firm, oval plums are available from May through September.

Damson should be selected at their peak of ripeness. Look for full bluish purple color, firm plumpness, smooth skin, and fresh appearance. For canning purposes choose mellow plums not quite ripe. An excellent fruit for cooking, Damson plums may be used for jams, jellies, pickles, preserves, puddings, and pies. (See also *Plum.*)

DANDELION—A delectable spring green of the chicory family cultivated for its bitter, toothed or pinnated leaves which are used as a vegetable and in salads, and the roots used for wine and coffee. The sharply indented leaves influenced the French name *dent de lion* or "lion's tooth."

Grown and used not only in the United States, but in France, England, and Italy as well, the dandelion plant grows in the poorest soil and should not be picked before the yellow flower appears.

Two types of dandelions, cultivated and wild, are found on the market in early spring. Cultivated dandelions, with a bleached appearance, are more tender.

Select both types of dandelion greens carefully, avoiding the slightest bit of yellow bud as this causes an undesirable acrid taste. Choose young plants with tender, delicately flavored leaves.

Prepare the greens for cooking or for use in salads by first removing the root and quartering the base of the plant with a knife. Sand may be found among the leaves, so a thorough washing and cleaning is important. Drain and crisp the greens for salads in the refrigerator.

If the dandelion is to be used as a vegetable, it is cooked like spinach. Add dandelion greens to a small amount of salted water in saucepan and cook till completely wilted. Drain and discard the water which will have become quite strong. Formerly, boiling the greens for a long time with several changes of water was recommended to remove bitterness. Today, however, authorities say that this process results in a loss of the rich vitamin and mineral nutritive value of the vegetable greens.

The humble dandelion may be served raw, eaten as a vegetable, or made into several unique beverages. Pour a tart French dressing over a dandelion salad of thinly sliced scallions, radishes, and cooked beets. Cook the greens like spinach and serve with a creamy sauce. Dried, ground dandelion roots make a delicious European coffee substitute, and the flowers make a delectable wine. Dandelions are made into refreshing European and Oriental soups, and are blended in with fritters and omelets. (See also *Vegetable.*)

DANISH BLUE CHEESE—A pungent, blue-veined mold-ripened cheese made with homogenized milk, very rich in cream. Danish Blue Cheese can be recognized by its off-white color with blue green mold and a buttery paste consistency. This cheese was invented in 1914 by a Danish cheesemaker, Marius Boel, who produced a mold on a barley bread baked for that purpose.

The rich, creamy milk from which Danish Blue Cheese is made accounts for its buttery consistency. Roquefort, Norwegian, and other domestic blues contain less fat than the buttery Danish blue. The liberal number of penlike blue vein markings make this rich-flavored cheese look like a delicate work of art. The cheeses made for local Danish consumption are lower in cream content, even more densely veined, and are sharper in flavor with a slight peppermint taste. (See also Blue *Cheese.*)

DANISH COOKERY—Food and drink influenced by the southernmost Scandinavian country—Denmark. Foods characteristic of this land of rich agricultural heritage and abundance include tiny artistic open-face sandwiches, buttery-rich pastries and desserts, steaming loaves of yeast bread, ground fish dishes, flavorful meatballs, fruit soups, and rice porridge. Rich foods, such as butter, cream, and eggs, are used lavishly in preparing dishes to satisfy the hearty appetites of Danish eaters.

Traditional recipes, handed down for generations, are the basis for Danish cuisine. Some are simple country-style recipes, while others, tinged with French cooking, are more sophisticated. The thrifty Danes treat their food with respect, as every scrap finds its way into a delectable dish such as open-faced sandwiches.

A Danish open-face sandwich is a small sandwich, or *Smörrebröd* of thinly sliced buttered bread topped with the main ingredient, artistically arranged, and tastefully garnished. The sandwich can be found almost anywhere in Denmark and is sold on street corners, boats, trains, and in restaurants. One restaurant has a yard-long menu listing some 175 choices.

The bread is usually buttered and may be white, rye, or a crisp bread. The main ingredient is carefully arranged and garnished keeping texture and color in mind. A leaf green is sometimes tucked under a filling corner. The lovely little meal is eaten with a knife and a fork.

Shrimp-Capers Sandwich

For each sandwich, butter 1 slice French bread generously. Cover with a ruffly leaf of lettuce. Arrange canned tiny shrimp, overlapping, in two rows atop lettuce. Pipe mayonnaise or salad dressing from pastry tube down sandwich center. Top with capers.

Danish open-face sandwiches

←Artistic Danish cookery consists of an open-face sandwich buffet of Shrimp-Capers, Ham Pinwheel, and Egg-Sardine-Tomato.

Ham Pinwheel Sandwiches

    8 slices whole wheat bread
    ⅓ cup mayonnaise or salad
         dressing
  1⅓ cups shredded lettuce
    1 3-ounce package cream cheese,
         softened
    1 teaspoon horseradish
    4 slices Danish-style boiled ham

Spread bread with mayonnaise; top with shredded lettuce. Blend cream cheese and horseradish, adding milk if necessary to make mixture of spreading consistency. Spread evenly on ham slices. Roll up tightly. (To make slicing easier, refrigerate the rolls a short time.) Slice each ham roll into tiny pinwheels. Arrange pinwheels on shredded lettuce in diagonal line, 5 per sandwich. Makes 8 sandwiches.

Egg-Tomato-Sardine Sandwiches

Butter 1 slice rye bread generously for each sandwich. Mix chopped hard-cooked egg with mayonnaise or salad dressing to moisten; spread on buttered bread. Arrange canned sardines and small tomato wedges atop egg. Garnish with parsley or dill sprigs.

In this dairy country excellent cheeses are made and enjoyed in every possible way. Cream is used generously in cooking, and butter is the shortening used in most baked foods. Buttermilk soup, delectably flavored with sugar, raisins, and lemon peel, is enriched with cream. Salads are preferred with a sour cream sauce, vegetables are usually served with a cream sauce, and whipped cream is used to top puddings, cakes, and desserts.

The Danish also are great lovers of rye breads. Hearty white and satisfying dark rye Danish breads are integral parts of meal courses. Rye bread crusts are used with beer in a simple brown soup. Rye bread crumbs, with milk and sugar, are used in an apple whipped cream dessert garnished with grated chocolate. World famous Danish coffee bread, *Wienerbröd* (Vienna bread), is produced by steaming the yeast loaves in the oven while baking.

Danish Coffee Ring

Tender Danish pastry ring with sugar icing and raisin-nut filling—

- **1 package active dry yeast**
- **2½ to 3 cups sifted all-purpose flour**
- **¾ cup milk, scalded**
- **¼ cup shortening**
- **¼ cup sugar**
- **½ teaspoon salt**

. . .

- **1 slightly beaten egg**
- **½ teaspoon vanilla**
- **1 teaspoon grated lemon peel**

. . .

- **2 tablespoons butter, melted**
- **½ cup raisins**
- **½ cup slivered almonds, toasted**
- **⅓ cup sugar**
- **½ teaspoon ground mace or**
-   **1½ teaspoons ground cinnamon**
- **Icing**

In large bowl combine yeast and 1½ *cups* flour. Heat milk, shortening, sugar, and ½ teaspoon salt just till warm, stirring occasionally to melt shortening. Add to dry mixture in bowl; add egg, vanilla, and lemon peel. Beat at low speed with electric mixer for ½ minute, scraping sides of bowl constantly. Beat 3 minutes at high speed. By hand, stir in enough of remaining flour to make soft dough.

Knead on floured surface till smooth and elastic. Place in greased bowl, turning once to grease surface of dough. Cover and let rest till double, about 1½ hours. Punch down. Cover and let rest 10 minutes. Roll to 21x7 inches, ¼ inch thick. (Or, divide dough in half and roll to 13x6 inches to make two smaller rings.)

Brush dough with melted butter. Combine remaining ingredients; spread on dough. Roll from long edge; seal. Shape ring on greased baking sheet. With scissors, snip almost to center at 1-inch intervals. Pull sections apart; twist slightly. Cover, let rise till double, about 50 minutes. Bake at 375° for 20 minutes. Frost with *Icing:* Mix 1 cup sifted confectioners' sugar, 4 teaspoons milk, ½ teaspoon vanilla, and dash salt. Makes 1 large ring.

As befits a country of many islands and available fresh fish markets, the Danish are great fishermen and are fond of fish dishes. Ground white fish baked with bread crumbs may be served to the family hot at dinner time, or sliced and served cold at a buffet party with garnishes of sliced hard-cooked eggs, tomatoes, cucumber, and dill. Skinned eel, and other such seafoods, may be jellied with carrots and peppercorns or fried in butter and served with apple-curry sauce or other such accompaniments.

A Danish Kringle becomes a special treat for family and friends when stuffed with a sweet and spicy raisin or pecan filling. Serve the flaky coffee bread, adorned with toasted almond pieces, with tiny butter curls and steaming hot cups of coffee.

Danish cooks make ground beef, veal, or pork into flavorful meatballs called *Frikadeller*. Similar mixtures may be the stuffing for cabbage or the heart of broth cooked dumplings. Fresh pork is delectably stuffed with prunes and apples for roasting, chicken is often stuffed with a handful of parsley, and the Christmas roast goose has a stuffing of prunes. Also at holiday times, a reindeer roast, imported from Iceland, may be the special treat.

Pickling, a meat preservation technique of the past, is now an important flavor addition. Pickled duck served with horseradish cream sauce is one such specialty.

Traditional in Denmark is a rice porridge, served piping hot with a chunk of cold butter in the center. At Christmas time it is a "must," served with sugar, cinnamon, and cream. Typically Danish, too, are the dainty apple puffs called *Abelskiver*, baked in a special iron utensil with numerous rounded cups. As in other Scandinavian countries, fruit soups are made in Denmark and often are served as a dessert. Danish cooks are experts at making thin, dainty pancakes to be served with a filling of rich ice cream or cool fruit. (See *Danish Pastry, Scandinavian Cookery* for additional information.)

DANISH HAM—An imported specialty ham weighing up to 12 to 14 pounds. These boneless, fully cooked hams are packed in cans and weigh from 1½ to 6 or 7 pounds or are marketed in 4- to 6-ounce packages. These hams come from animals that have been fed on a milk and grain diet, the reason for the tender, succulent, juicy meat.

As with all fully cooked hams, Danish hams may be thinly sliced, or baked to heat through, garnished, and served hot or cold. Uniformly sliced, fully cooked Danish ham is available in 4- to 6-ounce packets in markets. (See also *Ham*.)

DANISH PASTRY—Traditional Danish sweet, buttery-rich, yeast-raised rolls and coffee cakes. Dough is spread with chilled butter or margarine and folded into three layers and rolled. The technique is similar to puff pastry. Fillings of dried fruit, jelly, or soft cheese are placed in the center. Delightful individual pastries or masterfully shaped large, holiday breads can be formed from the rich dough. Occasionally the dough is chilled before baking, and an egg and water mixture is brushed on the raised surface to give it a glazed appearance.

As part of the cooking process, the delicate pastries are sometimes put into a preheated hot oven, which is reduced quickly to moderate to bake evenly. Mouth-watering garnishes and flavor additions, such as sugar, candied fruits, nuts, spices, and icing add the finishing touch. (See also *Scandinavian Cookery*.)

Danish Kringle

Roll ¾ cup softened butter or margarine out between two sheets of wax paper to 10x6-inch rectangle. Chill. Soften 1 package active dry yeast in ¼ cup *warm* water. Combine 1 slightly beaten egg, ¼ cup sugar, 1 teaspoon salt, and ¾ cup cold milk in large mixing bowl. Stir in softened yeast and 3 cups sifted all-purpose flour. Mix well to form a moderately stiff dough. Roll dough out on a lightly floured surface to a 12-inch square.

Place chilled butter in center of dough square. Overlap dough; pinch to seal center seam and ends. Cover and let rest 10 minutes. Roll out again to 12-inch square. Fold in thirds. Wrap in foil and chill 30 to 60 minutes; repeat rolling, chilling and folding twice more. Cut dough lengthwise into 3 strips, 12-inches long. Roll first strip out to an 18x4-inch rectangle. Combine 1 beaten egg with 1 tablespoon water; brush on strip with pastry brush. Sprinkle strip with ⅓ of the Sweet Filling. Seal edges together to form 18-inch long roll. Shape into an oval, placing seam side down in greased baking sheet.

Seal ends together and flatten dough with rolling pin or palm of hand to ½-inch thickness. Brush flattened surface with remaining egg-water mixture. Using ¼ cup finely chopped blanched almonds and ¼ cup sugar, sprinkle a third over the top. Repeat with remaining dough, filling, and topping. Let dough rest at room temperature for 30 minutes. Bake at 375° till golden brown, about 25 minutes. Remove to rack; cool. Makes 3 kringles.

Sweet filling: In small bowl cream together ½ cup butter or margarine and 1½ cups sugar till fluffy. Stir in 1½ cups golden raisins or 1½ cups coarsely chopped pecans.

DARJEELING TEA (*där je' ling*)—A variety of black tea grown at altitudes of from 1,000 to 7,000 feet in the Himalaya Mountains near Darjeeling, India. Considered to be India's finest tea, its pungent, distinctive flavor permeates the flavor of other teas. This black tea is blended into many American tea brands for that reason. Prized as a "straight" brew, Darjeeling tea produces an attractive, handsome reddish color when brewed. (See also *Tea.*)

DASHEEN (*da shēn'*)—A starchy root vegetable grown in southern United States and in tropical climates as a substitute for potatoes. A variety of taro, it has grown as a commercial crop in the Southern states since 1913. The nutlike-flavored vegetable grows in a warmer, more moist climate than does the potato and is a staple food for the people of southeastern Asia, Polynesia, an the Pacific Islands.

The vegetable consists of one large bulbous root with many smaller attached tubers. The larger root, called the corm, can weigh up to 6 pounds. The light tan vegetable is characterized by heavy, circumference rings; shaggy, fibrous skin; and a tapering, round, stem end. The small roots called tubers or cormels, often irregular in shape, may be cream-colored or run from gray to lavender shades.

Being a starch tuber, the dasheen has more carbohydrates and proteins than do potatoes and is easily digested. The roots are most readily available in Spanish neighborhoods in vegetable shops.

When purchasing dasheens, select a heavy, full-bodied vegetable with a firm, fresh-looking skin. It will keep 4 to 5 days if it is stored in a cool, dark, well-ventilated storage place.

Before cooking, scrub, but do not peel the vegetable as its raw juice irritates the skin. They should then be cooked like potatoes in boiling salted water until tender, usually about 15 to 30 minutes. After cooking they should be peeled and mashed or put through a ricer. Season cooked dasheens with salt and pepper to taste and plenty of butter or margarine.

Dasheens may be baked by first boiling and then adding a thin oil coat to prevent a hard rind. Hollow out corm interior. Par-boil hollowed dasheens for 10 minutes in salted water, and stuff with meat, fish, or green vegetables. Slice raw dasheens and onions in greased baking dish, sprinkle with cheese and buttered crumbs, and bake. Prepare a pie filling of boiled, riced dasheens with butter, sugar, egg, milk, and spices. Drop dasheen fritters in hot fat, sprinkling with powdered sugar after cooking. Any potato recipe may be used for this potato substitute if the homemaker remembers that dasheens need added moisture and fat because they are drier than are potatoes. (See also *Taro.*)

DATE—A one-seeded berry fruit growing in thick clusters on a tall date palm tree. Dates are sweet and flavorful, plump and lustrous, golden brown to deep amber in color, and smooth skinned.

In its long history dating back more than 8000 years to Mesopotamia (now Iraq) in an area commonly associated with the Garden of Eden, the brown fruit has had many uses. It has been used as a fruit, to make bread and wine, and has saved many a wanderer in the deserts of the Middle East and Africa from starvation.

Records show that the Egyptian queen, Cleopatra, ate dates and drank wine made from them. A kind of bread containing dates was also eaten by the Egyptians and the Greeks. Greeks dedicated the date to the god of music and poetry because it was thought of as a symbol of light, fertility, and riches. The plump dates were favorite sweets in Ancient Persia, and palm branches became symbolic of Jesus' march to Jerusalem on Palm Sunday.

Had it not been for dates and their ability to thrive in hot, dry climates, the desert populations and camels of the Middle East and Africa might not have survived the torrid climate. Fortunately, the sight of a palm tree offered welcome shade relief and food to the people who lived in or traveled through the scorching hot and barren desert countries.

Because of the abundance of dates in these desert regions, the fruit has become a principal source of wealth in those countries where they grow abundantly.

Early Spanish missionaries introduced dates to the Western world. Some of the original palm offshoots may still be found in parts of Southern California and Mexico where their missions were first established. The Department of Agriculture, in 1890, shipped in date varieties from Egypt. Commercial firm representatives began visiting date growing countries bringing back better shoots from the date palms. By the middle of the nineteenth century, a climate best suited for large-scale production of dates was found to be the warm valleys of California and Arizona. Today, California and Arizona are still America's leading date-producing states. Dates are also grown in Texas, Florida, and the Gulf States, but the fruit does not ripen as well in these states as it does in the climatic conditions of California and Arizona.

How dates are produced: The slender trunked date palm may reach a height of a hundred feet and have 10- to 20-foot long leaves that grow into a stiff, green crown. Palm trees must be hand-pollinated as the female blossoms have no scent to attract bees. The date clusters may weigh from 15 to 25 pounds and produce over 1000 dates. Date palms bear 300 to 400 pounds of fruit per season for one or two centuries. This long-lived tree, sometimes existing for more than 200 years, requires a hot climate and low humidity.

Dates begin to ripen during the late summer and early fall. The green, unripe dates are crisp, smooth, firm, and astringent. Mature size and full sugar content is attained before it turns to a red or yellow colored (depending on variety), sweet, thick-fleshed fruit. The date ripens to a glossy brown and the flesh softens and partially dries. Curing, the natural process of drying out, occurs as the fruit ripens.

Because the individual fruits do not ripen at the same time, harvesting usually continues from September through February. The ripe dates should be picked several times during the growing season to insure prime ripeness and proper curing. Trees are covered for protection from rain, birds, and insects during ripening.

Nutritional value: Dates have differing characteristics. The oblong fruit varies in shape, size, color, quality, and flesh consistency according to variety and environmental conditions. Age and ripeness of the fruit when picked determine the composition. Because dates are 60 to 65 percent sugar, they are high in calories and often are called "candy that grows on trees." Nutritionally valuable, dates contain vitamin A, some of the B vitamins, and are a good source for minerals—calcium, iron, phosphorus, and copper.

Kinds of dates: Dates are classified commercially as soft, semidry, and dry, depending upon the softness of the ripe fruit. They are also classified according to sugar content. Soft varieties are invert-sugar dates (containing mostly dextrose and levulose) and dry varieties are cane-sugar dates (containing mostly cane sugar). Semidry varieties may contain either.

Common invert-sugar soft varieties include Hayany, Barhee, Khadrawy, Rhars, Kustawy, Halawy, Sayer, Saidy, and Maktoom. The common cane-sugar dry dates include Kenta and Thoory. Semidry varieties include Zahidi and Deglet Noor. Deglet Noor is a cane-sugar date and Zahidi an invert-sugar type.

The nonperishable dry varieties contain very little moisture when ripe. Soft varieties are dehydrated after being sized and separated to bring them to the desired moisture content. Semidry dates are sold in their natural state as fresh dates.

The most popular date variety grown in the Coachella Valley of California is the semidry Deglet Noor, a native of Algeria. Other leading varieties of dates grown and used in the United States are the Egyptian Khadrawy, Zahidi, and Halawy.

How to select: Even though the date harvest season is from September through February, refrigeration makes it possible for dates to be available all year long. They are most plentiful around holiday seasons. Choose the black, sweet, meaty, thin-skinned date or the golden brown date with a coarse texture and larger seed.

Dates are sold pitted or unpitted in assorted sizes in overwrapped paper trays, jars, and film bags. As a convenience item, chopped or diced dates are also available. Regular and spiced dates, and canned date nut rolls are available in most markets and gift and mail order shops.

How to store: Moisture and odors are absorbed easily by fresh dates; therefore, they should be tightly covered and stored at a cool temperature between 32° and 40°. Shelf life of packaged dates is four to six months. An opened package of dates will keep only for two months.

How to prepare: Use pitted dates when a recipe calls for a measured amount of dates. Using a small paring knife, cut a lengthwise slit in the date, rolling out the pit with the tip of the knife. For those recipes which require dates to be diced or cubed, cut the fruit on a wooden cutting board with a knife or kitchen shears frequently dipped in cold water. Avoid mincing dates or chopping in fine pieces as they will bind together in a sticky mass.

How to use: Eat dates right from the package as a delicious confection; or, pit, cut up, and toss into a breakfast cereal, fruit salad, or fruit cup. Serve dates in malted milk shakes or ice cream sodas, or sprinkle some of them over a pudding.

Use packaged dates in baked goods, candies, and to make mouth-watering desserts. Bake snipped or chopped dates in muffins, cookies, pies, and cakes. Stuff dates with such delectable delights as fondants, maraschino-flavored marzipan, or a chopped hazelnut, honey, and sugar mixture. For dessert, roll stuffed dates in crushed macaroon or cereal crumbs, fry quickly in deep fat, and serve with a creamy vanilla sauce.

The wholesome fruit, when served with milk, is believed to be a nearly perfect meal. Athletes rely on sweet dates as a source of quick energy.

The stately date palm has many uses besides bearing fruit. In tropical climates the palm leaves are woven into roofs, walls, and baskets, and the fibrous tree bark is twisted into a type of rope. The date pits may be roasted and made into a beverage brewed like coffee, or the mashed pulp made into wine. The Arabs still use dates as feed for livestock by mashing the pitted pulps into cakes. (See also *Fruit.*)

Sweet Potato-Date Puffs

Golden sweet potatoes and date bits form honey-glazed potato balls atop thick pineapple slices—

  1 17-ounce can sweet potatoes, drained
  ¾ cup snipped dates
  6 slices canned pineapple
  • • •
  ¼ cup butter or margarine
  ¼ cup brown sugar
  2 tablespoons honey

Mash sweet potatoes; stir in ¼ *cup* of the dates. Shape into six balls. Drain pineapple, reserving 2 tablespoons syrup. Melt butter or margarine in medium skillet; stir in brown sugar, honey, reserved pineapple syrup, and the remaining dates. Heat till sugar is dissolved.

Place 6 slices pineapple into syrup in skillet; top each with a potato ball. Cover; simmer over low heat for 10 to 12 minutes, spooning pineapple syrup over potatoes several times during cooking. Makes 6 servings.

Ginger-Date Triangles

Easy party sandwiches of canned date-nut roll sliced and spread with ginger-flavored filling—

  1 3-ounce package cream cheese, softened
  1 tablespoon milk
  1 tablespoon finely snipped candied ginger
  • • •
  1 8-ounce can date-nut roll

Blend together cheese and milk; stir in candied ginger. Slice date-nut roll into slices about ⅜ inch thick. Spread half the slices with cream cheese mixture. Top with remaining date-nut slices. Cut each sandwich in quarters. Chill thoroughly. Makes about 20 triangles.

Hot braided coffee cake

Build a good cook's reputation with this→ date Braided Coffee Cake. Rich date filling and nut topper makes it a special feast.

Stuffed Date Drops

Dates stuffed with nuts and dropped in cookie dough become golden delights topped with icing—

½ pound (about 39) pitted dates
About 39 pecan or walnut halves
¼ cup shortening
¾ cup brown sugar
1 egg
½ cup dairy sour cream
1¼ cups sifted all-purpose flour
½ teaspoon baking powder
½ teaspoon baking soda
¼ teaspoon salt
. . .
6 tablespoons butter
2 cups sifted confectioners' sugar
¼ teaspoon vanilla
Hot water

Stuff pitted dates with walnuts or pecan halves. Cream shortening and brown sugar till light and fluffy; beat in egg. Stir in dairy sour cream. Sift all-purpose flour, baking powder, baking soda, and salt; add to creamed mixture. Stir in stuffed dates. Drop onto greased cookie sheet, using one date for each cookie. Bake at 400° for 6 to 8 minutes. Remove immediately; cool. Spread creamy icing over each date drop.

Dates combine with banana, pineapple, and nuts to make a glamorous freeze-ahead salad. Date Soufflé Salads are frozen in paper cups.

To make icing, lightly brown butter in a saucepan. Remove from heat and cool. Gradually beat in confectioners' sugar and vanilla. Slowly add hot water till of spreading consistency (about 2 tablespoons). If necessary, add hot water to thin. Makes about 3 dozen.

Stuffed Dates

A mouth-watering candy treat of dates and nuts—

3 tablespoons butter, softened
3 tablespoons light corn syrup
½ teaspoon shredded orange peel
½ teaspoon vanilla
¼ teaspoon salt
2⅓ cups sifted confectioners' sugar
. . .
Walnut halves
48 pitted dates

Cream butter; blend in corn syrup, shredded orange peel, vanilla, and salt. Add confectioners' sugar all at once; mix in, first with spoon, then by kneading with hands. Place mixture on board; knead till smooth. Wrap in foil; chill 24 hours. Wrap each nut about ½ teaspoon candy and stuff into date. Makes 48.

Date Soufflé Salads

1 8-ounce package cream cheese, softened
¼ cup maple syrup
1 tablespoon lemon juice
1 medium banana, mashed (½ cup)
1 8¾-ounce can crushed pineapple, drained
½ cup finely chopped dates
½ cup chopped pecans
1 cup whipping cream

Cream the cheese; beat in maple syrup, lemon juice, and mashed banana. Stir in crushed pineapple, chopped dates, and pecans. Whip cream; fold in. Line 6 to 8 muffin cups with paper bake cups; fill with salad. Freeze till firm. Remove bake cups. If desired, arrange on pineapple and greens; top with maraschino cherry. Let salads stand 15 minutes at room temperature before serving. Makes 6 to 8 servings.

Date Chiffon Pie studded with snipped dates offers an unusual
prepare-ahead dessert. The magnificent filling is turned into
a cooled cheese pastry for double flavor eating.

Date Chiffon Pie

    1 cup sifted all-purpose flour
    ½ teaspoon salt
    ⅓ cup shortening
    ½ cup shredded sharp process
        American cheese
    3 tablespoons cold water

            • • •

    1 envelope unflavored
        gelatin (1 tablespoon)
    ¼ cup sugar
    2 egg yolks
    ½ cup orange juice
    ⅓ cup lemon juice
    ½ cup light cream
    2 egg whites
    ¼ cup sugar
    1½ cups snipped dates

Prepare cheese pastry by sifting together flour
and salt. Cut in ⅓ cup shortening. Add shredded sharp process American cheese; toss lightly.
Gradually sprinkle cold water over mixture,
tossing with fork till moistened. Roll out on
floured surface to ⅛ inch. Fit into 8-inch pie
plate, being careful not to stretch the pastry;
crimp edges. Prick crust with a fork. Bake at
450° for 8 to 10 minutes.

In a saucepan mix the gelatin and ¼ cup
sugar. Beat together the egg yolks and fruit
juices; stir into gelatin mixture. Cook and stir
over medium heat just till mixture comes to
boiling and is slightly thickened. Cool. Stir in
cream; chill till slightly thickened. Beat egg
whites with dash salt till soft peaks form. Add
¼ cup sugar gradually; beat till stiff peaks
form. Fold in gelatin mixture, then dates. Turn
into cooled pastry. Chill firm.

Date Cake

½ pound pitted dates, coarsely
    chopped (1½ cups)
½ cup shortening
1 cup sugar
1 teaspoon vanilla
1 egg
1½ cups sifted all-purpose flour
1 teaspoon baking soda
½ cup chopped walnuts

Combine chopped dates with 1 cup boiling water; cool to room temperature. Cream shortening and sugar till light. Add vanilla and egg; beat well. Sift flour, baking soda, and ¼ teaspoon salt together; add to creamed mixture alternately with date mixture, beating after each addition. Stir in chopped walnuts. Bake in greased and lightly floured 13x9x2-inch baking pan at 350° about 25 to 30 minutes. If desired, serve with a dollop of whipped cream.

Easy Date Crumble Torte

1 14-ounce package date bar mix
½ cup chopped walnuts
2 tablespoons melted butter
    or margarine
1 cup frozen whipped dessert
    topping, thawed

Combine the crumb portion of the date bar mix and chopped walnuts; stir in melted butter or margarine, mixing well. Spread in 13x9x2-inch baking pan. Bake at 400° for 10 minutes. Break up with a fork, cool and crumble.

Prepare date filling according to package directions; cool. Place *half* the crumb mixture in bottom of 10x6x1¾-inch baking dish. Cover with ½ cup thawed whipped dessert topping, then with date mixture. Repeat crumb and whipped topping layers. Chill several hours or overnight. Top each serving with a walnut half, if desired. Makes 8 servings.

A fast dessert idea

← Make Easy Date Crumble Torte using a package date bar mix and frozen dessert topping. Garnish with whole walnuts.

Braided Coffee Cake

1 package active dry yeast
4 to 4¼ cups sifted all-purpose
    flour
1¼ cups milk
½ cup butter or margarine
½ cup granulated sugar
1 egg

· · ·

1½ cups snipped dates
½ cup brown sugar
½ cup chopped walnuts
2 tablespoons lemon juice
1 egg yolk
2 tablespoons milk

· · ·

⅓ cup all-purpose flour
¼ cup butter or margarine
2 tablespoons granulated sugar
½ teaspoon ground cinnamon

In large bowl combine yeast and 2½ *cups* flour. Heat together 1¼ cups milk, ½ cup butter, ½ cup granulated sugar, and 1 teaspoon salt till warm, stirring to melt butter. Add to dry mixture in bowl; add egg. Beat at low speed with electric mixer for ½ minute, scraping sides of bowl. Beat 3 minutes at high speed. By hand, stir in enough remaining 1½ to 1¾ cups flour to make moderately stiff dough. Cover and refrigerate at least 2 hours or overnight.

Divide dough in half. On lightly floured surface, roll each half to 14x8-inch rectangle. Place rectangles on greased baking sheets. Spread half the Date Filling lengthwise down center third of each rectangle. Cut 12 slits, about 1 inch apart, in dough along each side of filling. Fold strips at an angle across filling, alternating from side to side. Cover; let rise till double, about 1 hour. Combine egg yolk and 2 tablespoons milk. Brush dough with egg mixture using a pastry brush. Sprinkle half the Topping on top of each coffee cake. Bake at 350° for 30 to 35 minutes. Makes 2 coffee cakes.

Date Filling: In a saucepan combine dates, brown sugar, 1 cup water, walnuts, and lemon juice. Bring to boil over medium heat, stirring constantly. Continue boiling gently, stirring occasionally, till mixture is thick enough to spread, about 8 minutes. Cool.

Topping: Combine ⅓ cup flour, ¼ cup butter or margarine, 2 tablespoons sugar, and ground cinnamon; mix well.

DAUBE *(dōb)*—A French stew of braised meat, vegetables, herbs and seasonings, and sometimes red wine. Different regions in France have specialty daubes, such as *Daube a l'Avignonnaise,* which is lamb cubes cooked in red wine with onions and bacon, and *Daube a la Provencale,* which is a beef stew containing olives, mushrooms, onions, and tomatoes.

Deep, covered earthenware, a heavy braising pot, or Dutch oven is used to cook the stew slowly on top of the range or in the oven. The procedure resembles braising. The stew is better when made a day in advance because the flavors develop more and may be served hot or cold.

DECAFFEINATED COFFEE *(dē kaf' uh nāt' uhd, - kaf' ē uh -)*—Regular, instant, or freeze-dried coffee from which almost all caffein has been extracted. Decaffeinated coffee was developed in the early 1920s to provide a coffee beverage for those people who are affected by caffeine present in regular coffee. Although the caffeine is removed from the coffee before roasting the coffee beans, manufacturers have developed special processing techniques so that the desired coffee flavor is maintained. Decaffeinated coffee is available in several forms for brewing in a coffeemaker or preparing instantly in the cup with the addition of water. (See also *Coffee.*)

DECANT *(di kant')*—The process of gently pouring red wine from its bottle into another container, leaving the sediment behind. (White wines do not collect a heavy sediment so decanting is not necessary for them.) Traditionally, a lighted candle was placed behind the bottle so that when the wine was poured out, the movement of the sediment could be observed.

Sometimes the wine is poured through a cloth to screen out the sediment, cork particles, and other impurities. Decanting should be completed at least an hour before the wine is to be served.

DECANTER—A container made of ceramic, glass, plastic, or metal in which wines, liquors, and liqueurs may be kept. These decorative vessels became popular because it was believed that the label exposing the manufacturer's or shipper's name was commercial and not a gracious way to serve guests. Most fine decanters are made of crystal and topped with an elaborate stopper. By custom, shapes vary according to use: short, squatty ones with long necks for port or sherry, sturdy taller ones for whiskies, and dainty ones for liqueurs. (See also *Wines* and *Spirits.*)

DECORETTE—This is the overall term for the tiny candies used to garnish cakes and cookies, such as chocolate shot, silver and gold dragees, and varicolored dots, shreds, and assorted shapes.

DEEP-DISH PIE—A one-crust pie (top crust only) with sliced, diced, or whole fruit filling. The sweetened, spiced fruit is placed in a deep pie pan, shallow baking pan, or individual dishes and then covered with pastry. To prevent boiling over during baking, a custard cup or small inverted cup is sometimes placed in the center to draw up some of the juices. Slashes should be made in the pastry to allow for steam to escape during baking.

In some recipes, the pie is baked in a 450° oven for 10 to 15 minutes, then reduced to 350° so both fruit and crust will bake. The result is a cross between a

The old "as American as apple pie" slogan takes on special note with this Deep-Dish Apple Pie served with Custard Sauce.

"spoon dessert" and a regular pie. A deep-dish pie is somewhat like a fruit cobbler made with a pastry rather than biscuit crust. (See also *Pie*.)

Custard-Sauced Deep-Dish Apple Pie

      8 large tart apples, peeled,
           cored, and sliced (8 cups)
    ¾ to 1 cup sugar
      1 teaspoon ground nutmeg
      1 tablespooon butter or margarine
         Plain pastry for 1-crust
           9-inch pie (See *Pastry*)
      1 cup light cream
      2 slightly beaten egg yolks
    ¼ cup sugar

Place apples in 9x9x2-inch baking dish. Combine sugar and nutmeg; sprinkle atop apples. Dot with butter. Prepare pastry; roll into a 10-inch square ⅛ inch thick. Place over filling, cutting slits for escape of steam. Crimp to edges of dish. Bake at 425° for 40 minutes.

Serve with *Custard Sauce:* Combine cream, egg yolks, and sugar in top of double boiler. Cook over hot water, stirring constantly, till mixture coats a metal spoon.

Deep-Dish Orange-Peach Pie

    ¾ cup sugar
      3 tablespoons all-purpose flour
      1 teaspoon grated orange peel
         Dash ground nutmeg
      2 cups orange sections, cut up
      1 29-ounce can sliced peaches,
           drained
      2 tablespoons butter or margarine
         Plain pastry for 1-crust 9-inch
           pie (See *Pastry*)

Combine sugar, flour, orange peel, and nutmeg. Mix with orange sections and canned peaches. Turn into 8x8x2-inch baking dish. Dot with butter or margarine.

Prepare pastry. Roll into a square, ⅛ inch thick; cut in 9-inch square. Place atop orange-peach filling, cutting slits for escape of steam. Crimp pastry to edges of baking dish. Bake at 400° about 40 minutes. Serve warm.

DEEP-FAT FRY — A cookery method in which food is completely immersed in hot fat.

One of the oldest recorded cookery methods, deep-fat frying in olive oil was used by ancient Romans. Oriental tempura dishes were also early successful beginnings of the deep-fat frying technique.

The eating quality of the food is largely dependent on the way the food is readied for frying, the type of fat used, and the frying temperature of the fat. A properly cooked deep-fat fried food has a crisp outside and a moist, tender interior. Less fat is absorbed by the product than when cooking in a smaller amount of fat because deep-fat frying is faster.

A longer cooking period and larger pieces increase the fat absorption, so pre-cooking is sometimes necessary. Cut food into small pieces (two to three inches in diameter) and fry only a few at a time so fat absorption will not be lowered and excessive bubbling will be avoided. The pieces should be somewhat uniform in size so they will fry evenly and brown nicely at the same time. Be sure to dry moist foods, such as potatoes, with paper toweling before frying, to minimize spattering.

Many kinds of foods are suited to deep frying. These include vegetables, such as potatoes, eggplant, cauliflower, squash, or onion rings; any kind of croquettes; meats and fish, such as veal, chicken, fish, or shrimp; doughnuts and crullers; fruits; and hearty and sweet fritters.

Most foods prepared for frying are coated to give them a pleasing, crunchy texture. Fine crumbs or crushed cereals adhere well to the surface during cooking. Before rolling the food in crumbs, dip in milk and egg batter. When food pieces are dipped in egg before the crumbs, let excess egg drip off, then crumb the pieces evenly. Drain batter-dipped foods on a wire cake rack before frying.

Croquettes are made by combining meats with vegetables and then coating with eggs and crumbs and fried. Excess crumbs floating in the fat will lower the temperature so make sure crumbs adhere.

Fritters are made by mixing the basic food, such as corn kernels or fruit pieces, right into a batter which is dropped into the pot from a spoon.

Dip shrimp butterflies in a curried flour mixture and then into bubbling hot fat till golden brown. Keep controlled frying temperature by frying a few shrimp at a time and removing loose particles in the fat with a slotted spoon. Drain shrimp on paper toweling. Foods prepared in this manner are sometimes called French-fried.

Remove French-Fried Butterfly Shrimp from absorbent paper to heated platter. Serve at once. Eat the crisp shrimp by picking up by the tail and biting into the meat part of shrimp. For hors d'oeuvres, serve with chutney and lemon wedges. For a main course, serve with chili or tartar sauce.

> **Fats for deep-fat frying**
>
> Fats with a high smoking point such as salad oils and all-purpose shortenings are best for deep-fat frying. Do not use olive oil, butter, or margarine. At high temperatures they give off irritating aromas and fumes.

Maintain a constant frying temperature for uniform, evenly browned food. Use tongs or a long-handled fork to remove food and place on absorbent paper toweling. Cool, strain, and refrigerate oil for future frying use. If oil has absorbed a strong flavor, such as fish, reuse it again for future frying use. (See also *Fry*.)

French-Fried Butterfly Shrimp

Peel shells from 2 pounds large raw shrimp, leaving tails. Slit shrimp along back; remove sand vein, flatten shrimp. Make cut in center back; pull tail through. Pat shrimp dry. Combine 1 cup sifted all-purpose flour, ½ teaspoon sugar, ½ teaspoon salt, and dash curry powder; add 1 egg, 1 cup water, and 2 tablespoons salad oil; beat well. Dip shrimp in batter; fry in deep hot fat (375°) till brown. Remove cooked shrimp to paper toweling to drain; serve at once. Makes 4 to 6 servings.

DEEP-FAT FRYER—A deep, heavy, three- to four-quart kettle used to fry foods in deep fat. It may be a deep saucepan, Dutch oven, electric skillet, or saucepan fitted with a long-handled wire basket and hooks to catch on pan edge, keeping basket off the bottom. A deep-fat thermometer, clipped to pan side, indicates temperature.

There is a portable electric deep-fat fryer with thermostatic temperature regulator to be used on counter or table. Besides frying, it's used for stewing, braising, pot roasting, soup making, or corn-popping. Use it to blanch vegetables for home freezing or to steam puddings, to stew dried fruits, to make applesauce, or to heat punch or chocolate drink.

Take good care of the deep-fat fryer by cleaning thoroughly after every use. Empty out fat, wipe inside with paper toweling, then wash it with hot sudsy water. Scrub out stains. Rinse thoroughly with clear water; dry well. Follow manufacturers' directions for cleaning and care instructions. (See also *Equipment*.)

DEER—A type of wild game whose edible flesh is called venison. The age of the animal is important to the meat flavor and texture. A fawn is not more than six months old and a stag is five years or older. The hunting season with regard to age and sex of deer and limit is state regulated.

Fresh deer should be hung in a cool place to age from 5 days to a month depending on age and condition of the animal. Deer cuts are the same as for beef and can be cut by a butcher. Also similar to beef cuts as far as tenderness is concerned, deer can be cooked like any other meat. Recipe for deer, moose, and elk are interchangeable. (See also *Venison*.)

DEGLAZE—Adding liquid to a roasting pan after meat and fat have been removed to loosen adhering meat bits. Wine, soup stock, or other liquid is used to remove the succulent browned particles so that they can add flavor to a gravy or sauce.

DEHYDRATION *(dē hĭ drā' shun)*—Removal of water from fruits and vegetables for preservation purposes.

A berry or fruit shriveled by the sun was probably man's first encounter with dehydrated food. People dried food thousands of years ago—Stone Age people dried legumes and Persians dried figs. Greeks and Romans used dried peas, and the early American Indian settlers dried corn.

Dehydration may be carried out in three separate ways. 1. Sun-drying is done with fruits picked at the peak of ripeness, spread on trays, and sunned for a limited time. They are moved to a shady place to cure, where the minute amount of moisture left spreads throughout the piece. 2. Dehydration is also carried out by drying food in mechanically circulated air currents, some heated then cooled; in a variety of machines; and drying chambers. Dried fruits, dried beans, and dried corn products are some of the most common dehydrated goods. 3. A recently introduced

dehydration process, known as freeze-drying, concerns the removal of water from frozen food in a vacuum. Familiar examples include camping supplies, dry soup mixes containing vegetable, and instant coffee crystals. (See also *Dried Fruit*.)

DELICIOUS APPLE—An apple discovered by Jesse Hiatt of Peru, Iowa, in 1872. Named the *Hawkeye*, it was purchased by Stark Brothers in 1895 and introduced commercially as *Delicious*. In 1900, a man named Mullins discovered a golden-yellow apple in his West Virginia orchard. Purchased also by the Stark Brothers in 1916, it was named the *Golden Delicious*. Now Delicious apples lead the national apple production with Washington state the top commercial grower of this variety.

Both varieties are recognized by the five points on the bottom. The Red Delicious apple with thick red strips against a yellow background and a pleasant subacid taste is best used for salads and desserts.

The popular Golden Delicious is more firm and tart than the Red Delicious. It can be used for pies, sauces, and baking, but remember that it is sweeter than most cooking apples so little sugar is needed. It does not brown when cut so is excellent for fruit salads. (See also *Apple*.)

DEMERARA *(de' muh ruh)*—A region in Guiana, South America, where dark, heavy, and high-proof rum is distilled, and where a special sugar is refined. (See *Rum, Sugar* for additional information.)

DEMI-GLAZE—A French term for a brown sauce simmered slowly to reduce its volume and concentrate its flavor. Flavored with wine, it is used as a base in making other sauces. (See also *Sauce*.)

DEMI-SEC—A French term for a sweet champagne or wine which is drier than sweet *doux* but sweeter than *sec* which is dry but not as dry as brut. (See also *Champagne*.)

DEMI-SEL CHEESE—A soft, creamy, lightly salted cream cheese made in Normandy, France. The fragile cheese is consumed where it is made because it is so highly perishable. (See also *Cream Cheese*.)

This delightful entertaining idea gives just reason to bring out tiny demitasse cup collections. Frosted petits fours served with the double-strength Demitasse gives miniature elegance to special occasions.

DEMITASSE *(dem' i tas', täs')* — 1. A dark, fragrant coffee usually served after dinner. 2. The small half-size cup used for serving the dark coffee. Demi means half and tasse means cup. Demitasse was traditionally served black, but cream and sugar are now acceptable additions.

The stronger brew is made by reducing the amount of water used for each standard measuring cup. Enhance the afterdinner coffee by pouring it from a handsome silver pot. Offer elegant toppings such as crushed cinnamon or peppermint candies, shredded orange peel, and fat curls of sweet baking chocolate in separate little individual bowls. Offer whipped cream and make demitasse a special dessert. Add flavor and a bit of color to the tiny drink with a teaspoon of lemon or orange juice and a twist of peel.

Demitasse may be served at cocktail time for those not wishing alcoholic drinks. However, hot demitasse mixes well with brandies and liqueurs, such as white crème de menthe, curacao, kummel, anisette, and Cointreau. (See also *Coffee*.)

Demitasse

Brew coffee as usual but use only ½ cup water, instead of usual ¾ cup, for each 2 level measuring tablespoons of coffee. (A standard coffee measure holds 2 level measuring tablespoons.)

DENVER SANDWICH — A sandwich made of eggs scrambled with ham, chopped onions, and green peppers. Also called the Western Sandwich, it was invented by the pioneers. As eggs were being transported over long, hot trails, they would start to decompose and become tainted. The alert pioneer woman would salvage the eggs and kill the strong flavor with onions, bacon fat, and any available seasonings on hand. The mixture was then served as a sandwich filling on bread.

A sophisticated version of the Denver sandwich might be an egg omelet combined with sautéed ham, onion, and green pepper. Sometimes bacon bits are used instead of ham, and the bread may or may not be toasted. (See also *Sandwich*.)

Dad's Denvers

A quick snack sandwich using canned ham, topped with eggs and broiled for hearty goodness—

Split and toast 6 hamburger buns. Spread lower half of buns with one 4½-ounce can deviled ham. Combine 4 eggs, ¼ cup milk, and dash pepper. Beat slightly for gold-and-white effect, thoroughly for all-yellow effect. Add ¼ cup chopped green onion; mix well.

Heat 2 tablespoons butter or bacon drippings in skillet till just hot enough to make water drop sizzle. Pour in beaten egg mixture. Reduce heat and cook, lifting and folding occasionally, till eggs are set, but still moist. Pile cooked eggs atop deviled ham.

Place sandwiches on baking sheet; broil about 4 inches from heat 3 to 4 minutes. Top *each* sandwich with 1 thin tomato slice and then 1 slice sharp process American cheese. Broil just till cheese melts. Cover hot sandwiches with bun tops. Makes 6 servings.

Denver Sandwich

  ¼ cup finely chopped onion
  2 tablespoons finely chopped
    green pepper
  1 tablespoon butter or margarine
  4 slightly beaten eggs
  ½ cup finely chopped fully
    cooked ham
  ¼ cup milk
  1 tablespoon chopped canned
    pimiento
  4 buns, split, buttered, and toasted,
    or 8 slices bread, buttered
    and toasted, if desired

In skillet cook onion and green pepper in butter till tender. Combine eggs, ham, milk, pimiento, dash salt, and dash pepper. Pour into skillet with onion mixture. Cook over low heat, lifting and folding occasionally, just until set. Spoon mixture between bun halves or between bread or toast slices. Makes 4 servings.

Delicious Dad's Denvers become special treats to all family members. Eggs scrambled with deviled ham and onions sport a tomato and melted cheese topper. Serve with soup or salad.

DESSERT

A guide to a delicious final course—either quick and simple or elegant and impressive.

Traditionally, the dessert is the final course served at a noonday or evening meal, but it need not be an afterthought. You can make it the course to remember.

The name is derived from the French word *desservir* meaning "to clear the table," for at one time the dessert was served after everything had been removed from the table, including the tablecloth. Later, it was served before removing the tablecloth and was accompanied by a small cup of coffee, a glass of brandy, and several cigarettes placed on a small silver tray to the right of each dinner guest.

During the nineteenth century, elaborate meals staged by the French included a spectacular array of fresh fruit arranged in decorative baskets and used as a part of the table decoration. In addition, an assortment of mouth-watering sweets surrounded the fruit baskets. Near the close of the meal, cheese was passed to accompany the wine and this was followed by a dessert of fresh fruit and sweets.

Today, national custom dictates to a large degree the pattern followed in serving dessert. In some European countries, a cheese course still precedes the sweet, which in turn is followed with fresh fruit. The English, however, prefer to serve cheese after the sweet. The traditional American dessert offers any of these— cheese, fruit, or sweet—singly or in combination, as typified by the favorite fresh apple pie with cheese wedge.

A spectacular ending

←Strawberry Meringue Cake tempts guests for second helpings. Meringue-topped cake mix sports strawberries and whipped cream.

Some desserts are linked traditionally to special celebrations or holidays. Pumpkin pie tops off the bountiful Thanksgiving Day feast, while fruitcake adds a festive air to the Christmas holiday. Cake, decorated or plain, is popular fare for birthdays, weddings, and anniversaries. In addition, fresh fruit pies and homemade ice cream mark summertime socials.

The dessert course serves many functions, one of them being the hostess's opportunity to leave a favorable impression with her dinner guests. If well planned, the dessert completes an enjoyable, yet satisfying meal. It should not dominate the food which precedes it; neither should it be lost or ignored. If the meal is hearty, a light dessert is in order; if the meal is light, a more filling dessert provides needed contrast. Thus, dessert may vary from a simple fruit cup to a dramatic flaming fruit combination served in a chafing dish.

Some desserts are rich in vitamins, minerals, and/or calories. Among the more nutritious meal-endings are those prepared with fruit, milk, and eggs. The well-planned menu takes advantage of the final course to add important nutrients to the meal—not just calories. However, in too many cases, dessert is synonymous with calories. Yet, the weight-conscious individual need not despair. Low-calorie ingredients make possible a wide variety of desserts. A further control of calories is possible with the wise selection of dessert garnishes, such as fresh fruit slices, flavored-gelatin cutouts, shredded citrus peel, ground cinnamon, ground nutmeg, or low-calorie dessert toppings.

The abundance of convenience dessert items on the market, both partially prepared and ready-to-eat, attest to the popularity of dessert in the American home.

Many homemakers prefer to devote most of the meal preparation time to the main dish; thus, convenience dessert mixes not only simplify meal preparation, but also are a boon to the cook who wishes to add variety to her repertoire of desserts.

Mixes, such as cake, cookie, frosting, piecrust, custard, dessert topping, and pudding, make possible a wide variety of desserts which can be prepared on short notice. Variations of commercial mixes are used to prepare a grand assortment of delicious desserts which often mask their simplicity. In addition, ready-to-eat canned puddings and frozen cakes, pies, and cheesecakes eliminate all preparation.

Types of desserts

The classification of desserts into types is at best overlapping. Some desserts are frozen or chilled, while others are baked, steamed, broiled, or fried. The texture may be rich and creamy, soft and delicate, light and foamy, or crisp and chewy. Flavor varies from very sweet to slightly tart. Despite these differences, certain characteristics are apparent among many desserts due to the similarity of ingredients and methods of mixing used in preparation.

Fruit desserts: Many desserts are made with fruit, fruit-flavored ingredients, or are served with fruit. However, fruit is an excellent dessert served alone and provides a simple, yet refreshing ending for lunch or dinner. In addition, it is one of the most nutritious desserts since it is relatively high in many of the essential vitamins and minerals and low in calories.

Some of the more popular desserts are a mixture of several fruits. Fruit ambrosia, in which coconut is tossed with assorted fruits, makes an attractive dessert. Likewise, compotes, made by cooking fruits in a sugary syrup, are delicious. Fruit soups may be served either as an appetizer or as a dessert. Although fruit fritters are most often served with the main course in American homes, they are popular served as the dessert course in Europe and many other sections of the world.

Fruits such as apples and rhubarb may be cooked in water till tender and then sweetened to make a dessert sauce. Other fruit sauces are served over ice cream or cake and are made by thickening the fruit syrup with a little cornstarch. The whole fruit is then stirred into the thickened liquid for an attractive sauce.

Fruit is often baked to prepare such favorites as apple dumplings, apple crisp, and apple betty. The combination of fruit with pastry is excellent as evidenced by the popularity of fruit pies, cobblers, tarts, turnovers, and shortcakes.

The different forms of fruit available—fresh, canned, frozen, and dried—as well as the wide variety of fruits make fruit desserts possible year-round. Fruit lends itself to many methods of preparation including baking, stewing, broiling, and frying. Thus, fruit may be served as simply as "an apple a day," or as elegantly as flaming Cherries Jubilee.

Cherry Melange

An elegant dessert for an evening buffet—

    1 14½-ounce can pitted dark sweet
        cherries, drained and halved *or*
        2 cups fresh dark sweet
        cherries, pitted and halved
    1 cup fresh strawberries, sliced
    1 cup cantaloupe balls (about
        ⅓ of a cantaloupe)
    1 13½-ounce can frozen pineapple
        chunks, thawed and drained
                . . .
    ½ cup orange marmalade
    ¼ cup hot water
    1 teaspoon snipped candied ginger
    1 medium-large banana, sliced
        Fresh mint

Chill dark sweet cherries, sliced strawberries, and cantaloupe balls. Layer chilled fruits and drained pineapple chunks in compote, glass bowl, or 8 sherbet glasses. Combine orange marmalade, hot water, and candied ginger. Drizzle mixture over fruit. Chill.

When ready to serve, arrange banana slices atop fruit. (To prevent banana slices from darkening, dip in lemon juice or ascorbic acid color keeper.) Garnish fruit with sprigs of fresh mint. Makes 8 servings.

Strawberry Cream

    1 3-ounce package cream cheese,
        softened
    2 tablespoons sugar
    1 cup whipping cream
      Fresh whole strawberries,
        hulled

In small mixing bowl combine cheese, sugar, dash salt, and *2 tablespoons* of the whipping cream; beat till fluffy. Whip remaining cream; carefully fold cream into cheese mixture. Spoon over berries. Makes 1¾ cups sauce.

Custard desserts: Custard provides a simple, yet versatile dessert. Often flavored with vanilla, custard is delicious served alone or topped with fruit. A delicate custard sauce is a good substitute for cream, whipped cream, or ice cream served over fruit pies, steamed puddings, or cakes. A flavorful custard dessert—crème brûlée—features stirred custard sprinkled with brown sugar; just before serving, it is placed under the broiler to caramelize the sugar. Baked custard is an equally satisfying and nutritious dessert accompanied with fruit or baked in a pastry shell.

Pumpkin Crème Brûlée

    1 cup canned pumpkin
    3 slightly beaten eggs
    ½ cup granulated sugar
    ½ teaspoon grated orange peel
    ½ teaspoon ground cinnamon
    ¼ teaspoon ground allspice
    1 14-ounce can evaporated milk
        (1⅔ cups)
    ¼ cup brown sugar

Combine first 6 ingredients; slowly stir in milk. Fill six 5-ounce custard cups; set in shallow baking pan on oven rack. Pour hot water into pan 1 inch deep. Bake at 325° till knife inserted halfway between center and edge comes out clean, 50 to 55 minutes. Chill.

Sift brown sugar over custards. Set in shallow baking pan of ice cubes and cold water. Broil 5 inches from heat till bubbly crust forms, about 5 minutes. Chill. Serves 6.

Pudding desserts: Puddings are thickened with cornstarch, tapioca, rice, bread, or other cereal. Fruit, chocolate, caramel, and nuts are often added for variety. Some puddings are baked in the oven; others are stirred in a saucepan during cooking.

Puddings thickened with cornstarch have a smooth and creamy texture and many be served warm or chilled. In addition, they may be used as fillings for cakes, pies, cream puffs, and other desserts.

Unlike other types of puddings, steamed puddings have a cakelike texture. Usually served with a hard sauce or fruit sauce, they often contain dried, canned, or fresh fruit. Delicious served warm, steamed puddings are a favorite holiday dessert.

Blueberry Steamed Pudding

    ½ cup butter or margarine
    1 cup sugar
    2 eggs
    ½ teaspoon vanilla
    2 cups sifted all-purpose flour
    3 teaspoons baking powder
    ½ teaspoon salt
    ½ teaspoon ground cinnamon
    ¾ cup milk
    2 tablespoons lemon juice
   2½ cups fresh blueberries
      Blueberry Sauce

Cream butter or margarine and sugar. Add eggs and vanilla; mix well. Sift together flour, baking powder, salt, and cinnamon. Add alternately with milk to creamed mixture, beating well after each addition. Stir in lemon juice. Fold in 1½ cups of the blueberries.

Pour into well-greased and floured 5½-cup mold. Cover with foil; tie with string. Place on rack in deep kettle. Add boiling water, 1 inch deep. Cover; steam 2 hours, adding water, if needed. Cool 20 minutes; unmold. Slice, if desired; serve warm with sauce. Serves 8.

Blueberry Sauce: Mix ½ cup sugar, 1 tablespoon cornstarch, ⅛ teaspoon ground nutmeg, and dash salt. Stir in ½ cup boiling water. Cook and stir till bubbly; cook and stir 2 minutes more. Stir in remaining 1 cup blueberries. Return to boiling; cook mixture just till berries begin to pop. Remove from heat; stir in 1 tablespoon lemon juice. Makes 1½ cups.

Cookie desserts: Cookies provide a light dessert for lunch and are ideal for boxed lunches. Prepared ahead, they can be stored in a cookie jar or frozen until needed. For a more filling dessert, they are often served with fruit or ice cream.

Cookies may also be used in preparing refrigerated or baked desserts. They add flavor and crunch when crushed to make a crumb crust for pies. Likewise, crushed gingersnaps or macaroons make a flavorful garnish sprinkled over desserts.

Cherry Cookie Crisp

    1 16-ounce can pitted tart red
        cherries (water pack)
    1 teaspoon lemon juice
        Few drops red food coloring
    ⅓ cup sugar
    ½ teaspoon ground cinnamon
    1½ cups vanilla wafer crumbs
    ⅓ cup butter or margarine, melted

Drain tart red cherries, reserving 2 tablespoons juice. Mix cherries, reserved juice, lemon juice, and few drops red food coloring. Pour into 10x 6x1¾-inch baking dish. Sprinkle mixture of sugar and cinnamon atop dessert. Combine vanilla wafer crumbs and melted butter or margarine; pat over cherries. Bake at 400° for 25 minutes. Serve dessert warm. Serves 6.

Apricot-Scotch Cobbler

    1 21-ounce can apricot pie
        filling*
    1 roll refrigerated butterscotch-
        nut cookie dough, sliced ¼
        inch thick
    1 teaspoon sugar
        Dash ground cinnamon

Heat pie filling; pour into 8-inch pie plate. Slightly overlap cookie slices atop filling around edge of pie plate. (Bake any remaining cookies separately for snacks.) Sprinkle cookies on filling with mixture of sugar and cinnamon. Bake at 350° till cookies are done, about 25 minutes. Serve warm or cold; top with ice cream, if desired. Makes 5 servings.
    *Substitute any flavor pie filling as desired.

Cake desserts: Glamorous or plain, cake is an all-time dessert favorite. Texture varies from the light and airy chiffons to the fruit-laden holiday cakes. Made in assorted sizes, shapes, and flavors, cake is often accompanied with fruit or ice cream.

Cake makes possible countless desserts, such as baked Alaskas, tortes, upside-down cakes, and jelly rolls. Cake is also popular layered with a cream filling.

Strawberry-Meringue Cake

    1 package 2-layer-size yellow
        cake mix
    1 cup orange juice
    4 egg yolks
    1 teaspoon grated orange peel
        • • •
    4 egg whites
    ¼ teaspoon cream of tartar
    1 cup sugar
    1 quart fresh strawberries,
        hulled
    2 cups whipping cream
    ¼ cup sugar

Combine cake mix, orange juice, ⅓ cup water, egg yolks, and orange peel; beat 4 minutes on medium speed of electric mixer.

Pour into 2 greased and waxed paper-lined 9x1½-inch round cake pans. Beat egg whites with cream of tartar to soft peaks; gradually add the 1 cup sugar, beating to stiff peaks. Gently spread meringue evenly over batter. Bake at 350° for 35 to 40 minutes; cool.

With flexible spatulas, carefully remove cake from pans, keeping meringue sides up. Set aside a few berries for garnish; slice remainder.

Whip cream with the ¼ cup sugar. Spread ⅔ of the whipped cream over meringue on bottom cake layer. Arrange sliced berries on whipped cream. Add top layer, meringue side up. Garnish dessert with remaining whipped cream and reserved whole strawberries.

A dessert to remember

Quick and easy Peach-Pecan Mold presents → an ice cream sundae in a new version. Prepare ahead and assemble just before serving.

Refrigerator desserts: A variety of desserts that require refrigeration before serving. Often they are prepared with flavored or unflavored gelatin combined with a fruit mixture. Chilling the dessert mixture results in the formation of a gel.

Sometimes the mixture is whipped to produce a light and airy texture characteristic of whips, sponges, Bavarian creams, and snows. The addition of beaten egg whites, whipped cream, or whipped evaporated milk further increases the volume of the final dessert product.

Desserts such as cheesecakes and tortes are baked and then chilled before serving. Likewise, parfait and chiffon pies must be refrigerated until they are firm.

Refrigerator desserts are easy to serve since they can be prepared in advance. For added convenience, some may be chilled in individual serving dishes.

Snowflake Pudding

        1 cup sugar
     1½ tablespoons unflavored gelatin
     1¼ cups milk
        1 teaspoon vanilla
     1⅓ cups flaked coconut
        2 cups whipping cream
          Raspberry Sauce

In saucepan combine sugar, gelatin, and ½ teaspoon salt; add milk. Stir over medium heat till gelatin dissolves. Chill till partially set.

Stir in vanilla. Fold in coconut. Whip cream; fold into pudding. Pile into 6½-cup mold; chill till firm, at least 6 hours or overnight. Unmold; serve with Raspberry Sauce. Serves 8.

Raspberry Sauce: Thaw and crush one 10-ounce package frozen raspberries. Combine with 1 tablespoon cornstarch. Add ½ cup currant jelly. Cook, stirring constantly, till thick and bubbly; cook and stir 1 minute more. Strain sauce; cool. Makes 1¼ cups sauce.

Cool and refreshing

←Chilled Cherry Melange or frosty Strawberry Parfaits provide the perfect ending for a summertime luncheon or barbecue.

Frozen desserts: Ice cream, ice milk, and sherbet are favorite desserts served from the freezer. Their popularity is apparent by the wide variety of flavors available in supermarkets and ice cream shops. When prepared at home, they are considered a specialty. Other home-frozen desserts include mousses and parfaits.

Ice cream is a quick and easy dessert topped with fruit or sauce. Moreover, pies, cakes, and other desserts are sometimes served à la mode. Slightly lower in calories, sherbet provides a refreshing dessert at the end of a heavy meal.

Ice cream and sherbet may also be used in preparing baked Alaska. The meringue acts as an insulator to prevent the ice cream from melting during baking.

Strawberry Parfaits

        1 pint fresh strawberries, hulled
     1½ teaspoons unflavored gelatin
        2 tablespoons cold water
        2 cups buttermilk
     ¾ cup sugar
     ½ teaspoon vanilla
        1 to 2 drops red food coloring
              • • •
        2 egg whites
     ⅓ cup sugar
              • • •
        1 pint fresh strawberries, hulled

Put 1 pint strawberries through food mill or sieve to make puree. Soften gelatin in cold water; heat over hot water till gelatin dissolves. Combine buttermilk, ¾ cup sugar, strawberry puree, vanilla, food coloring, and gelatin; mix well. Turn into one 6-cup or two 3-cup refrigerator trays; freeze firm. Break into chunks; turn into chilled bowl.

Beat smooth with electric or rotary beater. Beat egg whites till soft peaks form. Gradually add ⅓ cup sugar, beating to stiff peaks.

Fold into strawberry mixture. Return mixture to cold refrigerator tray; freeze firm.

To serve, reserve a few whole strawberries from 1 pint strawberries; slice remaining berries and sweeten to taste. Spoon frozen mixture and sliced berries alternately into parfait glasses. Garnish with reserved whole berries. Serve immediately. Makes 7 or 8 servings.

Peach–Pecan Mold

　1 **quart vanilla ice cream**
　2 **teaspoons rum flavoring**
½ **cup chopped pecans**
　　Pecan halves
　　Peach Sauce

Stir ice cream to soften. Stir in flavoring and chopped nuts. Arrange a few pecan halves in top of 4½-cup mold. Add ice cream; freeze till firm, about 6 hours. To unmold, invert on serving plate; press hot damp towel around mold to loosen. If desired, garnish with pressurized dessert topping and thawed frozen sliced peaches. Serve with Peach Sauce.

Peach Sauce: In saucepan stir one 12-ounce can peach nectar (1½ cups) into 1 tablespoon cornstarch. Add ¼ cup light corn syrup. Cook and stir till thick and bubbly; cook and stir 2 minutes longer. Stir in 1 tablespoon butter, 1 tablespoon lemon juice, and dash ground mace; cool. Just before serving, add one 12-ounce package frozen peaches, thawed, drained, and coarsely chopped. Makes 6 to 8 servings.

Strawberry Squares

　1 **cup sifted all-purpose flour**
¼ **cup brown sugar**
½ **cup chopped walnuts**
½ **cup butter or margarine, melted**
　2 **egg whites**
　1 **cup granulated sugar**
　2 **cups sliced fresh strawberries***
　2 **tablespoons lemon juice**
　1 **cup whipping cream**

Stir together first 4 ingredients; spread evenly in shallow baking pan. Bake at 350° for 20 minutes; stir occasionally. Sprinkle ⅔ *of the crumbs* in 13x9x2-inch baking pan.

Combine egg whites, granulated sugar, berries, and lemon juice in large bowl. With electric mixer beat at high speed to stiff peaks, about 10 minutes. Whip cream; fold into berry mixture. Spoon over crumbs; top with remaining crumbs. Freeze 6 hours or overnight. Cut in squares. Trim with whole strawberries, if desired. Makes 10 to 12 servings.

*Or use one 10-ounce package frozen strawberries, partially thawed (undrained); reduce granulated sugar to ⅔ cup.

Pastry desserts: No doubt, pie is the all-American dessert. Prepared with a variety of fillings, pastry-filled desserts range from the light and airy chiffons to the more robust fruit or frozen ice cream pies. Cream-filled pies topped with meringue and custard-type pies are additional favorites. Pastry is also used for cobblers, tarts, turnovers, and dumplings.

Puff pastry, unlike pastry for pies, produces a rich, flaky dough which expands greatly as it bakes. Napoleons are made from puff pastry. The pastry is baked, then separated into layers and spread with a custard-type filling. The pastry layers are reassembled to complete the dessert. Turnovers and Danish kringle are also prepared from puff pastry.

Brazilian Pie

⅓ **cup sugar**
　1 **envelope unflavored gelatin**
　　(1 tablespoon)
　1 **tablespoon instant coffee**
　　powder
¼ **teaspoon ground nutmeg**
　　Dash salt
　3 **slightly beaten egg yolks**
　1 **14½-ounce can evaporated**
　　milk (1⅔ cups)
½ **teaspoon vanilla**
　　　　• • •
　3 **egg whites**
⅓ **cup sugar**
　1 *baked* **9-inch pastry shell,**
　　cooled
　　　　• • •
½ **cup whipping cream**
　3 **tablespoons grated unsweetened**
　　chocolate

In saucepan combine first 5 ingredients. In bowl combine beaten egg yolks and evaporated milk. Add to gelatin mixture. Cook and stir till gelatin dissolves and mixture thickens slightly. Stir in vanilla. Chill, stirring occasionally, till partially set. Beat smooth.

Beat egg whites till soft peaks form. Gradually add ⅓ cup sugar, beating to stiff peaks. Fold in gelatin mixture. Pile into pastry shell. Chill till firm. To serve, whip cream. Spread atop pie; sprinkle with grated chocolate.

Mile High Ice Cream Pie

1½ cups sifted all-purpose flour
½ teaspoon salt
½ cup shortening
4 to 5 tablespoons cold water

• • •

1 pint vanilla ice cream
1 pint chocolate ice cream

• • •

3 egg whites
½ teaspoon vanilla
¼ teaspoon cream of tartar
6 tablespoons sugar

• • •

4 1-ounce squares unsweetened
    chocolate
¾ cup water
1 cup sugar
    Dash salt
6 tablespoons butter or margarine
1 teaspoon vanilla

To prepare pastry, sift together flour and ½ teaspoon salt; cut in shortening with pastry blender till pieces are the size of small peas. Sprinkle 1 tablespoon cold water over part of mixture. Gently toss with fork; push to side of bowl. Repeat with remaining 3 to 4 tablespoons cold water till all is moistened.

Form into a ball. On lightly floured surface, roll to ⅛-inch thickness. Fit pastry into 9-inch pie plate; trim to 1 inch beyond edge. Fold edge under and flute. Prick bottom and sides with fork. Bake at 450° till golden, about 10 to 12 minutes. Cool pastry shell.

In cooled pie shell, layer vanilla ice cream, then chocolate ice cream.

To prepare meringue, beat egg whites with ½ teaspoon vanilla and cream of tartar till soft peaks form. Gradually add 6 tablespoons sugar, beating till stiff and glossy and sugar is dissolved. Spread meringue over ice cream, carefully sealing to edges of pastry. Bake at 475° till golden, about 4 to 5 minutes. Freeze pie several hours or overnight.

To prepare sauce, heat chocolate and ¾ cup water together over low heat, stirring constantly till melted and smooth. Stir in 1 cup sugar and dash salt; simmer till slightly thickened, about 5 minutes. Remove from heat; blend in butter and 1 teaspoon vanilla.

To serve, slice pie in wedges. Drizzle warm chocolate sauce over each serving.

Serving desserts

Always serve desserts attractively regardless of the occasion. With a little imagination, a plain dessert can often glamorize a meal for guests. You as a hostess will be much more at ease serving guests a favorite family dessert than if you prepare an unfamiliar dessert just because it may appear more elegant. For example, a simple fruit cup becomes a sophisticated dessert served in hollowed-out orange shells. And a simple fruit mixture is transformed into a flaming delight when served up in a chafing dish at the table. Likewise, individual tarts can replace the family's favorite pie for a company dessert.

Since dessert is served at the end of the meal, it is better to offer small helpings (with the invitation for seconds) than to serve too much to be enjoyed the first time around. Another important consideration for serving dessert is the temperature of the food. Some desserts are best served warm, while others should be eaten chilled; however, avoid extreme serving temperatures. Frozen desserts are best if allowed to stand at room temperature for a few minutes before they are served.

Desserts for mealtime: A well-planned menu includes a dessert compatible with the rest of the meal. Avoid repeating a food flavor which has already been served in the meal. Thus, if applesauce is served during the meal, it is better to select a dessert which doesn't include apples. Likewise, if two or more foods in the meal are accompanied with a sauce, plan a dessert which does not require a sauce.

The complexity of the meal determines to a great degree the type of dessert which is served. Many desserts can be prepared ahead of the meal so that more time can be devoted to the rest of the meal.

A simple dessert such as fruit or sherbet is an excellent way to end a heavy meal. Rich desserts are best served at the close of a light meal. Furthermore, respect for special diets and religious observances followed by family members or guests should be considered when planning the menu. Thus, dessert is a part of the total menu and provides a pleasant ending to the meal.

```
┌─────────────────────────────┐
│        ❦MENU❦               │
│                             │
│      SATURDAY LUNCH         │
│   Grilled Reuben Sandwiches │
│        Potato Chips         │
│    Celery and Carrot Sticks │
│ Baked Ambrosia or Hawaiian Fruit Crumble │
│  Coffee            Milk     │
└─────────────────────────────┘
```

```
┌─────────────────────────────┐
│        ❦MENU❦               │
│                             │
│        HAM DINNER           │
│      Broiled Ham Slice      │
│ Creamed Peas and New Potatoes │
│     Fresh Fruit Salad       │
│    Fast Crème Brûlée        │
│  Coffee            Milk     │
└─────────────────────────────┘
```

Baked Ambrosia

   1   16-ounce can apricot halves
   1   16-ounce can peach halves
   1   16-ounce can purple plums
   3 or 4 thin orange slices, halved
   ½   cup orange juice
   ¼   cup brown sugar
   ½   teaspoon shredded lemon peel
   2   tablespoons butter or margarine,
       melted
   ½   cup flaked coconut

Thoroughly drain apricots, peaches, and plums.
Arrange drained fruit with orange slices in a
shallow baking dish. In small bowl combine
orange juice, brown sugar, and shredded lemon
peel; pour mixture over fruit.

Drizzle melted butter or margarine over
plums; sprinkle flaked coconut over all fruit.
Bake at 425° till hot and coconut is toasted,
about 15 minutes. Serve warm. Serves 8.

Hawaiian Fruit Crumble

Toss 2 cups sliced, peeled tart apples with 1
tablespoon lemon juice; place in 10x6x1¾-inch
baking dish. Spoon one 8¾-ounce can crushed
pineapple, drained (¾ cup), evenly over
apples; spread one 16-ounce can whole cranberry sauce (2 cups) atop pineapple.

For topping, mix 1 cup quick-cooking rolled
oats, ¾ cup brown sugar, ½ cup all-purpose
flour, ½ teaspoon ground cinnamon, and dash
salt; cut in ⅓ cup butter or margarine till
crumbly. Sprinkle crumb mixture over fruit.
Bake at 350° till apples are tender, about 30
minutes. Serve warm. Makes 6 servings.

Fast Crème Brûlée

   1   3- or 3¼-ounce package *regular*
       vanilla pudding mix
   ½   cup whipping cream
   ½   cup brown sugar

Prepare pudding mix according to package
directions, *except use 1¾ cups milk*. Cool.

Whip cream. Fold into cooled pudding. Pour
mixture into 9-inch pie plate. Chill.

Sprinkle brown sugar evenly over top. Place
pie plate in shallow pan. Surround with ice
cubes and a little cold water; broil 5 inches
from heat till bubbly brown crust forms on
top, about 5 minutes. Chill. Serves 4 to 6.

Desserts for entertaining: Elegant and sophisticated desserts are often served when
entertaining guests. These desserts may
involve more preparation but should still
complement the rest of the meal.

Contemporary entertaining, however,
may not involve a complete meal. Thus,
desserts are a popular refreshment for
such occasions. More elaborate desserts
which may require last-minute preparation
are possible since the hostess is not in-
volved with the preparation of a meal.

Tortes, cheesecakes, shortcakes, parfaits, éclairs, Napoleons, baked Alaskas,
soufflés, dessert pancakes, and cream puffs
make impressive desserts for special occasions. For a large group, an assortment
of desserts may be offered buffet style.
Often very rich, these desserts are best
served in small portions and accompanied
by coffee, tea, or other suitable beverages.

Chocolate-Pecan Cornucopias

 2 sticks piecrust mix
 ¼ cup sugar
 1 tablespoon instant coffee
    powder
 1 cup whipping cream
 ½ cup grated sweet cooking
    chocolate
 ⅓ cup chopped pecans
    Pecan halves

Prepare pastry according to package directions. Roll to a 16x12-inch rectangle; cut into twelve 4-inch squares with pastry wheel. Roll each square to form a cone. For each pastry cone, fold a paper towel in quarters; shape into a cone. Insert paper cone in each pastry cone. Place on baking sheet; bake at 425° till golden brown, about 12 minutes. Remove paper toweling; cool cornucopias on rack.

Meanwhile, combine sugar, coffee powder, dash salt, and a little of the cream; stir till blended. Add remaining cream; chill. Whip till almost stiff. Fold in chocolate and chopped pecans. Spoon mixture into cornucopias; garnish with pecan halves. Makes 12 servings.

Heavenly Torte

 1 7-ounce jar marshmallow creme
 1 tablespoon hot water
 1½ teaspoons instant coffee powder
 1 teaspoon vanilla
 1 cup whipping cream
      •   •   •
 1 10-inch angel cake
 ½ 1-ounce square semisweet
    chocolate, shaved (3 tablespoons)
 2 tablespoons slivered almonds,
    toasted*

In small mixer bowl combine marshmallow creme, hot water, coffee powder, and vanilla. Beat at low speed of electric mixer till blended, then beat at high speed till fluffy.

Whip cream till soft peaks form. Fold whipped cream into marshmallow mixture.

Slice angel cake crosswise into three layers. Frost top of each layer with ⅓ of the marshmallow filling, then sprinkle with ⅓ of the shaved chocolate. Assemble frosted layers on cake plate; garnish top with toasted almonds.

*To toast, spread almonds on cookie sheet. Bake at 325° for 15 minutes; stir occasionally.

Chocolate-Pecan Cornucopias make a sophisticated dessert for entertaining. Cut and shaped from pastry mix, cornucopia shells boast a rich, mocha filling flecked with pecans.

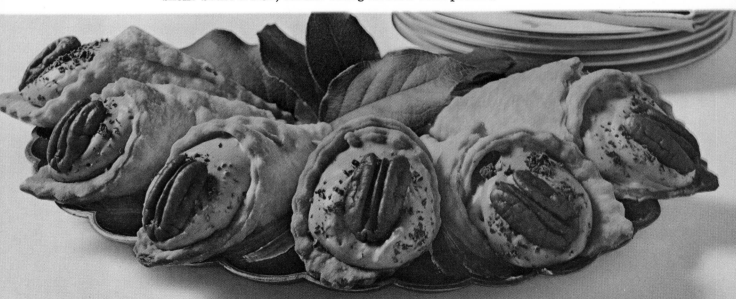

```
┌─────────────────────────────┐
│          ❦MENU❦             │
│      HOLIDAY DINNER          │
│    Standing Rib Roast        │
│ Oven-Browned Potatoes  Brussels Sprouts │
│   Molded Cranberry Salad     │
│ Brown-and-Serve Dinner Rolls  Butter │
│    Lemon Angel Torte         │
│        Coffee                │
└─────────────────────────────┘
```

```
┌─────────────────────────────┐
│          ❦MENU❦             │
│      COMPANY DINNER          │
│    Broiled T-Bone Steaks     │
│  Baked Potatoes with Sour Cream │
│    Tossed Green Salad        │
│      Garlic Bread            │
│ Cherries Portofino or Company Cheesecake │
│        Coffee                │
└─────────────────────────────┘
```

Lemon Angel Torte

    4 egg whites
    ¼ teaspoon cream of tartar
    ¾ cup sugar
        . . .
    4 egg yolks
    1 tablespoon grated lemon peel
    3 tablespoons lemon juice
    ½ cup sugar
        . . .
    1 cup whipping cream

For shell: Preheat oven to 450°. Beat whites with electric mixer till foamy; add cream of tartar and ¼ teaspoon salt. Slowly add ¾ cup sugar; beat to stiff peaks, about 7 minutes. Spread in buttered 9-inch pie plate, forming edge. Place in preheated oven; turn off heat. Let stand in *closed* oven 4 hours or overnight.

For filling: In top of double boiler beat egg yolks till thick and lemon-colored. Gradually beat in lemon peel, lemon juice, ½ cup sugar, and dash salt. Cook and stir over gently boiling water till thick, about 8 minutes. Remove from heat; cover and cool.

To assemble: Whip cream. Spread *half* of the whipped cream in shell; cover with filling. Top with remaining whipped cream, covering edges. Wrap loosely; chill 3 hours or overnight.

Easy and elegant

← Creamy coffee-flavored filling dotted with shaved chocolate oozes from between layers of angel cake in Heavenly Torte dessert.

Cherries Portofino

    1 16-ounce can pitted dark sweet cherries
    ½ cup port
    2 3-ounce packages raspberry-flavored gelatin
    2 cups boiling water
    1 quart vanilla ice cream, softened

Drain cherries, reserving syrup. Combine drained cherries and wine; let stand 3 hours.

Dissolve gelatin in boiling water. Drain cherries, reserving wine. Combine wine with reserved cherry juice and enough cold water to make 1½ cups. Stir into dissolved gelatin. Chill till partially set. Stir in cherries. Pour into 11¾x7½x1¾-inch dish. Chill till firm.

To serve, cut into cubes; spoon into sherbet glasses. Top with ice cream. Serves 8.

Company Cheesecake

Combine 1¾ cups fine graham cracker crumbs; ¼ cup finely chopped walnuts; ½ teaspoon ground cinnamon; and ½ cup butter or margarine, melted. Press on bottom and ⅔ of the way up sides of 9-inch springform pan.

Combine 3 well-beaten eggs; two 8-ounce packages cream cheese, softened; 1 cup sugar; ¼ teaspoon salt; 2 teaspoons vanilla; and ¼ teaspoon almond extract. Beat till smooth.

Blend in 3 cups dairy sour cream. Pour into crust. Bake at 375° till set, about 35 minutes; cool. Chill 4 to 5 hours. (Filling will be soft.) Makes 12 to 16 servings.

DESSERT SAUCE—A thickened sauce, usually sweetened, that tops a dessert.

Dessert sauces can spark a wide array of dessert foods by providing the extra touch that turns an ordinary dessert into a dazzling delight. Ice creams and sherbets, pies, cakes, and fruits or fruit-based desserts are frequently dressed up with a sauce. In fact, an intriguing sauce served over a simple base, such as vanilla ice cream or yellow cake, often develops into the star course of a menu.

The most common dessert foods served with a sauce are ice cream and sherbet. Often a spectacular display is created by spooning flaming sauces over each portion. Chocolate or fruit-filled sauces can be the beginnings for rich ice cream sundaes and multi-layered parfaits.

Cakes, particularly when unfrosted, and pies can also be glamorized with the addition of a sauce. Cake that has started to dry is revived to moistening goodness by spooning a sauce over each slice. A luscious fruit sauce with a dollop of whipped cream atop is an attractive finish to a serving of light lemon chiffon pie.

Don't forget the easy way to brighten fruit desserts either. A thick custard or lemon sauce transforms a fresh fruit cup finale into a rare treat. Lemon and custard sauces are also traditional crowning touches for fruit-filled steamed puddings and oven-fresh cottage puddings.

Sauces not only give desserts a more glamorous touch but also are a quick and convenient way to create a last-minute refreshment. Many sauces are prepared in advance, then stored in the refrigerator. These sauces are then served right from the refrigerator; a quick reheating brings the sauces back to their original delicious state. (See also *Sauce*.)

Marshmallow Sauce

½ 1-pint jar marshmallow creme
¼ cup pineapple juice

Spoon marshmallow creme into small mixer bowl. Gradually add pineapple juice, beating at high speed of electric mixer till thickened, about 5 minutes. Makes 1 cup.

Golden Raisin Flambé

A chafing dish specialty that's easy to fix, yet decidedly glamorous and delicious—

½ cup light raisins

• • •

¼ cup brandy
3 tablespoons brown sugar
¼ teaspoon grated lemon peel
1 tablespoon lemon juice

• • •

¼ cup brandy
   Vanilla ice cream

In saucepan cover raisins with water. Bring to boiling; simmer 5 minutes. Drain. Add the first ¼ cup brandy, brown sugar, lemon peel, and lemon juice. Cover; let stand at least 1 hour.

At serving time transfer raisin mixture to blazer pan of small chafing dish. Bring to boiling over direct heat. In small saucepan heat remaining ¼ cup brandy. Ignite; spoon over sauce. Serve raisin sauce over vanilla ice cream. Makes 6 servings.

Melted peppermint-flavored marshmallows impart a creamy smoothness and refreshing flavor to Mallow-Mint Sauce.

Mallow-Mint Sauce

- 3 cups peppermint-flavored marshmallows (29 marshmallows)
- 1 tablespoon butter or margarine
- 1 6-ounce can evaporated milk
  (⅔ cup)
- ¼ teaspoon vanilla
- 2 or 3 drops red food coloring
  Vanilla ice cream

In top of double boiler combine marshmallows, butter, and ¼ *cup* of the evaporated milk. Cook and stir over hot water till marshmallows melt and mixture is smooth; remove from heat. Stir in remaining evaporated milk, vanilla, and red food coloring; mix well. Serve sauce warm over vanilla ice cream. Garnish with mint sprigs, if desired. Makes 1¼ cups.

Candied Ginger Sauce

- ½ cup sugar
- ¼ cup orange-flavored breakfast
  drink powder
- 2 tablespoons cornstarch
- 2 tablespoons finely snipped
  candied ginger
  Dash salt
- 1½ cups water
- 2 tablespoons butter or margarine

In saucepan combine sugar, drink powder, cornstarch, candied ginger, and salt. Gradually stir in water, blending well. Bring to boiling; boil for 2 minutes, stirring constantly. Remove from heat. Blend in butter or margarine; cool. (If refrigerated, stir sauce well before serving.) Makes 1¾ cups.

Golden Apricot Sauce

- 1 30-ounce can apricot halves
- ¾ cup sugar
- ¼ cup orange juice
- ½ teaspoon almond extract

Drain apricots, reserving ½ cup syrup. Cut up apricots and stir in reserved syrup, sugar, orange juice, and dash salt. Simmer 10 minutes, stirring occasionally. Stir in extract; chill. Serve over ice cream. Makes 2 cups.

Cherry Sauce

- ¾ cup sugar
- 2 tablespoons cornstarch
  Dash salt
- 1 20-ounce can pitted tart
  red cherries, undrained
- 10 drops red food coloring

Combine sugar, cornstarch, and salt. Stir in undrained cherries. Cook quickly, stirring constantly, till mixture is thickened and bubbly. Reduce heat; cook 1 minute more. Add food coloring. Serve warm. Makes 2¾ cups.

Mocha Sauce

- 1 cup sugar
- ⅓ cup unsweetened cocoa powder
- 1 tablespoon cornstarch
- 1 tablespoon instant coffee powder

  • • •

- 1 14½-ounce can evaporated milk
- ¼ teaspoon vanilla
  Vanilla ice cream

In saucepan combine sugar, cocoa, cornstarch, and coffee powder. Gradually stir in milk. Cook, stirring constantly, till mixture is thickened and bubbly. Remove from heat; stir in vanilla. Spoon over ice cream. Makes 6 servings.

Nutmeg-Pineapple Sauce

- ½ cup granulated sugar
- ½ cup brown sugar
- ½ cup light corn syrup
- ¼ cup butter or margarine
- ½ teaspoon ground nutmeg

  • • •

- 1 13½-ounce can pineapple
  tidbits, drained
- ¼ teaspoon vanilla
- 10 slices sponge cake, angel cake,
  pound cake, *or* vanilla
  ice cream

In saucepan combine granulated sugar, brown sugar, corn syrup, butter, and nutmeg. Cook, stirring constantly, till mixture boils. Stir in pineapple and vanilla. Spoon hot pineapple sauce over cake or ice cream. Makes 10 servings.

Quick Fudge Sauce

1 6-ounce package semisweet
   chocolate pieces (1 cup)
1 6-ounce can evaporated milk
   (⅔ cup)
½ 1-pint jar marshmallow creme

In saucepan combine chocolate pieces and evaporated milk. Cook and stir over low heat till well combined. Beat in marshmallow creme till mixture is thoroughly blended. Serve warm or cool. Makes 2 cups.

Peanut Butter-Marshmallow Sauce

1 5½-ounce package peanut butter
   pieces (1 cup)
½ cup light cream
½ cup miniature marshmallows
1 teaspoon vanilla
   Toasted coconut

Melt peanut butter pieces in light cream over low heat, stirring constantly. Add marshmallows, stirring till melted. Remove from heat; add vanilla. Serve warm or chilled. Top each serving with coconut. Makes 1½ cups.

Creamy Butterscotch Sauce

½ cup butter or margarine
2 cups brown sugar
1 cup light corn syrup
1 15-ounce can sweetened
   condensed milk (1⅓ cups)
1 teaspoon vanilla

In saucepan melt butter; stir in sugar, corn syrup, and 2 tablespoons water. Bring to boiling. Stir in milk; simmer, stirring constantly, till mixture reaches thread stage (230°). Add vanilla. Serve warm over ice cream or cake.

DESSERT TOPPING—A light, fluffy foam whipped from a dairy or non-dairy base and used like whipped cream. Dessert toppings may be purchased in several forms: in the prewhipped and frozen state, in aerosol cans, as a dry mix, or as a liquid. The first two types require no pre-preparation. The dry mix, on the other hand, must be combined with milk prior to whipping, while the liquid dessert topping is simply whipped to soft peaks.

Dessert toppings have gained considerably in popularity because they are low in cost. Many maintain a stable foam for many days when refrigerated. And others are pleasingly light in calorie content.

Banana Split Pie

3 medium bananas
1 tablespoon lemon juice
1 9-inch *baked* pastry shell, cooled
   (see *Pastry*)
1 pint strawberry ice cream
   • • •
1 cup frozen whipped dessert
   topping, thawed
   Whole maraschino cherries
2 tablespoons finely chopped
   walnuts
   Canned chocolate sauce

Thinly slice bananas; sprinkle with lemon juice and arrange on bottom of baked pastry shell. Stir strawberry ice cream to soften slightly; spread atop bananas. Freeze till firm. Spread dessert topping over ice cream. Top with cherries; sprinkle with nuts. Freeze firm.

Let frozen pie stand 30 minutes at room temperature before serving. Spoon canned chocolate sauce over each serving.

Mocha-Velvet Torte

1 12-ounce loaf pound cake
1 4½-ounce package *instant*
   chocolate pudding mix
1 2-ounce package dessert topping
   mix
1 tablespoon instant coffee powder
1¼ cups cold milk

Slice cake horizontally in 4 layers. For frosting combine pudding mix, dessert topping mix, instant coffee powder, and milk in mixing bowl. Beat till fluffy and of spreading consistency. Spread three layers of cake with frosting; stack together and top with fourth layer. Frost top and sides of cake. Chill. Serves 10.

Lime-Pear Mold

Drain one 16-ounce can pear halves, reserving pear syrup; add enough water to syrup to make 1 cup liquid. Dissolve one 3-ounce package lime-flavored gelatin in 1 cup boiling water; stir in reserved pear syrup. Chill gelatin mixture till partially set.

Slice 3 pear halves and arrange around side of 5½- or 6½-cup mold, pointed end down; pour in ½ *cup* lime gelatin. Chill till *almost* firm. Dice remaining pear halves and add to remaining lime gelatin; let stand at room temperature. Spoon gelatin-pear mixture gently over chilled gelatin; chill again till *almost* firm.

Prepare one 2-ounce package dessert topping mix according to package directions. Beat 1½ cups small curd cream-style cottage cheese with electric mixer till smooth; fold into whipped topping. In small saucepan soften 1 envelope unflavored gelatin (1 tablespoon) in ¼ cup cold water; heat and stir over low heat till gelatin is dissolved. Stir into cottage cheese mixture. Pour gelatin-cottage cheese mixture over almost firm gelatin in mold. Chill till firm. Makes 8 servings.

Chocolate Angel with Lime Fluff

Prepare 1 package angel cake mix, stirring ⅓ cup unsweetened cocoa powder into dry mix for a one-step cake or into flour mixture for a two-step cake. In saucepan beat 2 eggs; stir in ½ of 6-ounce can frozen limeade concentrate, thawed, and ⅓ cup sugar. Cook and stir till mixture is thickened; add 2 drops green food coloring and cool lime mixture thoroughly.

Prepare ½ of 2½-ounce package low-calorie dessert topping mix (1 envelope) according to package directions. Fold in lime mixture; chill. Serve over angel cake wedges. Serves 12.

DEVEIN—To remove the black vein which runs down the back of a shrimp. Deveining is easily accomplished by making a slit down the shrimp's back with a sharp knife. Under cold running water, carefully scrape the vein away with the knife.

DEVILED—1. A broiled version of poultry. 2. A highly seasoned mixture that is most generally finely chopped.

Frilly radish roses, ripe olives, and Classic Deviled Eggs make an eye-appealing garnish for Chaud-Froid of Turkey (See *Chaud-Froid*). Leaf lettuce liners facilitate serving.

When deviled refers to the way in which poultry is cooked, the recipe usually includes the title *à la Diable*. To prepare poultry in this manner, the bird is slit down the back, spread flat, and pounded. The exposed surfaces are brushed with butter or oil, seasoned, and then the bird is broiled. Just before the end of the cooking period, soft bread crumbs are liberally sprinkled over the bird. Broiling continues until the topping is browned.

The more familiar usage of deviled implies a highly seasoned food. A zippy flavor is achieved by the use of hot seasonings, such as black and cayenne pepper, hot pepper sauce, Worcestershire sauce, mustard, horseradish, or garlic. Classic Deviled Eggs is probably the best-known recipe illustrating this term.

Classic Deviled Eggs

    6 hard-cooked eggs, halved
        lengthwise
    ¼ cup mayonnaise or salad
        dressing
    1 tablespoon finely chopped onion
    1 tablespoon finely chopped
        pimiento-stuffed green
        olives (optional)*
    1½ teaspoons prepared mustard

Remove egg yolks from whites. Mash yolks; blend with mayonnaise, onion, olives, mustard, ⅛ teaspoon salt, and dash pepper. Refill whites, using pastry tube, if desired. Chill. Garnish with paprika, if desired. Makes 12.

*Or, substitute crisp-cooked and crumbled bacon, chopped canned pimiento, snipped chives, sweet pickle, *or* snipped parsley.

Baked Deviled Tomatoes

Place 8 large tomato halves, cut side up, in baking dish. Sprinkle with a little salt. Spread tops with 1 tablespoon prepared mustard. Combine 2 tablespoons chopped green pepper; 2 tablespoons chopped celery; 1 tablespoon chopped green onion; and 2 tablespoons butter or margarine, melted. Spoon over tomatoes. Bake at 425° for 8 to 10 minutes. Makes 8 servings.

Red Deviled Eggs

    6 hard-cooked eggs
    2 tablespoons mayonnaise or
        salad dressing
    1 teaspoon grated onion
    1 teaspoon prepared mustard
    ½ teaspoon Worcestershire sauce
    1 2¼-ounce can deviled ham
      Salt
      Pepper

Cut tops off eggs; remove yolks and mash. Mix with mayonnaise, onion, mustard, Worcestershire sauce, and deviled ham. Add salt and pepper to taste. Fill eggs with deviled mixture, using pastry tube, if desired. Makes 12.

Deviled Hamburgers

    ⅓ cup chili sauce
    1 tablespoon chopped onion
    1 teaspoon prepared horseradish
    1 teaspoon prepared mustard
    ½ teaspoon Worcestershire sauce
    1 pound ground beef
    8 slices bread

Combine first 5 ingredients and ¾ teaspoon salt. Add ground beef; mix well. Trim crusts from bread slices; toast one side. Spread each untoasted side with ¼ cup meat; spread to edges. Broil 5 to 6 minutes. Serves 4.

Hot Deviled Potatoes

      Packaged instant mashed
        potatoes (enough for 4
        servings)
    ½ cup dairy sour cream
              • • •
    2 teaspoons prepared mustard
    ½ teaspoon salt
    ½ teaspoon sugar
    2 tablespoons chopped green onion

Prepare potatoes according to package directions. Heat sour cream (do not boil). Add mustard, salt, and sugar; stir to blend. Mix into hot potatoes with onion. Turn into 1-quart casserole. Sprinkle with paprika, if desired. Bake at 350° about 10 minutes. Serves 5.

Deviled Swiss Steak

¼ cup all-purpose flour
1½ teaspoons dry mustard
1 3-pound beef round steak,
  1½ inches thick
¼ cup salad oil
1 tablespoon Worcestershire sauce
1 3-ounce can mushroom crowns,
  drained (½ cup)
Butter or margarine

Combine flour, 2 teaspoons salt, mustard, and ¼ teaspoon pepper. Sprinkle mixture over meat; pound in with meat mallet. In heavy skillet brown steak slowly on both sides in hot oil. Combine ½ cup water and Worcestershire; add to meat. Cover tightly and cook over very low heat till tender, about 1¾ to 2 hours.

Remove steak to platter. Heat mushrooms in a little butter; serve with steak. Skim fat from meat juices; serve juices with steak. Garnish with parsley, if desired. Serves 6 to 8.

DEVILED HAM — A canned mixture of ground or minced fully cooked ham and seasonings. Deviled ham makes a convenient sandwich spread, or it can be the basis for appetizers and main dishes.

Deviled Ham-Bean Bake

1 16-ounce can pork and beans
  in tomato sauce
1 8-ounce can tomatoes, well
  drained (½ cup)
1 4½-ounce can deviled ham
½ cup chopped onion
1 tablespoon molasses
1 teaspoon prepared mustard
Dash salt

Combine pork and beans, tomatoes, ham, onion, molasses, mustard, and salt in a 1-quart casserole and bake, uncovered, at 350° for 1½ hours. Makes 6 servings.

Deviled Swiss Steak cooks to ideal juiciness and tenderness due to slow braising in a Worcestershire sauce and dry mustard-spiced liquid. Garnish with mushroom crowns and parsley.

Deviled Ham contains ground cooked ham and seasonings.

Deviled Ham Dip

This zesty dip, studded with onion and olives, also makes a delicious sandwich filling—

    2 4½-ounce cans deviled ham
    1 8-ounce package cream cheese
    2 tablespoons chopped pimiento-
       stuffed green olives
    1 tablespoon catsup
    1 to 2 teaspoons finely chopped onion

Combine deviled ham, cream cheese, olives, catsup, and onion; chill till serving time. Garnish with additional chopped pimiento-stuffed green olives, if desired. Serve with assorted crackers.

Dual-purpose Deviled Ham Dip can fill pinwheel tea sandwiches or can be a serve-yourself spread for assorted crackers.

Ham and Hamburgers

    1 beaten egg
    ¼ cup milk
    ¼ cup fine dry bread crumbs
    ¼ teaspoon salt
       Dash pepper
    1½ pounds ground beef
    1 4½-ounce can deviled ham
    ½ cup red Burgundy
    2 tablespoons salad oil
    2 tablespoons snipped parsley
    8 hamburger buns, split and
       toasted

Combine egg, milk, bread crumbs, salt, and pepper. Add ground beef and deviled ham; mix thoroughly. Shape into 8 patties, ½ inch thick. Place in 12x7½x2-inch baking dish.

Combine Burgundy, salad oil, and parsley for marinade. Pour over patties; let stand at room temperature about 1 hour, turning once or twice. Drain, reserving marinade. Grill patties over *medium* coals for 8 to 10 minutes, brushing occasionally with marinade. Turn; grill for 6 to 8 minutes more, brushing occasionally with marinade. Serve in toasted hamburger buns. Makes 8 servings.

Pepper Cups

    6 large green peppers
    ½ cup chopped onion
    2 tablespoons butter or margarine
    2 cups cooked long-grain rice
    1 10½-ounce can condensed cream
       of celery soup
    ½ teaspoon salt
       Few drops bottled hot pepper
       sauce
    1 4½-ounce can deviled ham

Remove tops, seeds, and membranes from green peppers. Precook peppers in boiling, salted water for 5 minutes; drain. In skillet cook onion in butter till tender; add cooked rice, celery soup, salt, and hot pepper sauce. Spoon rice mixture into peppers.

In each pepper, form a well in rice mixture. Divide deviled ham to fill wells. Stand peppers upright in shallow baking dish; add water just to cover bottom of dish. Bake at 350° about 30 minutes. Makes 6 servings.

Deviled Ham and Tuna Sandwiches

A hearty sandwich filling—

   1 6½- or 7-ounce can tuna, drained
     and flaked
   1 4½-ounce can deviled ham
   3 hard-cooked eggs, chopped
   ¼ cup finely chopped celery
   2 tablespoons chopped dill pickle
   ½ teaspoon grated onion
   ⅓ cup mayonnaise or salad
     dressing
  16 slices white bread
     Softened butter or margarine
     Lettuce leaves

Combine tuna, deviled ham, eggs, celery, dill
pickle, and onion; blend in mayonnaise. Chill.
Spread bread on one side with softened butter;
spread 8 of the slices on buttered side with tuna
mixture. Top each with lettuce leaf, then bread,
buttered side down. Makes 8 servings.

DEVIL'S FOOD CAKE—A light-textured
chocolate cake with a deep mahogany col-
or. The name seems to have been attached
to this cake in order to contrast its dark
chocolate color with the delicate white-
ness of an angel food cake. Devil's food
cake differs from regular chocolate cake
in that it contains more baking soda and
has a more pronounced chocolate flavor
and a darker chocolate color.

Many homemakers marvel at the rich,
red appearance achieved from some devil's
food cake recipes. This redness can be influenced by several ingredients. A deeper
red is attained by using sweet rather than
sour milk. Although an increase in baking
soda darkens the color, an excess will make
the cake taste alkaline and bitter. The
quantity of chocolate used as well as its
brand will also affect devil's food cake
color. Some recipes, furthermore, include
a small amount of red food coloring to
enhance color. (See also *Cake.*)

The long-time favorite Devil's Food Cake wears a party-pretty
boiled frosting variation, Peppermint-Stick Frosting. A splash
of crunchy candy tidbits dresses the frosty top and sides.

Devil's Food Cake

⅔ cup shortening
2¼ cups sifted cake flour
1¾ cups sugar
1 teaspoon salt
1 teaspoon baking soda
1 teaspoon baking powder
1 cup milk

• • •

¼ cup milk
3 eggs
3 1-ounce squares unsweetened
   chocolate, melted and cooled
1 teaspoon red food coloring
   Peppermint-Stick Frosting

Place shortening in mixer bowl. Sift cake flour, sugar, salt, baking soda, and baking powder. Add the 1 cup milk; mix batter until flour is moistened. Beat mixture 2 minutes at medium speed on electric mixer.

Add remaining ¼ cup milk, eggs, chocolate, and red food coloring. Beat 2 minutes longer. Bake in 2 greased and lightly floured 9x1½-inch round pans at 350° for 35 to 40 minutes. Cool. Frost with *Peppermint-Stick Frosting:* Place 2 unbeaten egg whites, 1½ cups sugar, 2 teaspoons light corn syrup *or* ¼ teaspoon cream of tartar, ⅓ cup cold water, and dash salt in top of double boiler (don't place over boiling water); beat ½ minute at low speed on electric mixer. Place over boiling water, but not touching water. Cook, beating constantly, till frosting forms stiff peaks, *about 7* minutes (*don't overcook*). Remove from boiling water.

If desired, pour into mixing bowl. Add 1 teaspoon vanilla and few drops red food coloring; beat till of spreading consistency, about 2 minutes. Frost tops and sides of cake layers. Trim cake with crushed peppermint-stick candy.

Red Devil's Food Cake

½ cup shortening
1¾ cups sugar
1 teaspoon vanilla
3 eggs, separated
2½ cups sifted cake flour
½ cup unsweetened cocoa powder
1½ teaspoons baking soda
1 teaspoon salt
1⅓ cups cold water

Cream shortening and *1 cup* of the sugar till light and fluffy. Add vanilla and egg yolks, one at a time, beating well after each. Sift together sifted cake flour, unsweetened cocoa powder, baking soda, and salt; add to creamed mixture alternately with cold water, beating well after each addition.

Beat egg whites till soft peaks form; gradually add the remaining ¾ cup sugar, beating till stiff peaks form. Fold egg whites into cake batter; blend well. Pour into 2 greased and lightly floured 8x1½-inch round pans. Bake at 350° for 35 to 40 minutes.

Devilicious Cherry Cake

A fluffy cream cheese topping and wine-sparked cherry sauce round out this elegant dessert—

1 package 2-layer-size devil's
   food cake mix

• • •

1 16-ounce can pitted dark sweet
   cherries
¼ cup sugar
2 tablespoons cornstarch
¼ cup red Burgundy

• • •

1 8-ounce package cream cheese,
   softened
¼ cup sugar
2 tablespoons milk
¼ teaspoon vanilla

Prepare devil's food cake mix and bake in a 13x9x2-inch baking pan following package directions. Cool thoroughly.

Drain dark sweet cherries, reserving syrup. In saucepan blend the first ¼ cup sugar and cornstarch; gradually add reserved cherry syrup, mixing well. Cook and stir over medium heat till syrup mixture is thickened and bubbly. Remove cherry sauce from heat; stir in red Burgundy wine and drained dark sweet cherries. Keep sauce warm while the topping is being prepared.

Beat softened cream cheese till fluffy. Add remaining ¼ cup sugar, milk, and vanilla; beat with rotary beater or electric mixer till fluffy. Cut devil's food cake into squares. Top with a small mound of cream cheese mixture. Then spoon warm sweet cherry sauce over each serving. Makes 12 servings.

DEVONSHIRE CREAM *(dev' uhn shir)*—A clotted cream that was originally made in Devonshire County, England. The thick clots are obtained after fresh non-homogenized milk is left to stand for up to six hours, then slowly heated for one hour. The top layer of cream which forms is then skimmed off.

Devonshire cream is a highly regarded complement for fresh fruits, toast, and desserts. It is appropriately served at breakfast, lunch, or dinner and as the appetizer or dessert course.

Mock Strawberries Devonshire

    1 3-ounce package cream cheese,
        softened
    2 tablespoons sugar
    1 cup whipping cream
      Fresh whole strawberries

In small mixer bowl combine cream cheese, sugar, dash salt, and *2 tablespoons* of the whipping cream; beat till fluffy. Whip remaining cream; fold into cream cheese mixture. Serve with fresh strawberries. Good for appetizer or dessert. Makes 1¾ cups.

DEWBERRY—A type of blackberry that grows on trailing rather than the traditional climbing vines. Although native to North America, species of dewberries are now found in many other parts of the world. Dewberries ripen a few weeks before their relatives, the standard blackberries. (See also *Blackberry*.)

DEXTRIN—An edible substance that possesses characteristics partway between starch and sugar. Dextrins are formed by the chemical action of heat, enzymes, or acids on starch. When starch or flour is pan-browned (heated without liquid), dextrins are formed. In the digestion of starches to sugar, starches are first changed to dextrins by enzymes. Corn syrup, commercially produced by allowing cornstarch and acid to react, contains numerous dextrins.

Pure dextrins are white, but those used in most home cooking are yellow to brown. Dextrins prepared by pan-browning flour or starch are often used when making gravy to improve the sauce color. The gravy mixture will not, however, be as thick as when plain flour or starch is used.

DEXTROSE—A simple sugar that is found widely in fruits, honey, and some vegetables. Dextrose may be called glucose or fruit sugar interchangeably.

Dextrose is only about three-fourths as sweet as table sugar. Because it is easy to digest, dextrose is used for intravenous feeding. (See also *Sugar*.)

DHAL, DHALL *(däl)*—A purée, thick or thin in consistency, made from legumes or beans. *Dhal* is a common food eaten as a vegetable in India and the East Indies. Its appearance is reminiscent of a porridge. (See also *Indian Cookery*.)

DIABLE *(dē ä' bl)*—1. The French word for deviled. 2. A cooking utensil made of two earthenware pans, one of which rests inside the other. 3. An accompaniment sauce for meat, poultry, or fish. Diable sauce is made by adding white wine, vinegar, onion, and spices to a basic brown sauce.

Sauce Diable

    ¼ cup snipped green onion
    3 tablespoons dry white wine
    8 to 10 whole peppercorns,
        crushed
    ½ cup Brown Sauce
    ½ teaspoon snipped parsley
    ½ teaspoon Worcestershire sauce

Combine green onion, wine, and peppercorns in saucepan. Reduce mixture to ½ its volume by boiling. Add Brown Sauce, parsley, and Worcestershire sauce. Heat through. Makes about ⅔ cup.

Brown Sauce: Melt 1½ tablespoons butter or margarine in saucepan; blend in 1½ tablespoons all-purpose flour. Cook and stir over low heat till browned. Stir in one 10½-ounce can condensed beef broth diluted with water to make 2 cups. Bring to boiling and cook 3 to 5 minutes. Reduce heat and simmer 30 minutes; stir occasionally. Makes 1⅛ cups. Use ½ cup as above. Refrigerate remainder; use as gravy.

DICE—To cut food into cubes about ⅛ to ¼ inch thick. A sharp knife is employed first to cut food into slices and then into strips. The strips are piled together and cut crosswise into small cubes. The diced food size may be indicated in a recipe ingredient list as "finely diced."

DIET—1. A person's daily food consumption. 2. The regulation of food consumption commonly associated with a trim figure.

For most people the word "diet" spells a horrendous picture of niggardly meals, watercress sandwiches, grapefruit, weak tea, and an absence of pastries. A diet, in fact, is a necessary balance of nutrients to maintain good health for everyone.

The nutrients come from foods of the Basic 4 Food Groups. The groups include meat, milk, vegetable-fruit, and bread-cereal. When these food groups are used by the body, they form heat energy in measured units called calories. Individual body build and daily activity influence the amount of calories which can be used up satisfactorily in one day. If the body consumes too much food, the calories formed are not used and, instead, form fatty tissue. Likewise, when too little food is consumed, the body uses up any fatty tissue it can, thus resulting in weight loss.

The principal food nutrients found within the Basic 4 Groups consist of carbohydrates, fats, proteins, vitamins, minerals, and water. Carbohydrates and fats are the energy foods, with fat contributing about twice as many calories as either carbohydrates or protein. The body building nutrient is protein of two sources—animal and vegetable. Vitamins and minerals are important to general body metabolism and operation. Water, furnishing no calories but some minerals, is important for body regulatory processes, so at least six glasses should be drunk each day.

Special weight programs and diets set up for health purposes require the guidance of a physician. Diets involving the gain or loss of weight are important to individuals learning to adopt better dietary habits. Nutrient diets, such as low-sodium, high-protein, or others must be guided by a physician so too much or too little of another nutrient is not being consumed.

Diced foods add contrast in shape to usual dishes. Use a French knife and wooden cutting board to cut food strips crosswise.

Complete formula diets, both solid and liquid, have become popular since their introduction by pharmaceutical companies and food manufacturers. Low-residue foods such as celery or lettuce should accompany formula diets to maintain bulk.

Dietary standards have been set up to quantitatively summarize nutritional requirements. A diet for good health can easily be established, but before going on a weight loss or weight gain diet, consult your physician. (See also *Nutrition*.)

DIETETIC FOOD *(di' i tet' ik)*—Commercially prepared food used in special diets. Examples of dietetic foods include low-sodium cheese and bread, tuna packed in water (without salt) instead of oil, and low-calorie dessert powders made with noncaloric sweeteners. Diabetic foods, not to be confused with dietetic foods, refer to a type of food that is sugar free, such as some artificial sweeteners.

DIGESTION—A body process occurring in the digestive tract by which food is broken into substances that can be absorbed and assimilated by the body. Digestion starts in the mouth where the food is chewed and mixed with saliva. This process continues as the food is acted upon chemically by digestive juices. The digested food reaches all tissues of the body by way of the bloodstream, thus furnishing body-building and maintenance materials.

Food temperatures have an effect on rate of digestion; warm foods speed up the process, while cold foods slow it down. Emotional stress and strain impede digestion; tranquility and happiness help digestion on its normal course.

DIJON MUSTARD *(dē zhön′)*—A French-style mustard containing dry mustard, herbs, spices, and white wine. It originated in Dijon, France, and is considered by connoisseurs to be one of the finest mustards. Dijon mustard is available in jars at specialty food stores and markets. Its smooth, tart, yet pleasing, flavor is an excellent seasoning for eggs, soups, roasts, steaks, chops, and fish. (See also *Mustard.*)

Mustard 'n Ham Dip

Combine one 4-ounce package whipped **cream cheese,** one 2¼-ounce can deviled **ham,** 1½ teaspoons Dijon-style **mustard,** 1 tablespoon chopped **chives,** and 2 teaspoons **milk.** Chill well; serve with relishes, chips, and crackers.

DILL—An aromatic herb related to the parsley family. The word dill is derived from the Norse *dilla* meaning "to lull to sleep," and it was formerly given to infants for that reason. Dill was used by Babylonian and Assyrian doctors as a drug, and the pungent seed was also said to remedy a stomachache and other such ailments.

The Romans made crowns of the dillweed. Colonial settlers chewed dillseed during long church services to delay hunger. Bad breath was also believed to be eliminated by chewing dillseed, and ground dillseed was recommended for use to those on salt-free diets.

Native to the Mediterranean countries and southern Russia, dill still grows wild in parts of Asia and Africa and is widely cultivated in England, India, Germany, and Romania. Dill, popular in the United States, is grown commercially in the southern and eastern parts of the country and also in some midwestern states. Dillweed is grown mainly in and around California.

The dill plant bears yellow blossoms which turn into tiny seeds. The mature plant is available, usually tied in bunches, in food stores and markets during the late summer and early autumn. The feathery, bright green leaves are dried, bottled, and labeled dillweed, and are found with bottled whole dillseed in the market.

Ground dill is bottled in ½- to 1-ounce containers and blends more easily with food than either the seed or dillweed. Dillseeds, in ½- to 2-ounce containers, have a warm, slightly sharp taste serving to stimulate the appetite, thus making them suitable for salad seasonings. Dillweed, either fresh or bottled, may garnish or enhance the flavor of mild foods.

Dill leaves are natural flavor additions to many foods. Add chopped dill to buttered new potatoes and to cream sauce for fish or shellfish; blend with cream or cottage cheese; sprinkle a bit on broiled meats or fish; or put a dash of dill in green salads or cooked green beans. If dillweed is used instead of fresh dill as a garnish, moisten it with a little lemon juice or water to revive its aromatic flavor.

Use dillseed with potatoes to flavor cabbage, in vegetable salads or slaws, or in

Tantalize guests with crisp zucchini sticks dipped in Dill Dip. As appetizer or relish, it will be the topic of conversation.

Spoon zesty Dill Sauce over Corned Beef Squares and cabbage wedges. The popular everyday dish becomes a new favorite.

soups and stews. Dill is the obvious flavor given to dill pickles. A few seeds add subtle flavor to the liquid in which fish is simmered or poached. The flavor of dillseed is found in a number of sausage and luncheon meats. (See also *Herbs.*)

Dill Dip

In small bowl combine one 3-ounce package cream cheese, softened; 1 tablespoon finely chopped pimiento-stuffed green olives; 1 teaspoon grated onion; ¼ teaspoon dried dillweed; and dash salt. Mix well. Stir in 1 to 2 tablespoons light cream to make mixture of dipping consistency. Chill. Serve with zucchini sticks as an appetizer. Makes about ⅔ cup.

Corned Beef Squares with Dill Sauce

In medium mixing bowl combine 1 cup milk, 2 eggs, 1 cup coarsely crushed saltine crackers (about 22 crackers), ½ cup chopped onion, 1 tablespoon prepared horseradish, and 1 teaspoon dry mustard. Add two 12-ounce cans corned beef, chopped (4 cups) to mixture; mix thoroughly. Turn corned beef mixture into 10x6x1½-inch baking dish. Bake at 375° for 30

to 35 minutes. Meanwhile, cut 1 medium head cabbage into 6 to 8 wedges. Prepare Dill Sauce. Cut corned beef into squares. Serve with cabbage and Dill Sauce. Serves 6 to 8.

Dill Sauce: In medium saucepan combine one 10½-ounce can condensed cream of mushroom soup, ½ cup milk, 1 teaspoon dried dillweed, and 1 teaspoon dry mustard. Cook, stirring frequently, over medium heat till bubbly.

Dill Potatoes

Peel 1½ pounds tiny new potatoes (about 15); cook in boiling salted water till tender, about 15 to 20 minutes; drain thoroughly. Melt 1 tablespoon butter or margarine; blend in 2 teaspoons all-purpose flour, ½ teaspoon salt, and 1 teaspoon snipped fresh dillweed. Add ⅓ cup milk and ¾ cup light cream all at once. Cook and stir over medium heat till mixture thickens and bubbles. Reduce heat. Add cooked potatoes; heat through. Sprinkle with additional dillweed. Makes 4 or 5 servings.

Dublin Potato Salad

  2 tablespoons vinegar
  1 teaspoon celery seed
  1 teaspoon mustard seed
  3 medium-large potatoes
  2 teaspoons sugar
  2 cups finely shredded cabbage
  1 12-ounce can corned beef,
      chilled and cubed
  ¼ cup sliced green onion
  ¼ cup finely chopped dill pickle
  1 cup mayonnaise or salad
      dressing
  ¼ cup milk

Combine vinegar, celery seed, and mustard seed; set aside. Meanwhile, peel and cook potatoes in enough boiling salted water to cover till done, 30 to 40 minutes; drain and cube. While potatoes are still warm, drizzle with vinegar mixture. Sprinkle with sugar and ½ teaspoon salt; chill before serving.

Before serving, add cabbage, corned beef, onion, and pickle to potatoes. Combine mayonnaise, milk, and ½ teaspoon salt. Pour mayonnaise mixture over corned beef mixture and toss lightly. Makes 6 to 8 servings.

Dilly Hamburgers

In small bowl combine 1 cup dairy sour cream, 1 teaspoon prepared mustard, and 3 tablespoons snipped fresh dillweed. Form 1 to 1½ pounds ground beef into 4 to 6 patties, ½ inch thick. Broil patties over *hot* coals about 9 minutes; turn and sprinkle with salt and pepper to taste. Broil to desired doneness, about 6 minutes longer. Season again with salt and pepper. Serve on hot toasted buns. Top with Dill Sauce. Makes 6 to 8 servings.

DILUTE—To thin or to weaken the strength or flavor of a food substance by adding a liquid such as water to it.

DIP—1. Immersing food in a liquid or in a dry mixture, such as flour. 2. Savory soft or semiliquid food mixtures into which crisp crackers, potato chips, raw vegetables, or special snack foods are dipped. Typically American, dips became popular shortly after the end of World War II.

The dip base may be cream cheese, sour cream, sweet cream or prepared baby foods already chopped and puréed to save time and work. Flavor the creamy dip mixture with bacon bits, seafood, onions, pickles, dried soups, relish, dill, favorite herbs and spices, or delicacies, such as minced clams, avocados, or Roquefort cheese.

Dips, although similar to canapé fillings, have a softer consistency. They should be thick enough not to drip on clothing or carpet when food sticks or chips are dipped into them, but not so thick that the dip needs to be scooped out. Dips may be served hot or cold.

Beat additional sour cream, sweet cream, or milk into the dip if it becomes thick upon standing. Add the amount needed to bring the dip back to its proper consistency. Crackers, toast sticks, potato chips, corn chips, pretzels, or melba toast are ready-made, convenient scoops. Cut narrow toast strips or cookie cutter shapes for unusual bread variations.

Crisp, cold, raw vegetables, such as carrot and celery sticks, cauliflowerets, iced cucumber rounds, green pepper strips, mushrooms, and radishes, make delicious appetizer accompaniments to the dip. For party refreshments, surround a dip bowl with cooked shrimp or cocktail frankfurters. There are many uses for dips. They are most satisfactorily served to small, informal adult groups, such as a casual get-together, centered around a buffet meal, and as cocktail accompaniments. And the leftover dips make excellent dressings for a mixed green salad or the topping for hot vegetables. When mixed with minced meat, they are a good choice for use in sandwiches. (See also *Appetizer.*)

It is great snacking for weight watchers with Dieter's Dip. The quick-to-fix dip is served with chilled, cooked shrimp.

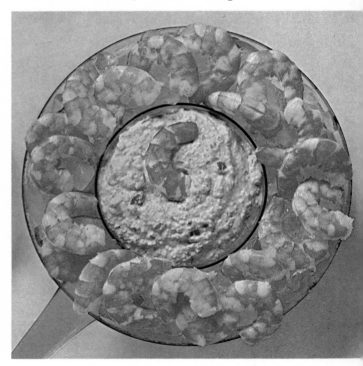

Make-ahead dip tips

So that the flavorings can mingle and mellow properly, prepare dips several hours before serving and refrigerate. Use strong spices such as garlic, onion, and chili powder sparingly because they intensify on standing.

Dieter's Dip

1 12-ounce carton cottage
    cheese (1½ cups)
½ envelope dill dip mix
    (about 1 teaspoon)
     • • •
1 tablespoon finely diced
    canned pimiento
1 tablespoon snipped parsley
    Chilled cooked shrimp

Beat cottage cheese and dill dip mix together
with electric mixer. Stir in pimiento and
snipped parsley. Serve with chilled shrimp.

Hot Cheese and Crab Dip

10 ounces sharp natural
    Cheddar cheese
 8 ounces sharp process
    American cheese
⅓ cup milk
½ cup dry white wine
1 7½-ounce can crab meat, drained,
    flaked, and cartilage removed

Cut cheeses in small pieces; combine in a
saucepan with milk. Stir over low heat till
cheeses melt. Stir in wine and crab; heat
through. Serve in chafing dish with shredded
wheat wafers, if desired. Makes 3 cups.

Dip à la Spaghetti

1 tablespoon dry spaghetti
    sauce mix
1 tablespoon finely chopped
    green pepper
1 cup dairy sour cream

Stir spaghetti sauce mix and green pepper into
dairy sour cream. Chill. Serve with crisp vegetables or corn chips, if desired.

Special late evening snack

←Surround piping Hot Cheese and Crab Dip
with shredded wheat wafers, garnished with
parsley and crab, and tempt your guests.

Lobster Dip Elegante

*Crisp crackers or toast dunked in hot lobster dip
are a welcome change-of-pace party treat—*

1 8-ounce package cream cheese
¼ cup mayonnaise or salad
    dressing
1 clove garlic, crushed
1 teaspoon grated onion
1 teaspoon prepared mustard
1 teaspoon sugar
    Dash seasoned salt
1 5-ounce can lobster, flaked
    (about 1 cup)
3 tablespoons sauterne

Melt cream cheese over low heat, stirring constantly. Blend in mayonnaise or salad dressing,
garlic, onion, mustard, sugar, and salt. Stir in
flaked lobster and sauterne; heat through.
Serve hot with melba toast and assorted crackers, if desired. Makes 1¾ cups.

Chicken Liver-Onion Dip

*Easy onion soup and liver dip served with crack-
ers will delight any dip-loving crowd—*

¼ cup water
2 tablespoons dry onion soup mix
½ pound chicken livers
1 hard-cooked egg, sliced
¼ cup mayonnaise or salad
    dressing
½ teaspoon Worcestershire sauce
3 slices bacon, crisp-cooked,
    drained, and crumbled

Combine water and dry onion soup mix; set
aside. Meanwhile, in small saucepan simmer
chicken livers in water till tender, about 8 to 10
minutes. Drain; cool. Place onion soup mixture, livers, egg, mayonnaise, and Worcestershire sauce in electric blender container; cover
and blend till almost smooth.

    Or, put livers and egg through meat grinder.
Combine onion soup mixture, Worcestershire
sauce, and mayonnaise or salad dressing. Stir
in liver mixture; mix well. Stir in about two-
thirds of the bacon; chill thoroughly. Top mixture with remaining crumbled bacon; serve
with assorted crackers or corn chips.

DISSOLVE—To release a dry substance into a liquid, thus forming a solution. A food ingredient may be stirred or melted into the liquid as part of a food preparation procedure. Examples include: stirring sugar in water to make syrup, sugar dissolved in hot coffee for flavor, gelatin in water, salt in a sauce, or yeast in water.

DISTILLED LIQUOR—Beverages of high alcoholic content produced by separating alcohol from another product. This is achieved by heating an alcohol-water mixture to a temperature between the boiling point of alcohol and water at which time the alcohol vaporizes. The vapors may be recondensed into a pure alcohol liquid form with special equipment.

Although distillation is based on the fact that the boiling point of water is lower than that of alcohol, the distillation of liquors involves more than just heating the alcohol-water mixture. This is especially true of brandy, distilled from wine; rum from molasses or other sugar-cane products; whiskey distilled from grain; and gin and vodka which are produced from any one of a number of products including wheat or rye. (See also *Liquor*.)

DISTILLED WATER—Purified water made by condensing the steam of boiling water. The vapor is condensed into pure water and has a flat taste due to the absence of air and natural chemical salts. The distilled product can be aerated to remove this flat taste for drinking purposes.

Distilled water is used on steamships for drinking purposes. It is also used extensively in steam irons and for cleaning equipment and glassware used in factories and chemical laboratories. Doctors recommend distilled water to make baby's formula. The water should be stored in tightly covered containers to avoid contamination and to retain its purity.

DIVAN (*dī' van*)—A recipe style created in a New York restaurant for a luscious, baked dish of chicken breasts, broccoli, and a rich, creamy sauce. The name is now given to similar mixtures with meats used instead of chicken breasts, such as veal or ham. It closely resembles a casserole.

Classic Chicken Divan

      2 10-ounce packages frozen
         broccoli spears
    1/4 cup butter or margarine
      6 tablespoons all-purpose flour
      2 cups chicken broth
    1/2 cup whipping cream
      3 tablespoons dry white wine
           . . .
      3 chicken breasts, halved
         and cooked
    1/4 cup grated Parmesan cheese

Cook broccoli according to package directions; drain. Melt butter or margarine; blend in flour, 1/2 teaspoon salt, and dash pepper. Add chicken broth; cook and stir till mixture thickens and bubbles. Stir in cream and wine.

Place broccoli crosswise in 12x7 1/2 x2-inch baking dish. Pour *half* the sauce over. Top with chicken. To remaining sauce, add cheese; pour over chicken; sprinkle with additional Parmesan cheese. Bake at 350° till heated through, about 20 minutes. Then broil just till sauce is golden, about 5 minutes. Serves 6.

Easy Chicken Divan

      2 10-ounce packages frozen
         broccoli spears
      2 cups sliced cooked chicken
         or 3 chicken breasts,
         cooked and boned
      2 10 1/2-ounce cans condensed
         cream of chicken soup
    3/4 cup mayonnaise or salad
         dressing
      1 teaspoon lemon juice
      2 ounces sharp process American
         cheese, shredded (1/2 cup)
      1 cup soft bread crumbs
      1 tablespoon butter, melted

Cook broccoli according to package directions in salted water till tender; drain. Arrange broccoli in greased 12x7 1/2 x2-inch baking dish. Layer chicken atop the broccoli.

Combine next 3 ingredients; pour over chicken. Sprinkle with cheese. Combine crumbs and butter; sprinkle over all. Bake at 350° till heated, about 35 minutes. Trim with pimiento strips, if desired. Makes 6 to 8 servings.

Easy Chicken Divan, appropriately named as frozen broccoli
and mushroom soup, combines with chicken to make an easy
super-supper dish. Garnish with bright red pimiento strips.

DIVINITY—A fudgelike candy made with corn syrup, sugar, and water cooked to the hard-ball stage and then beaten into stiff-peaked egg whites. Divinity, sometimes called divinity fudge, is classified as a crystalline candy but is different from most crystalline candies because it contains egg whites. The candy is very similar to nougat which contains almonds and honey although nougat is heavier than divinity.

Because good divinity requires constant heavy beating (when electric mixer is not used) and since it sets very fast, it is more fun, and makes the job easier to make divinity with a partner.

Divinity may be stirred over hot water if it does not set. Hot water may be added to the candy if it becomes too hard to work. Candies using water instead of milk can be heated to a higher temperature as there is no danger of scorching. Reaching and maintaining the recommended candy temperature or cooking stage is very important to the consistency and texture of the cooked candy. Divinity should be cooked to the hard-ball stage, between 250° and 266°. The candy syrup will form a hard ball, yet will remain somewhat pliable.

High humidity or rainy weather may affect the setting up and keeping qualities of the candy. Cook the candy a degree or two higher if the humidity is high.

Wipe the sides of the pan occasionally with a damp brush to avoid crystal formation during cooking. Tint divinity with drops of food coloring to brighten dishes of assorted candy, and add nutmeats, candied fruits, or coconut during the last few strokes of beating before the divinity has a chance to cool and set thoroughly.

Fill up the candy plate with Remarkable Fudge squares topped with walnut half (See *Fudge*), white Divinity, Cherry Fluff Divinity, and Creamy Praline Patties (See *Praline*).

After all ingredients are mixed and beaten along with egg whites, drop divinity by spoonfuls onto waxed paper and leave it to cool. Additional nuts and toppings may be pressed into the top at this time. The light candy can also be turned into a buttered pan and cut into squares or pieces like fudge after it has set.

Eat divinity while it is fresh as it does not keep well and dries out quickly. Store fresh divinity in tightly covered containers. Divinities can be satisfactorily frozen.

Another candy made in the same way as divinity, but called seafoam, uses brown sugar instead of granulated sugar. This changes not only the flavor of the candy, but also its color. (See also *Candy*.)

Divinity

2½ cups sugar
½ cup light corn syrup
• • •
2 egg whites
1 teaspoon vanilla

In 2-quart saucepan combine sugar, corn syrup, ¼ teaspoon salt, and ½ cup water. Cook to hard-ball stage (260°) stirring only till sugar dissolves. Beat egg whites to stiff peaks. Gradually pour syrup over egg whites, beating at high speed on electric mixer. Add vanilla; beat till candy holds its shape, 4 to 5 minutes. Quickly drop from teaspoon onto waxed paper. Makes about 40 pieces of divinity.

Cherry Fluff Divinity

Sweet pink confections studded with candied cherries are bound to tempt any candy dish taster—

> 2 cups sugar
> ½ cup water
> ¼ cup light corn syrup
> 1 7¼-ounce package fluffy
>   cherry frosting mix
> 1 teaspoon vanilla
> ⅓ cup finely chopped red
>   candied cherries

In a heavy 2-quart saucepan, combine sugar, water, and corn syrup. Cook and stir over medium heat till sugar dissolves and mixture is boiling. Cook, without stirring, to hard-ball stage (265°). Remove from heat. Meanwhile, prepare frosting mix according to package directions; transfer to large mixer bowl. *Very slowly* pour hot syrup over frosting, beating constantly at high speed on electric mixer, about 5 minutes. Continue beating 5 minutes more; stir in vanilla and cherries. Cool, stirring occasionally, till mixture holds soft peaks and begins to lose gloss. Drop mixture from rounded tablespoons onto waxed paper, swirling tops with spoon. Makes about 30 pieces.

Rainbow Divinity

Delicate divinity made new and colorful with flavored gelatin and tinted coconut—

> 3 cups sugar
> ¾ cup light corn syrup
> ¾ cup hot water
> ¼ teaspoon salt
>   • • •
> 2 egg whites
> ½ 3-ounce package cherry- or lime-
>   flavored gelatin* (3 tablespoons)
> 1 teaspoon vanilla
> 1 cup chopped nuts (optional)
> ¾ cup flaked coconut, tinted
>   pink or green**

Butter sides of heavy 2-quart saucepan. In it combine sugar, corn syrup, water, and salt. Cook and stir till sugar dissolves and mixture reaches boiling point. Cook to hard-ball stage (250°) without stirring; remove from heat.

Push divinity from spoon onto waxed paper-lined baking sheet with the aid of another spoon. Candy is best when eaten fresh.

Meanwhile, beat egg whites to soft peaks; gradually add gelatin, beating to stiff peaks. Add vanilla and pour hot syrup slowly over egg white mixture, beating with mixer at high speed till soft peaks form and mixture starts to lose its gloss. Stir in nuts. Drop from teaspoon onto waxed paper. Sprinkle candy with tinted coconut. Makes about 54 pieces.

  *Add few drops green food coloring to lime-flavored gelatin, if desired.

  **Tint coconut by shaking with a few drops of food coloring in screw-top jar.

DOBOS TORTE *(dō' bōs, -bōsh)*—A Hungarian cake of butter cream-filled layers and a caramel topping. Josef Dobos, a Hungarian pastry chef, created this dessert confection, and is popular in Vienna.

The rich, butter cream filling, between each thin sponge cake layer, is usually chocolate. The topping may be whipped cream or a frosting but is most often a caramel glaze. Sometimes the whole cake is frosted, but this detracts from the superb torte attractiveness. Speed is necessary when making this Hungarian specialty with caramel topping. If the topping cools before servings have been cut, the caramel will crack and cannot be cut into even, neat slices. (See also *Torte*.)

Split cake layers in half using wooden picks as guides. Position picks in center of side all the way around. Slice.

Spread creamy chocolate filling with shaved chocolate between each cake layer. Position each layer with the cut side down.

Shortcut Dobos Torte

      5 eggs
    ½ teaspoon salt
      1 teaspoon vanilla
      1 cup granulated sugar
    1½ cups pancake mix
              . . .
      2 cups whipping cream
    ½ teaspoon vanilla
    ¼ cup sifted confectioners'
          sugar
    ¼ cup unsweetened cocoa powder
      2 1-ounce squares semisweet
          chocolate, shaved
    ¼ cup slivered almonds, toasted

Combine eggs, salt, and 1 teaspoon vanilla. Beat till thick and lemon-colored, about 5 minutes. Gradually beat in the granulated sugar; fold in pancake mix. Pour into 2 greased and waxed paper-lined 9x1½-inch round cake pans. Bake at 350° for 15 to 18 minutes. Cool; remove from pans. Split cake layers (see picture). To make filling, combine whipping cream, ½ teaspoon vanilla, confectioners' sugar, and cocoa powder; whip till thickened.

To assemble torte place cake layer on serving plate, *cut side down*. Spread with 1 cup of the whipped filling; sprinkle with about 1 tablespoon of the shaved chocolate. Top with second layer, cut side down; spread with same amounts of filling and shaved chocolate. Repeat with remaining 2 layers. Sprinkle toasted almonds on top layer. Chill before serving.

Elegant prepare-ahead dessert

New Shortcut Dobos Torte uses pancake→ mix to make spongy layers. Garnish with toasted almonds and shaved chocolate.

DOCK—A pungent herb, related to sorrel and buckwheat. The leaves are used in cooking to enhance and add to the flavor of foods.

Some varieties of dock plants grow wild and can, in fact, be a problem weed. The leaves are most desirable for cooking in the springtime when they still are young and tender. (See also *Herb*.)

DOLLOP—A recipe term describing a small amount, such as a scoop or spoonful, of semiliquid food used to garnish another food. A dollop of whipped cream can top a dessert or fruit salad. Likewise, a dollop of sour cream might dress and add flavor to a main dish, salad, or dessert.

DOLMA—A ground meat appetizer or main dish from the Near East. The word *dolma* literally means "something stuffed."

Traditionally, meat (usually lamb or mutton) together with rice, onion, and seasonings is wrapped in cabbage or grape leaves. However, other meat mixtures used as stuffing for vegetables, such as green peppers or squash, are frequently called *dolmas* also. The Greek form of *dolmas* wrapped in grape leaves are called *dolmades*. (See also *Greek Cookery*.)

Dollops of frozen whipped cream are helpful standbys for a quick topping. Freeze on cookie sheet, then transfer to a plastic bag.

Turkish Zucchini Dolmas

     1 **pound ground beef**
    ⅓ **cup uncooked packaged**
         precooked rice
    ¾ **cup milk**
    ½ **cup chopped onion**
     1 **teaspoon salt**
     1 **teaspoon chopped fresh mint**
         or ¼ teaspoon dried mint
         leaves, crushed, *or* 1 teaspoon
         chopped fresh dillweed, *or* ¼
         teaspoon dried dillweed
    ¼ **teaspoon pepper**
     2 **pounds zucchini squash**
         (5 medium)
     2 **8-ounce cans tomato sauce**
    ½ **teaspoon salt**

Combine ground beef, uncooked rice, milk, chopped onion, the 1 teaspoon salt, mint *or* dillweed, and pepper; mix well. Cut both ends from zucchini squash. With apple corer, scoop out centers of zucchini. (Chop centers and reserve.) Fill zucchini loosely with ground meat mixture. Make meatballs from leftover meat mixture.

In a large skillet combine tomato sauce, the ½ teaspoon salt, and reserved chopped zucchini centers; heat through. Add zucchini and ground meatballs. Cover and simmer till done, about 30 minutes. Makes 4 to 6 servings.

DOT—To cover the surface of food with small pieces of another food, for example, to place bits of butter over pie fruit filling.

DOUBLE-ACTING BAKING POWDER—A leavening compound which releases part of the carbon dioxide at room temperature and the remainder during baking. This is the most common type used in home kitchens. (See also *Baking Powder*.)

DOUBLE BOILER—A utensil comprised of two saucepans, one of which rests inside the other. The top pan contains the food; the bottom pan, water. (The water should not touch the bottom of the top pan.) Thus, the food cooks by indirect heat produced as the heated water changes to steam.

The double boiler cooking method is very satisfactory when controlled temperatures below boiling are needed. The water in the bottom pan is usually heated to just below boiling. Heat-sensitive sauces and egg mixtures such as hollandaise sauce or stirred custard are often cooked over hot water to prevent curdling. Semisweet chocolate pieces must be melted over hot water; if boiling water were used, steam from the water might cause the chocolate to solidify. To melt commercially made caramels, the candies must also be melted in a double boiler to avoid scorching.

DOUBLE CONSOMMÉ—1. A consommé that has been cooked down to concentrate and strengthen its flavor. 2. A standard consommé to which bouillon cubes are added. Canned condensed consommé, if left undiluted, may also be used as a double consommé. (See also *Consommé*.)

DOUBLE CRÈME CHEESE—A rich, soft cheese produced in France. Several varieties of double crèmes are made in different areas of France. All are high in milk fat—a 60 percent concentration by law. These high-fat cheeses are made by adding cream before and after the whey is removed from the milk.

Double crèmes may be purchased in the fresh or ripened form. Except for their double richness and prominent tangy taste, the fresh double crème varieties are very similar to American cream cheeses.

Cured or ripened double crèmes undergo more processing than do the fresh cheeses. They are brushed with special molds and then allowed to ripen from exterior to interior. This ripening action takes from 10 days to 2 weeks. The resulting products are again rich and tangy in taste but are heavier in texture, somewhat reminiscent of rich cheesecake.

Because of the increased milk fat present, double crème cheeses deteriorate rapidly even with refrigeration. For this reason, only a few varieties are available in the United States, frequently only at specialty cheese shops or delicatessens.

Be very careful when selecting double crèmes. First, choose a reputable store. Second, check the wrapping; it should look clean and fresh, not brown and sticky. Third, check for odor. A strong odor indicates that the cheese is old.

DOUBLE GLOUCESTER CHEESE (*glos' tuhr*)—A hard, satiny cheese. Golden in color and mellow, but slightly piquant in flavor, double Gloucester cheese was originally made from the rich milk of Gloucester cows only. Today, however, milk from other breeds of cows is used.

Double Gloucester is a centuries-old English favorite formed into large circles called millstones. These millstones are thick and heavy, and are aged six months to one year. (Regular Gloucester is made in thinner circles that are aged six weeks.) The millstones are cut generally into small wedges for retail sale.

Double Gloucester makes a delightfully different addition to a cheese appetizer or dessert tray. (See also *Gloucester Cheese*.)

DOUGH—A mixture containing flour, liquid, seasonings, and usually a leavening agent. A dough is firm enough to work with the hands or knead. In fact, the word dough comes from the Old English word *dah* meaning "to knead." This thick, nonpourable state distinguishes it from batters.

Doughs can be divided into two basic categories: soft and stiff doughs. Soft doughs contain about one part liquid to three parts flour. They feel soft but can still be handled on a floured surface. Typical soft dough recipes are baking powder biscuits, yeast rolls, and yeast breads.

The composition of stiff doughs, on the other hand, is approximately one part liquid to four parts flour. The high proportion of flour produces a dough that is firm to the touch and can be rolled easily. Piecrust, homemade noodle, and rolled cookie doughs all fall in the stiff dough classification. (See also *Batter*.)

Double
Gloucester, an
English cheese.

DOUGHNUT — Small, individual sweet cakes leavened with baking powder or yeast and cooked by deep-fat frying or baking. They are often dusted with sugar, glazed with a sweet icing, or filled.

Light, puffy fried cakes with holes have been eaten since the earliest of times. Some have even been found in petrified form among prehistoric Indian ruins.

A product of pioneer cooking, the first real doughnuts were introduced to America by the Dutch settlers in New England. These were yeast-raised spherical doughnuts. Because they were called fried cakes by the early New Englanders, upstate New Yorkers still refer to doughnuts as fried cakes. Today, doughnut specialty shops are popular all over the country.

The doughnuts, called oil cakes by the Dutch, became an integral part of pre-fasting activity. The Pennsylvania Dutch served triangular yeast-raised doughnuts called *fastnacht kuche* the day before Lent, Fastnacht Day or Shrove Tuesday. The custom developed with the thrifty Dutch woman who used up all the butters and fats, which were not allowed during the Lenten season, in the doughnut recipe. The last person down to breakfast in the morning on Fastnacht Day was called a "lazy fastnacht," assigned extra work duties for the day, and only received one large *fastnacht kuche* to eat.

A sea captain is credited with cutting the hole in the doughnut, sometime during the middle of the nineteenth century. He complained of the doughy uncooked center and how difficult it was to digest. The sea captain asked that the center of the doughnut be cut out. The cook liked the easier method of cooking and the captain enjoyed the holed doughnut. Thus, to the delight of children and coffee drinkers, the warm, holed doughnut was born. Or so the story goes of how the hole was cut in the doughnut and still remains.

Before airtight wrappings and containers were developed, leftover doughnuts became hard and dried out in a very short time. Thrifty homemakers found that dunking doughnuts in coffee softened them and made an excellent snack. This led to the widespread popularity of the doughnut and coffee companionship.

Types of doughnuts: The basic doughnut can take on round, square, triangular, and braided shapes. These shapes are often a part of the doughnut's name.

Crullers, or twisted doughnuts, are made with more eggs than the usual doughnut recipe, producing a lighter, richer product with a moist texture.

Round or square doughnuts without a hole in the center are actually breads fried in deep fat on the range. Jelly-filled Bismarcks were named after a German politician. French doughnuts differ from basic doughnut recipes in that cream puff dough rather than a yeast dough is used to form the doughnut rings in the hot fat.

Purchase packaged ready-made doughnuts at the supermarket or buy the exact amount wanted at a local bakery or specialty shop. There is usually a selection of plain, glazed, sugared, and filled types.

How to store: Keep fresh doughnuts in a tightly covered container to avoid drying out. To make leftover doughnuts soft and fresh, place them in a paper bag or covered container and heat in a warm oven. Package the number of doughnuts to be eaten at one time in moisture-vaporproof material and freeze for future use.

Basic preparation: The proportion of the ingredients to each other has a great effect upon the finished doughnut. The most important variations include the liquid, fat, and sugar. Too much of any one of these, particularly the sugar, causes greater fat absorption by the doughnut during the deep-fat frying process.

Whole eggs as well as egg yolks are required in most doughnut recipes. Whole eggs make light, puffy doughnuts, while additional egg yolks contribute extra richness. The best flour with which to make ideal doughnuts is a blend of bread flour and cake or pastry flour.

Pick a favorite doughnut

Choose New Orleans Square Doughnuts, →
Coconut Cake or Potato Doughnuts, Doughnut Balls or Filled Doughnuts, or Crullers.

When making doughnuts, keep dough soft and pliable by using as little flour as possible during rolling. Avoid overhandling the dough at all times to eliminate the possibility of producing a tough product with a compact texture. The dough may be chilled slightly in the refrigerator before rolling to make the cutting easier.

Roll the chilled dough to one-third inch thickness and cut with a floured doughnut cutter. Cookie and biscuit cutters can be used to make interesting shapes. A quick and easy way to make doughnuts is to cut the centers from convenient refrigerated biscuits and deep-fat fry as usual. Drop the centers in to fry for the youngsters.

A baking powder dough may be allowed to stand, uncovered, for a few minutes before frying to allow a delicate thin crust to form. This will inhibit the immediate absorption of fat. Doughnuts made with yeast must be allowed to double in size after cutting before they are fried.

When the doughnuts are dropped into the hot fat, they will sink to the bottom and then rise and float. After the doughnut has risen to the top, turn with fork

---

Doughnut frying pointers

Maintaining the hot fat at a temperature between 350° and 375° is best for frying doughnuts. When the fat is below this temperature, the doughnuts may become fat soaked, making them greasy to the taste and difficult to digest. Too hot a deep-fat temperature will cook the outside of the doughnut too quickly while leaving the inside of it uncooked.

If a fat thermometer, automatic fryer, or temperature-regulated skillet is not available, frying temperature may be estimated by dropping a bread cube into the hot fat. When the temperature is correct, the bread will be delicately browned within one minute.

Cook only a few doughnuts at one time for the best results. Too many doughnuts in the pan will lower the temperature and cause a greater amount of fat to be absorbed. Overcrowding will also distort the shape of the products where they touch and makes turning considerably more difficult.

---

till both sides are evenly browned. Turn some doughnuts several times to prevent surface from cracking. The complete frying time should not be over three minutes. Remove doughnut from hot fat with fork or slotted spoon. Lay doughnuts on paper toweling to absorb excess fat. The cooked doughnut should be evenly browned and have a light texture throughout.

A wide variety of choices exist at this point as to whether the doughnut should be served filled, spiced, or frosted. Serve jelly-filled Bismarcks to the morning coffee group or for Sunday breakfast. Make a slit in the side of the uncooked doughnut that has been cut with a biscuit cutter. Insert the jam with a spoon or squirt the jelly in with a long, narrow pastry tube. Jelly can also be sandwiched between two dough rounds and deep-fat fried.

For afternoon or evening eating, prepare whipped cream doughnuts or frosted, twisted crullers. Cut doughnuts in half spreading one half with whipped cream and top with the second half. Garnish whipped cream doughnuts with fruits and nuts. They can also be filled with jelly or custard. The Danish use a special aebleskiver pan for making their round doughnuts and then use applesauce and cream for the rich filling to serve for dessert.

Make interesting shapes with rich cruller dough and spread with mouth-watering frostings. Dunk the frosted doughnuts in little dishes containing coconut or small decorative colored candies.

Doughnuts can be sprinkled with granulated sugar, confectioners' sugar, or a cinnamon and sugar mixture. An easy way to completely cover the doughnuts is to drop them, one at a time, in a paper bag with sugar, then shake gently.

Aside from the traditional warm, sugary doughnut, many doughnut variations can be concocted with fillings and unusual ingredients. Fold the doughnut dough over a pitted prune or other dried fruit before deep-fat frying. Mix snipped dates and raisins into dough to make fruited balls. Added mashed potatoes or sweet potatoes give an interesting flavor to the balls.

Leftover doughnuts make an excellent coffee companion, or serve them with hot apple cider for a change. Perfect for dunking, the doughnuts can be split, toasted, and buttered. The doughnut halves may be topped with jelly and broiled till the jam is hot and bubbly. (See also *Bread*.)

Cake Doughnuts

Delight your family and friends with warm dough-nuts smelling of sweet sugar and cinnamon—

- 3¼ cups sifted all-purpose flour
- 2 teaspoons baking powder
- ½ teaspoon ground cinnamon
- ¼ teaspoon ground nutmeg
- Dash salt
- 2 eggs
- ⅔ cup sugar
- 1 teaspoon vanilla
- ⅔ cup cream
- ¼ cup butter or margarine, melted
- ½ cup sugar
- ½ teaspoon ground cinnamon

Sift together all-purpose flour, baking powder, ½ teaspoon ground cinnamon, the ground nut-meg, and salt. Beat eggs, ⅔ cup sugar, and the vanilla till thick and lemon-colored. Combine cream and butter; add alternately to egg mixture with flour mixture, beating till just blended after each addition. Cover and chill dough in the refrigerator about 2 hours.

Roll dough ⅜ inch thick on lightly floured surface. Cut out doughnuts with floured 2½-inch doughnut cutter. Fry in deep hot fat (375°) till golden brown, turning once (about 1 minute per side). Drain. While warm, shake in mixture of ½ cup sugar and ½ teaspoon ground cinnamon. Makes about 20 doughnuts.

Jiffy Doughnuts

In a hurry? Pop open a tube of refrigerated bis-cuits to make a quick and easy doughnut treat—

Stretch and slightly flatten with palm of hand each biscuit from 1 tube refrigerated biscuits (10 biscuits). With finger, punch hole in center of biscuit and shape into doughnut. Fry in deep hot fat (375°) about 2 minutes; turn once. Drain cooked doughnuts on paper toweling. Roll in mixture of ground cinnamon and sugar. Serve warm. Makes 10 doughnuts.

Apricot jam bubbles atop Apricot Split-Ups. Sprinkle broken nuts over doughnut halves and serve with steaming coffee.

Apricot Split-Ups

Cut plain doughnuts in half. Broil cut side down 3 to 4 inches from heat ½ to 1 minute. Spread cut surface with apricot jam; sprinkle with broken nuts. Broil till jam is bubbly.

Shaggy Mochas

- 2 teaspoons instant coffee powder
- ½ cup flaked coconut
- 1 cup sifted confectioners' sugar
- 2 tablespoons light cream *or* milk
- 12 plain doughnuts

In pint jars dissolve coffee powder in 2 table-spoons water; add coconut. Cover and shake until coconut is coffee color. Spread coconut on *ungreased* baking sheet; dry in 300° oven for about 25 minutes, stirring occasionally. To make icing, combine confectioners' sugar and cream. Frost tops of doughnuts and sprinkle with coffee-flavored coconut.

Coconut Cake Doughnuts

Flaked coconut makes this doughnut different—

>   2 eggs
>   ½ cup sugar
>   ¼ cup milk
>   2 tablespoons melted shortening
>   2⅓ cups sifted all-purpose flour
>   2 teaspoons baking powder
>   ½ teaspoon salt
>   ¾ cup flaked coconut
>   • • •
>   Sugar

Beat eggs with sugar till light; add milk and cooled shortening. Sift flour, baking powder, and salt together. Add dry ingredients and coconut to eggs; stir just till blended. Cover and chill mixture several hours. Roll on lightly floured surface to ½ inch thick. Cut out doughnuts with 2½-inch doughnut cutter. Fry in deep hot fat (375°) till brown; turn and brown other side (about 1 minute per side). Drain on paper toweling. While warm, shake in bag with sugar to coat. Makes 1 dozen.

Doughnut Twists

>   4 beaten eggs
>   ⅔ cup sugar
>   ⅓ cup milk
>   ⅓ cup salad oil
>   3½ cups sifted all-purpose flour
>   3 teaspoons baking powder
>   ¾ teaspoon salt
>   1 teaspoon ground cinnamon
>   ½ teaspoon ground nutmeg
>   • • •
>   ½ cup sugar
>   1 to 2 teaspoons ground cinnamon

Beat eggs and sugar till light; add milk and salad oil. Sift together flour, baking powder, salt, ground cinnamon, and ground nutmeg; add to egg mixture and mix well. Chill dough. On lightly floured surface, roll dough ¼ inch thick into a 12x16-inch rectangle. Cut strips ¾ inch wide and 6 inches long. Twist or form in knots. Let rest 15 minutes. Fry in deep hot fat (375°). Drain. Shake warm doughnuts in bag containing ½ cup sugar and 1 to 2 teaspoons ground cinnamon. Makes 2½ dozen.

Doughnut Balls

>   2 cups sifted all-purpose flour
>   ¼ cup sugar
>   3 teaspoons baking powder
>   1 teaspoon salt
>   1 beaten egg
>   ½ cup milk
>   ¼ cup orange juice
>   ¼ cup salad oil
>   1 teaspoon grated orange peel
>   ½ cup coarsely chopped pecans
>   Sugar

Sift flour, ¼ cup sugar, baking powder, and salt together into mixing bowl. Combine egg, milk, orange juice, salad oil, and orange peel. Stir into dry ingredients. Add nuts. Stir to blend.

Drop by teaspoons into deep hot fat (about 360°) and fry till brown, about 3 minutes, on all sides, turning once. Drain on paper toweling. Roll in sugar. Makes about 2½ dozen.

Potato Doughnuts

>   3 eggs
>   1⅓ cups sugar
>   ½ teaspoon vanilla
>   1 cup mashed potatoes, cooled*
>   2 tablespoons melted shortening
>   4 cups sifted all-purpose flour
>   6 teaspoons baking powder
>   2 teaspoons ground nutmeg
>   1 teaspoon salt
>   ⅓ cup milk
>   Sugar

Beat eggs with 1⅓ cups sugar and vanilla till light. Add potatoes and shortening. Sift together dry ingredients; add alternately with milk to potato mixture, beating well after each addition. Chill 3 hours in the refrigerator.

Roll out half of dough at a time, keeping other half chilled. Roll on floured surface to ⅜ inch thick. Cut dough with floured 2-inch biscuit cutter; chill cut doughnuts for 15 minutes.

Fry in deep hot fat (375°) till brown, about 3 to 4 minutes, turning once; drain. Dip cooked doughnuts in sugar. Makes about 3 dozen.

*Cook 2 medium potatoes; mash potatoes with butter to make light and fluffy. Or use instant mashed potatoes and prepare potatoes according to package directions.

Raised Doughnuts

In large mixer bowl combine 2 packages active dry yeast and 2 cups flour. Heat 1 cup milk, 1/3 cup shortening, 1/3 cup sugar, and 1 teaspoon salt just till warm, stirring occasionally to melt shortening. Add to dry mixture in mixing bowl; add 2 eggs. Beat at low speed with electric mixer for 1/2 minute, scraping sides of bowl constantly. Beat 3 minutes at high speed. By hand, stir in 1 1/2 to 2 cups flour to make moderately soft dough; mix the dough mixture well.

Place dough in greased bowl; turning once to grease surface. Cover and chill in the refrigerator about 3 hours or overnight. (If dough rises in refrigerator, punch down with fist.) Turn out on lightly floured surface and roll 1/3 inch thick. Cut with floured doughnut cutter. Set cut doughnuts aside and let rise till very light, about 30 to 40 minutes.

Fry in deep hot fat (375°) about 2 minutes or till browned, turning once. Drain on paper toweling. Drizzle warm doughnuts with Orange Glaze. Makes about 2 dozen.

Orange Glaze: In small mixing bowl thoroughly combine 1 teaspoon grated orange peel, 3 tablespoons orange juice, and 2 cups sifted confectioners' sugar. Mix well.

New Orleans Square Doughnuts

Dip in sugar and serve warm with coffee—

In large mixer bowl combine 1 package active dry yeast and 1 1/2 cups flour. Heat together 1 cup milk, 1/4 cup sugar, 1/2 cup shortening, and 1 teaspoon salt just till warm, stirring to melt shortening. Add to dry mixture in bowl; add 1 egg. Beat at low speed with electric mixer for 1/2 minute, scraping sides of bowl. Beat 3 minutes at high speed. By hand, stir in 1 1/2 to 2 cups flour to make a moderately soft dough.

Turn out on lightly floured surface; knead smooth, about 8 minutes. Place in greased bowl, turning once to grease surface. Cover; let rise till double (1 1/4 hours). Punch down. Cover and let rest 10 minutes.

On lightly floured surface, roll out dough to 14x10-inch rectangle. Cut in 2-inch squares. Cover and let rise till light (30 to 40 minutes). Fry in deep hot fat (375°) about 3 minutes, turning once. Drain. While warm, dip in sugar, if desired. Makes about 3 dozen doughnuts.

Filled Doughnuts

      4 to 4 1/2 cups sifted all-purpose
        flour
      2 packages active dry yeast
   1 1/4 cups milk
      1/3 cup shortening
      1/4 cup sugar
      1 teaspoon salt
      2 eggs
        •   •   •
     18 prunes *or* 36 apricots
      1/3 cup sugar
        Sugar

In large mixer bowl combine the yeast and *2 cups* of the flour. Heat milk, shortening, 1/4 cup sugar, and salt just till warm, stirring occasionally to melt shortening. Add to dry mixture in mixing bowl; add eggs. Beat at low speed with electric mixer, scraping sides of bowl constantly. Beat 3 minutes at high speed. By hand, stir in enough remaining flour to make a soft dough.

Turn out on floured surface and knead till smooth and elastic, about 5 to 8 minutes. Place in greased bowl, turning to grease surface. Cover; let rise till double, about 45 to 60 minutes.

Meanwhile, cook fruit following package directions, adding 1/3 cup sugar at beginning of cooking. Cool; halve and pit prunes but leave apricots whole. Cut dough in half for easy handling. Roll 3/8 inch thick; cut with a 2 1/2-inch round cutter. Place prune half or apricot in each round of dough; fold dough over fruit and seal edges. Cover and let rise in warm place till double, about 20 minutes. Fry in deep hot fat (375°) till golden, about 1 minute on each side. Drain on paper toweling. Roll in sugar. Makes about 3 dozen doughnuts.

Cinnamon Doughnuts

Taste almost like freshly baked—

     12 plain doughnuts
      1/2 cup sugar
      1 to 2 teaspoons ground cinnamon

Heat doughnuts on baking sheet at 375° till very hot, about 5 minutes. Remove hot doughnuts from oven and shake in paper or plastic sack containing mixture of sugar and ground cinnamon till coated. Serve warm.

Broken nuts perch atop chocolate-dipped Rocky-Road Rings—an easy snack to be served with fresh fruit and coffee.

Orange Doughnuts

        1 package active dry yeast
        4 to 4½ cups sifted all-purpose
            flour
        1 cup orange juice
        ½ cup sugar
        ¼ cup butter
        2 teaspoons grated orange peel
        1 egg

In large mixer bowl combine yeast and *2 cups* flour. Heat orange juice, sugar, butter, orange peel, and ¾ teaspoon salt just till warm, stirring occasionally to melt butter. Add to dry mixture in mixing bowl; add egg. Beat at low speed with electric mixer for ½ minute, scraping sides of bowl constantly. Beat 3 minutes at high speed. By hand, stir in enough of the remaining flour to make soft dough.

Turn out on floured surface; knead till smooth. Place in greased bowl, turning to grease surface. Chill dough 1½ to 2 hours. Roll to ½ inch thick. Cut with floured doughnut cutter. Let rise about 1¼ hours. Fry in deep hot fat (375°). Drain. Dust with confectioners' sugar, if desired. Makes about 1½ dozen.

Rocky-Road Rings

Another time drizzle with confectioners' sugar icing and top with coconut—

        ½ cup semisweet chocolate pieces
        8 plain doughnuts
          Coarsely broken walnuts

Melt semisweet chocolate pieces over hot, not boiling, water. Dip tops of plain doughnuts in melted chocolate, then in coarsely broken walnuts. Makes 8 servings.

Crullers

Let the children twist the sweet doughnut dough into other interesting shapes—

        2 packages active dry yeast
     3¼ to 3¾ cups sifted all-purpose
            flour
              •   •   •
        1 cup milk
        ¼ cup shortening
        ⅓ cup sugar
       1½ teaspoons salt
              •   •   •
        1 egg

In large mixer bowl combine yeast and 1¾ *cups* of the flour. Heat together milk, shortening, sugar, and salt just till warm, stirring occasionally to melt shortening. Add to dry mixture in mixing bowl; add egg. Beat at low speed with electric mixer for ½ minute, scraping sides of bowl constantly. Beat 3 minutes at high speed. By hand, stir in enough of the remaining flour to make a moderately stiff dough.

Turn out on lightly floured surface; knead till smooth, about 8 minutes. Place in greased bowl, turning once to grease the surface; cover and let rise till double, about 1 to 1½ hours. Punch down. Let rest 10 minutes. On lightly floured surface roll into 12x9-inch rectangle, ½ inch thick. Cut in half crosswise; cut each half into 12 strips. Roll each strip under hands to make 10-inch strip; twist for crullers. Bring ends together. Seal ends; twist 3 times. Cover; let rise till almost double, about 45 minutes. Fry in deep hot fat (375°) about 1½ to 2 minutes, turning once; drain. Brush with a confectioners' icing, if desired. Makes 2 dozen.

DOVE—A young wild pigeon, small in size. A young dove has darker flesh and less fat than an old bird which makes the age of the dove important to its eating qualities.

Aging the bird by hanging by its feet in a cool, dry place for three to four days is important to the flavor of the dark, rich meat. Dressing procedures for a dove are the same as for domesticated birds.

Recipes used for preparing dove should suit the age and size of the bird. Recipes suitable for tame varieties of the pigeon family can be used for dove. A sophisticated and elegant meat to prepare, dove may be stuffed or braised in butter and white wine. (See also *Pigeon*.)

DRAIN—To draw off liquid from a food. Draining is usually that part of the cooking procedure which involves the gradual or complete removal of fat, water, or other liquid from another solid food.

A sieve or colander is often used to drain such foods as water from macaroni or spaghetti. A canned fruit or vegetable can be drained by pouring the liquid from the can. Excess fat is removed from deep-fat fried foods, such as doughnuts or French fried potatoes, by laying the food on paper toweling after cooking it.

DRAW—1. To eviscerate or disembowel, as when preparing poultry or fish; remove entrails. 2. To clarify butter. 3. To withdraw essence by steeping, as tea.

DRAWN BUTTER—1. Melted butter. 2. Clarified butter with seasonings added.

Drawn butter was a common ingredient listed in early day cook books. The butter was melted and mixed with hot water, flour, and seasonings. It was one way by which colonial homemakers made butter go farther. Today's classic butter sauce is also made with melted butter but with the addition of flour, seasonings, and lemon juice. Sometimes meat or fish stock is added instead of hot water to give flavor.

Drawn butter and drawn butter sauces are used with fish and meat dishes as well as with vegetables. Hot drawn butter served in individual sauce warmers enhances an elegant lobster dinner. Drizzle drawn butter sauces over other fish as well as meat dishes for rich flavor. Dress up vegetables with seasoned drawn butter sauce. (See also *Butter*.)

DREDGE—To coat or dust food with a dry ingredient. The food, such as meat or fish, can be rolled in crumbs or flour. Food pieces can be put in a paper or plastic bag with dry ingredients and shaken gently till coated completely with the mixture, as with sugar-coated doughnuts.

Dredging serves three useful purposes in connection with the cooking and palatability of food: adding flavor, facilitating browning, and improving the appearance of cooked food. Spices and seasonings may be added to the dry mixture before dredging to add additional flavor.

The dredging process also facilitates browning, such as vegetable pieces coated with flour or fish sprinkled with bread crumbs that are to be fried in fat or baked. The improved appearance of food is evidenced in the eye appeal of a crisp, golden chicken leg that has been rolled in cereal or cracker crumbs.

DRESSED—1. Poultry, fish, or game that has been cleaned and prepared for cooking. 2. Mixing a food with a seasoning or sauce before serving, such as when tossing a salad and its dressing.

Dressing procedures for meat differ from those used for fish. Fowl and poultry require plucking, drawing, trimming, and sometimes singeing. The trimming usually involves removing the head and cutting the legs off at the first joint. Singeing, or passing the bird over a flame, removes small feathers that are hard to pluck by hand. Game birds are larded to prevent drying out. This is done by tying bacon or salt pork around the bird before cooking.

Some fish need to be scaled, others skinned, and all drawn. Large game is skinned and drawn. Some birds are trussed, the legs being pulled close to the body and fastened with skewers or string, before cooking to retain the body juices.

When a salad is tossed with oil and vinegar, or vegetables are coated with melted butter before serving, they are said to be dressed. This is done to enhance the flavor of fresh or cooked food.

DRESSING — 1. A flavorful sauce-type topping, most often cold, used for salads, fruits, and meats. 2. A seasoned stuffing of a food, such as bread, rice, or potatoes, mixed with diced vegetables or fruits and used to fill the cavity of meat, poultry, or hollowed-out fruits and vegetables.

Salad dressings, most often mixtures of fats, acids, and seasonings, can be categorized into three basic types: French or basic pour dressings, basic thick mayonnaise, and cooked salad dressings.

Dressings used for stuffing usually begin with a starchy food base, such as bread, rice, or cornmeal, and then individual tastes and preferences take over with the addition of diced fruits and vegetables, zesty herbs and seasonings, and fats. A poultry or fish stuffing often serves to keep the meat moist, extend the number of servings, and retain the shape of the bird or fish during roasting period. Holiday poultry stuffings become almost as special as the bird itself. (See *Salad Dressing, Stuffing* for additional information.)

DRIED or DRYING — 1. The removal of moisture from a food as a means of food preservation. 2. Dehydration.

Spreading foods such as grapes, plums, figs, corn, and beans in the sun was man's earliest means of food preservation. Later, meat and fish were also dried. The pemmican of the American frontiersman was a mixture of dried meat and sun-dried berries sometimes mixed with fat. It was concentrated food which was easy to carry and did not need to be refrigerated.

Because modern processors can control temperature and humidity 365 days a year, few foods are dried by the idiosyncrasies of the sun's rays alone. Mechanical air circulation under carefully controlled conditions is the most frequent process, but freeze dehydration promises to be commercially important. In addition to the actual drying procedures, there are special techniques such as pasteurization which insure complete sterilization and the absence of harmful bacterial growth. Exposing the food to sulfur fumes prevents decaying and speeds the drying process.

The advantages of dried foods are: no refrigeration or special care is required before the package is opened; and being less bulky and thus easier to store, they are a concentrated form of energy.

The flavor and appearance as well as the aroma of a dried food is different from fresh food. Many dried foods such as fruit are delicious as they come from the package. Due to the concentration, color and flavor qualities are improved.

Though flavor is often concentrated, the nutritive content is sometimes altered by the drying process. Vitamin retention depends on the quality of the fresh food, the preparation of the food for drying, and the moisture-removing process. In fruits, for example, vitamin A is destroyed by prolonged sun-drying and, although sulfuring improves quality, it affects the thiamine content adversely. Ascorbic acid content varies both with the type of fruit and the drying processes applied.

There is more variation in the nutrient change in fruits than in vegetables. In vegetables the thiamine loss due to sulfuring is not serious although ascorbic acid is usually completely eliminated. Vegetables usually retain almost all of their vitamin A during the drying processes.

The principle dried vegetables include peas, beans, and lentils, and the most common dried fruits are apples, apricots, peaches, prunes, and raisins.

The same dried food advantages apply to commercial food products: 1. no refrigeration before package is opened, 2. less bulky and easier to store, and 3. concentrated energy source.

In addition to fruits and vegetables, other foods are commercially dried and include dried herbs and spices, such as dried parsley and onion flakes, thyme, celery, mint, and green pepper. Also included are dried soup mixes, dried egg, and dried milk. (See also *Dehydration*.)

DRIED BEEF — Cured top round beef that has been pickled, smoked, dried, and cut wafer-thin for packaging. Dried beef, often called chipped beef, is a preserved, salted meat distinguished by its dark red color and its concentrated smoky flavor. The pickling process, similar to that for corned beef, takes about eight weeks. The beef is then smoked for two days and subjected to a drying process for two weeks before being cut into thin slices.

Dried beef is available chipped or sliced and packaged in foil or jars. Smoked sliced beef, a different product entirely, can be distinguished from dried beef by its lighter color and less salty flavor.

When buying dried beef, check for the characteristic red beef color. The meat should be free from brown spots. The sliced, packaged meat usually has been cut in larger slices than those slices which come in small, glass jars.

Keep dried beef in refrigerator after opening. Unopened jars may be stored on the kitchen shelf up to six weeks if the room temperature is not too warm. Freezing dried beef is not recommended because undesirable flavors develop in cured meats stored at freezing temperatures.

Dried beef is packaged for use in sandwiches or as an ingredient. When used as an ingredient, some of the salty flavor can be removed by covering the meat with hot water for a minute and draining. When this is not done, little or no salt needs to be added to recipes using dried beef.

Dried beef is often served as creamed beef on toast; for variety drizzle creamed beef over baked potatoes or popovers. Or, pair it with potatoes, rice, or noodles in a casserole. Dried beef is also tasty when cooked in bacon drippings or butter and crumbled in scrambled eggs, salads, or vegetables. (See also *Beef*.)

Save time and utensils by snipping several slices dried beef right into measuring cup. Separate the pieces before using in recipe.

Dried Beef Log

    1 8-ounce package cream cheese,
          softened
 1/4 cup grated Parmesan cheese
    1 tablespoon prepared
          horseradish
 1/3 cup chopped pimiento-stuffed
          green olives
 2 1/2 ounces dried beef, finely
          snipped

Blend cream cheese, Parmesan cheese, and horseradish. Stir in olives. On waxed paper shape mixture in two 6-inch rolls. Wrap and chill several hours or overnight. Roll in snipped beef. Serve with crackers.

Chipped Beef Puff

    4 ounces dried beef, snipped
 1/4 cup butter or margarine
    3 tablespoons all-purpose flour
    2 cups milk
    2 tablespoons chopped canned
          pimiento
    1 3-ounce can sliced mushrooms,
          drained (1/2 cup)
       Cheese Topper

Cook dried beef in butter or margarine over low heat, stirring till slightly crisp and frizzled. Blend in flour and dash pepper. Stir in milk all at once; cook and stir till mixture thickens and bubbles. Stir in pimiento and drained mushrooms. Pour into 10x6x1 3/4-inch baking dish. Keep dried beef mixture hot in 375° oven while making the cheese topper.

Cheese Topper: Beat 3 egg whites with 1/4 teaspoon salt till stiff peaks form. Beat 3 egg yolks till thick and lemon-colored. Fold yolks into whites; fold in 1/3 cup shredded process American cheese. Pour over hot beef mixture. Bake at 375° till golden brown, about 15 to 20 minutes. Garnish with additional frizzled dried beef. Makes 4 or 5 servings.

Beef and Noodle Bake

Rinse 3 ounces, snipped (1 cup), dried beef with hot water; drain. In saucepan melt 2 tablespoons butter; blend in 2 tablespoons all-purpose flour, ½ teaspoon salt, and ¼ teaspoon pepper. Stir in 1½ cups milk. Cook and stir till mixture thickens and bubbles. Mix in dried beef; 1 teaspoon prepared mustard; ¼ cup chopped celery; 2 tablespoons chopped green pepper, 2 hard-cooked eggs, chopped; and 2 ounces (1 cup) medium noodles, cooked.

Turn into 1-quart casserole, or divide between four 8-ounce individual casseroles. Mix 1 cup soft bread crumbs with 2 tablespoons melted butter; sprinkle atop.

Bake at 350° for 15 to 20 minutes for individual casseroles or 30 to 35 minutes for 1-quart casserole. Makes 4 servings.

Creamed Dried Beef

**4 ounces dried or smoked dried
   beef*, torn
2 tablespoons butter
2 tablespoons all-purpose flour
1 cup milk**

    • • •

**½ teaspoon Worcestershire sauce
Toast points**

Cook dried beef in butter till edges frizzle. Push meat to one side; blend flour into butter. Stir in milk all at once. Cook, stirring constantly, till thick and bubbly, gradually incorporating dried beef. Add Worcestershire and dash pepper. Spoon over buttered toast. Serves 3.

*If dried beef is extra salty, let stand a few minutes in boiling water. Drain on paper toweling before cooking in the butter.

DRIED FRUIT—Ripe fruit that has been processed by sun-drying or mechanical-drying techniques. Dried fruits were eaten by everyday people before the Christian Era, being used extensively by the Egyptians. Before the twentieth century, dried fruits were imported to the United States.

How dried fruit is produced: Most dried fruit found in the markets today is processed in this country either by sun-drying or mechanical-drying techniques with the former being traditional and the latter the most convenient method.

The sun-dried fruits usually dry two to three weeks after ripening. Sulfuring (exposing the fruits to sulfur fumes) ensures color retention, serves as an insect repellent, prevents decaying, speeds drying, and influences vitamin retention.

Mechanical-drying techniques use artificial heat and often natural or forced air ventilation. Sulfuring is also part of the mechanical-drying method.

Fruits are dried in different ways depending on the particular fruit. Prunes, figs, and raisins are dried whole, while apples are peeled, cored, and sliced before drying processes. Ripe figs drop from the tree already partially dried.

Inspection and grading of dried fruits ensure uniform packaging. Good packaging is very important in maintaining the moist quality of the firm, meaty fruit.

Nutritional value: Although over 50 percent of the water is evaporated, many of the nutrients still remain after the drying process. Vitamin A is sometimes altered by extensive sun-drying periods, while ascorbic acid loss varies with the fruit as well as with the drying treatment.

If the dried fruit is eaten as purchased, the caloric value extends to four or five times that of the same fresh fruit. A pound and a half of dried fruits equals the mineral equivalent of six to eight pounds fresh fruit. All dried fruits are a good source of energy because of the simple fruit sugar which the body naturally assimilates. This fruit sugar requires no digestive action. Prunes and raisins are good iron suppliers. Apricots are rich in vitamins A and C.

How to select: Most dried fruits are available in sealed cartons or bags throughout the year. All dried fruits are graded and grouped according to their size. Five grades have been set up and are indicated on the package of dried fruit. The five grades are Extra Fancy, Fancy, Extra Choice, Choice, and Standard.

A label indicating that the fruit is "tenderized" means a shorter cooking period is required. Fruit is packaged according to

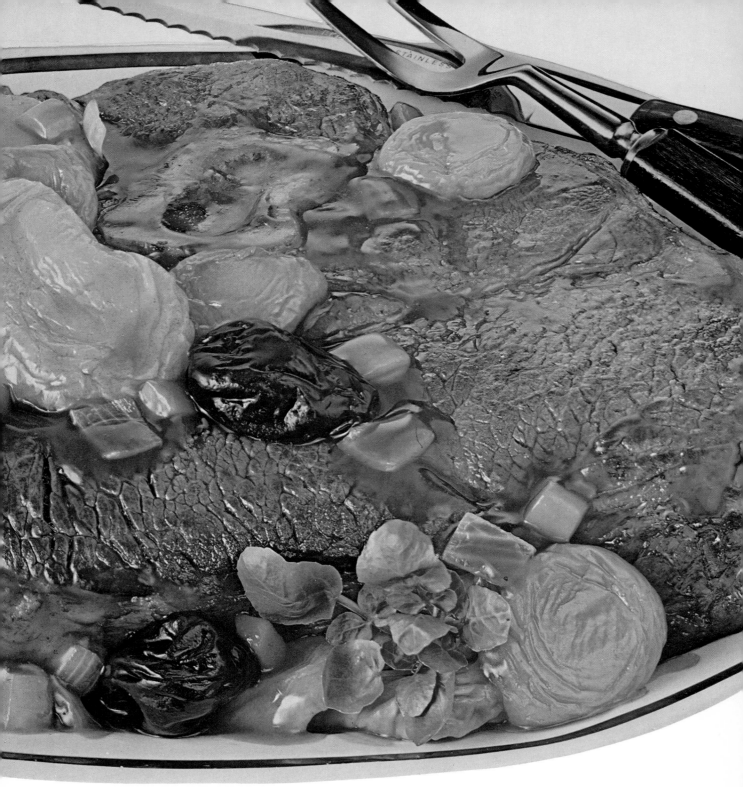

Add main dish color to the meal by combining dried fruit and tasty cider mixture to make mouth-watering Fruited Pot Roast.

individual type or in assorted mixtures suitable for use in recipes requiring combinations of fruits. Packaged dried fruit should be free of dirt, mold, insects, other foreign matter, and musty odor.

How to store: The concentrated simple sugars of dried fruit serve as a natural preservative, so caring for and storing the fruit is relatively simple. Vacuum-packed in cartons or transparent film bags, the fruit will keep up to six or eight months on the kitchen shelf or in the refrigerator.

Store leftover fruit from an opened package in a tightly covered container in a cool, dry place. Dried fruits need to be stored in the refrigerator during hot weather months to retain fruit quality.

How To Cook Dried Fruit

Rinse fruit and cover with water 1 inch above fruit in saucepan. Cover; simmer gently for time specified in chart. If desired, add sugar last 5 minutes of cooking.

To plump raisins, cover with water in saucepan. Bring to boiling. Remove from heat; let stand, covered, 5 minutes.

Dried fruit	Cooking time in minutes*	Sugar**
Apples	20 to 30	4
Apricots	20 to 25	3 to 4
Figs	40 to 45	1
Mixed Fruits	25 to 30	2 to 3
Peaches	30 to 35	3 to 4
Pears	30 to 35	3 to 4
Prunes	10 to 20	2

*Some dried fruits are processed to cut cooking time. See cooking directions on package.

**Sugar in tablespoons per cup uncooked fruit.

How to prepare: Formerly, drying techniques left fruits hard and withered, requiring tedious long soaking and cooking periods. Today, dried fruits require little or no soaking, and quick cooking is necessary to retain the delicate fruit pulps.

Oversoaking produces a watery, tasteless fruit. Hot water hastens soaking and leaves the fruit plumper than does cold water. Fruit should not be crowded in water so it has a chance to rehydrate and properly cook. Add sugar, if extra sweetness is desired, during the last five minutes of cooking as sugar inhibits the absorption of water. Fruits may be baked for dessert in the oven right along with other foods for a meal. The fruits will come out juicy and plump and will not require any additional preparation before serving.

Different dried fruits take up varying amounts of water during cooking. Apricots, figs, prunes, and raisins double in bulk by the end of cooking period. Peaches and pears triple in bulk and apples increase in bulk by five times.

The amount of fresh fruit needed to produce one pound of each type dried fruit helps explain the differing size increases of the cooked fruit. To make one pound of each fruit it takes seven to ten pounds of apples, six to seven pounds of peaches, six to seven pounds of pears, two and one half to three pounds of plums for prunes, and four pounds of grapes for raisins.

How to use: Dried fruits are delicious energy-givers eaten right out of the carton or bag. Make fruit purées by cooking fruits longer with added water and putting through sieve. Cook favorite dried fruit and serve as a sauce with dessert topping or as a meat accompaniment.

Add delectable flavors to pies, cakes, and cookies with chopped, cooked fruits. Bread puddings and stuffings for meat and fish acquire tasty flavor and new texture when dried fruits are added.

Colorful dried fruits make delightful meal garnishes and a wide assortment of tasty appetizers. Single fruits or assorted fruit mixtures are suitable for use in a simple compote or cold fruit soup served for wintertime desserts and snacks or at brunches. (See also *Fruit*.)

Fruited Pot Roast

Colorful meat accompaniment adds new flavor—

    12 dried apricots
    12 dried prunes
     1 3- to 4-pound beef chuck
          pot roast
     1 cup cider *or* apple juice
     2 tablespoons sugar
    ¼ teaspoon ground cinnamon
    ¼ teaspoon ground ginger
     3 whole cloves
    1½ cups sliced onions

Cover apricots and prunes with water. Soak several hours. Meanwhile, brown pot roast on both sides in a little hot fat; season with salt and pepper. Combine cider, sugar, cinnamon, ginger, and cloves; pour over meat. Add onions. Cover; simmer till meat is almost tender, about 2 hours. Drain fruits; place atop meat and cook 30 minutes longer. Thicken liquid in pan for gravy. Makes 6 to 8 servings.

Fruit Compote Pie

Fruit flavors blend in a refreshing dessert pie—

     1 cup mixed dried fruits, cut
          in pieces
    ½ cup orange juice
    ¼ cup raisins
    ¼ cup sugar
     1 tablespoon quick-cooking
          tapioca
     1 baked 9-inch pastry shell
              • • •
     1 3-ounce package no-bake
          custard mix
     2 cups milk
    ½ teaspoon shredded orange peel

In medium saucepan combine dried fruits, orange juice, ½ cup water, raisins, sugar, and tapioca; let stand 5 minues. Bring to full rolling boil; reduce heat and simmer till fruits are tender, about 10 minutes, stirring frequently. Cool; turn into baked pastry shell. Combine custard mix and milk; cook and cool according to package directions for custard pie. Pour carefully over fruit layer. Sprinkle with orange peel. Chill 3 to 4 hours before serving.

Fruit Confections

     1 cup raisins
    ¾ cup dried apricots
    ½ cup pitted dates
     1 cup walnuts
     2 tablespoons honey
              • • •
     2 tablespoons sugar
    ½ teaspoon ground cinnamon

Grind fruits and nuts with coarse blade of a food grinder. Mix with honey. Shape into 1-inch balls. Combine sugar and cinnamon. Roll balls in sugar mixture *or* sifted confectioners' sugar, if desired. Makes about 3 dozen 1-inch balls.

Fruit Balls

    1½ cups prunes, cooked and
          pitted
    1½ cups pitted dates
    ¾ cup dried apricots
    ½ cup raisins
     1 cup walnuts
    ¼ cup sugar
    ¼ cup orange juice concentrate,
          thawed
     1 3½-ounce can flaked
          coconut (1⅓ cups)

Grind prunes, dates, apricots, raisins, and walnuts with coarse blade of a food grinder. Add sugar and orange juice. Form into 1-inch balls; roll in coconut. Makes 10 dozen.

Harvest Fruit Compote

     1 16-ounce package dried prunes
    ½ of 11-ounce package dried
          apricots (1⅓ cups)
     1 13½-ounce can pineapple
          chunks, undrained (1⅔ cups)
              • • •
     1 21-ounce can cherry pie filling
     2 cups water
    ¼ cup dry sherry

In 9x2-inch baking dish, layer prunes, apricots, and pineapple. Combine remaining ingredients; pour over fruit. Cover and bake at 350° for 1½ hours. Serve warm. Serves 8.

DROP—1. A minute quantity of liquid that falls in a single globule. 2. A soft batter or dough shaped with a spoon into biscuits, cookies, or dumplings.

Liquid flavorings, such as peppermint or lemon, are often measured in number of drops or degree of flow as "drop by drop." An eye-dropper is used when the exact number of drops is vitally important.

Batter or dough of drop consistency, as in biscuits or cookies, indicates the liquid proportion is high and, therefore, makes it unlikely that the product can be shaped with the hands. A spoon is most frequently used for shaping and then the food is dropped directly from the spoon onto baking sheet or stew, or pushed off the spoon with the aid of another spoon.

DROP BISCUIT—Biscuit baked from standard biscuit dough to which more liquid has been added. The same basic flour, shortening, and milk ingredients are leavened with baking powder or baking soda as for standard biscuits. The added liquid gives the biscuit a softer consistency and a spoon is needed to shape it.

Biscuits can be dropped by rounded spoonfuls onto a greased baking sheet or into muffin cups. If biscuits are dropped close together, they will bake together and have soft sides. Baking biscuits farther apart or in the muffin cups will produce crisp, tender sides. Baked drop biscuits will have a somewhat pebbly browned top as compared to the smooth top of a standard biscuit. (See also *Biscuit*.)

Drop Biscuits

>   2 cups sifted all-purpose flour
>   3 teaspoons baking powder
>   ½ teaspoon salt
>   ¼ cup shortening
>   1 cup milk

Sift dry ingredients together into bowl. Cut in shortening with pastry blender or two forks till mixture looks like coarse crumbs. Make a well; add milk all at once. Stir quickly with fork till ingredients are moistened. Drop from teaspoon onto greased baking sheet. Bake at 450° for 12 to 15 minutes. Makes 16 biscuits.

DROP COOKIE—A soft-dough cookie shaped by dropping the dough from a spoon onto a baking sheet. One of the quickest and easiest types of cookies to make, drop cookies are acceptable in dainty sizes or as big, round sugar cookies.

A variety of shapes and forms can be achieved with drop cookie dough. If the dough is not lumpy, force some batters through a pastry bag. The dough is softer than a rolled cookie, yet stiff enough to be shaped and molded into balls or swirled shapes. Flatten some drop cookies with a glass that has been dipped in sugar, or make a crisscross pattern with a fork. Decorate drop cookies using raisins, assorted candies, and coconut. Stir candied fruits, nuts, or raisins into others.

Space drop cookies at regular intervals on the cookie sheet so they will not bake into each other and will bake evenly. Chill and mound the cookie dough before baking to prevent the cookie from spreading. Using a cool cookie sheet for each baking also eliminates spreading. Move cookies from cookie sheet to cooling rack immediately, as they continue to bake on sheet.

Drop cookies store well. Maintain moist qualities of the cookie by keeping them in a covered container. The drop cookie packs well and makes an excellent gift for mailing. (See also *Cookie*.)

Problems with drop cookies?

A doughy texture indicates that the cookie has not been baked long enough. A dry-textured cookie with dark brown edges means the cookie has been baked too long.

Brown-Eyed Susan Cookies

Combine 1½ cups packaged biscuit mix, two 3¾- or 3⅝-ounce packages *instant* vanilla pudding mix, ⅓ cup salad oil, and 2 eggs; mix well. Drop cookies from teaspoon onto *ungreased* cookie sheet. Flatten each cookie slightly. Top each with 6 or 7 mint-flavored chocolate pieces. Bake at 350° for 12 to 14 minutes. Spread melted chocolate over tops. Makes about 42.

Drop cookies are dropped from spoon or aided by another spoon or spatula onto greased baking sheet. Space cookies evenly apart.

Treat the family to spicy-rich Oatmeal Cookies. The pebbly topped, plump cookies are chock full of raisins and chopped nuts.

Oatmeal Cookies

    1 cup shortening
1½ cups brown sugar
    2 eggs
    ½ cup buttermilk or sour milk*
1¾ cups sifted all-purpose flour
    1 teaspoon baking soda*
    1 teaspoon baking powder*
    1 teaspoon ground cinnamon
    1 teaspoon ground nutmeg
    3 cups quick-cooking rolled oats
    1 cup raisins
    ½ cup chopped walnuts

Cream shortening, sugar, and eggs till light. Stir in buttermilk. Sift together dry ingredients and 1 teaspoon salt; stir into creamed mixture. Stir in oats, raisins, and nuts. Drop from tablespoon 2 inches apart on lightly greased cookie sheet. Bake at 400° about 8 minutes. Cool slightly; remove. Makes 60.

    *Or use sweet milk; reduce baking soda to ¼ teaspoon and use 2 teaspoons baking powder.

Butter Pecan Cookies

    1 cup butter or margarine
    ¾ cup brown sugar
    ¾ cup granulated sugar
    2 eggs
    1 teaspoon vanilla
2¼ cups sifted all-purpose flour
    1 teaspoon baking soda
    1 cup chopped pecans

Cream butter and sugars till light. Beat in eggs and vanilla. Sift together flour, soda, and ½ teaspoon salt; blend into creamed mixture. Stir in nuts. Drop from teaspoon on *ungreased* cookie sheet. Bake at 375° about 10 minutes. Makes about 4 dozen cookies.

Funny-Face Cookies

½ cup shortening
1 cup brown sugar
½ cup light molasses
½ cup milk
2 teaspoons vinegar
2½ cups sifted all-purpose flour
½ teaspoon baking soda
½ teaspoon salt
½ teaspoon ground ginger
½ teaspoon ground cinnamon
    Wooden skewers
    Raisins, assorted candies,
        coconut
    Corn syrup

Cream together shortening, brown sugar, and molasses. Stir in milk and vinegar. Sift together flour, soda, salt, ginger, and cinnamon; stir into molasses mixture. Drop by tablespoon about 2½ inches apart on lightly greased cookie sheet. Insert wooden skewer halfway into cookie dough mound. Stagger rows of cookies to leave room for the skewers. Use small spatula to spread dough around skewer if dough separates. Bake at 350° for 15 to 20 minutes. Decorate faces with raisins, candies, and coconut. Brush decorations with corn syrup to secure. Let stand before removing to rack.

DRY MILK — Whole or skim milk from which the water has been removed.

This convenient dairy product is produced and marketed in three forms: nonfat dry milk, instant nonfat dry milk, and dry whole milk. For each dry milk form, the manufacturing process is basically the same; only the products differ.

Nonfat dry milk: This starts out as fresh whole milk. The first step is the removal of milk fat from the fresh milk. The remaining nonfat portion is then put through a pasteurization process in which a large portion of the moisture is evaporated. Sprayed into a drying chamber, the milk is exposed to heated air filters which evaporate the remaining moisture and form the dry, white particles called dry milk.

The nutritional value of dry milk is not altered by these processes. In fact, the fat removal for the nonfat milk makes this milk form even more desirable for special diets and for weight watchers. The milk solids of lactose, milk protein, and minerals are readily available in dry milk.

Instant nonfat dry milk: This is the most popular of the three forms and can easily be found in supermarkets. Dry milk is instantized by moistening it, causing the dry milk particles to clump together, and then redrying. Instant nonfat dry milk is available in packages or jars. Buy the size to fit family and cooking needs.

Dry whole milk: Although this form is not often found in the United States, when it is, it is often used for infant feeding.

After milk has been reconstituted with water, it should be refrigerated in a manner similar to fresh milk. Dried whole milk, requiring special packaging because of the milk fat content, does not store easily.

Nonfat dry milk is used commercially in such foods as prepared mixes, bakery products, dairy foods, baby foods, and others. Use dry milk at home in place of fresh milk. Reconstitute milk according to package directions and add to recipe or add dry milk to dry ingredients and then add liquid. Use dry milk in desserts and toppings. Added to meat mixtures, dry milk holds in juices. (See also *Milk*.)

DRY WINE — A red or white unsweetened wine brought about by the fermentation of all of the sugar into alcohol. This results in the dry taste. Dry wines are perishable and should be consumed within 48 hours after opening. Dry wines are often served as appetizer or table wines when entertaining guests. (See also *Wines and Spirits*.)

DUCHESS POTATO — Mashed or puréed potatoes mixed with egg yolks and butter having salt, pepper, and sometimes nutmeg added. The fluffy, light potatoes, de-

Mashed potato elegance

Transform ordinary potatoes into a special→ surprise by mixing mashed potatoes, egg, and seasonings. Bake the Duchess Potatoes.

veloped by the French, can be shaped into many forms. Duchess potatoes may be forced through a pastry tube to pipe the edges of a steak or used as a fish or meat garnish. Decorate a casserole with potato rosettes. Pipe the potatoes onto a baking sheet, making individual servings; then broil them until they are done.

Duchess potatoes are often used as a beginning step for other potato and main dish recipes. Shaped potato croquettes are rolled in bread crumbs and deep fried. Serve creamed dishes in individual potato cases. Sometimes the potatoes are used as filling for stuffed baked potatoes or twice-baked potatoes. Glaze small portions of duchess potatoes and bake in oven to serve with a company meal instead of baked potatoes, which are the usual starch item at such affairs. (See also *Potato*.)

Duchess Potatoes

2 cups hot mashed potatoes
1 tablespoon butter or margarine
1 beaten egg yolk
  Salt
  Pepper
1 tablespoon butter or margarine, melted

To potatoes add 1 tablespoon butter or margarine, the egg yolk, and salt and pepper to taste; mix well. Push mounds from spoon onto greased baking sheet. Drizzle with remaining 1 tablespoon melted butter or margarine. Bake at 450° 10 to 12 minutes. Serves 4 to 6.

DUCK AND DUCKLING—Wild or domestic bird sought for its dark meat and distinctive flavor. Duck refers to the older duck, over eight weeks, and more specifically to the female bird. The male bird is called the drake. Duckling designates the young bird of less than eight weeks old. Both terms are used in the United States, but duckling is more correct as most birds sold in the United States are young.

The web-footed bird makes its home near fresh water. Various types of ducks exhibit different plumage colorings, but the basic down and feather covering is the same for all ducks. The soft down coat situated underneath the plumage protects the bird from cold weather. This soft down is often used for pillow filling. The duck uses an oil gland located at the base of the tail to keep the outer thick plumage groomed and cleaned at all times.

The birds' diets range from fish to grass and seeds, depending on the kind of bird and the water environment. The flavor of its meat is greatly affected by the diet of the bird as well as by its age and weight.

Ducks have been hunted as a major source of food since the earliest days of recorded time. The hieroglyphics of the ancient Egyptians show ducks being salted and dried for future use. The first people to actually breed and raise the ducks for food were the Chinese.

Domesticated ducks began to appear in Europe during the first century of the Christian Era. Romans fed figs to the ducks and then cooked them in delectable wine sauces. Ducks were an important meat source to the colonial Americans. They stored and cured the ducks in cellars, and sometimes canned them.

Types and kinds: There are over a hundred species of wild ducks found all over the world. One of the most widely known and delicately flavored is the canvasback. Getting its name from plumage coloring and a canvas bag shipment method of some years ago, the canvasback is regarded as the ultimate of wild duck dinners. The delightful, delicate flavor of the bird is contributed to by celery grass which the canvasback seeks out and thrives on.

The teal, including the green-winged, blue-winged, and cinnamon varieties, is another well-known freshwater duck. The loud whistling widgeon is a third freshwater duck known to most hunters.

The most beautiful of American ducks is the freshwater wood duck, or summer

A festive duck dinner

Carve tender duckling meat slices right at →
the table and pass tangy cranberry sauce. Guests will enjoy Cranberry Ducklings.

duck as it is sometimes called. The wood duck flies in noiseless, graceful motion. The duck is easily domesticated and it is bred on the Pacific Coast. Freshwater ducks, unlike saltwater ducks, prefer shallow, fresh waters where little diving is required to pick up fish and other edible substances from the pond bottom.

The mallard, found in all parts of the world, is probably one of the most important ducks as far as abundance and flavor are concerned. Being a river and pond duck, the mallard's diet consists of grains and small animal life. Many domestic varieties are descendants of the mallard.

The merganser ducks, with slender, cylindrical bills, dive for and feed on fish. The flavor of their meat is affected by this fish diet. Eight to ten types of merganser ducks, including the hooded merganser and red-breasted merganser in America, are found throughout the world.

In addition to the large number of wild ducks, commercially raised ducklings are also available. The largest percentage of commercially raised ducklings are descendants of the white Pekin duck brought from China in 1873. The white Pekin duck is a member of the mallard family.

Over one-half of the ducklings sold in America are raised on Long Island. The five million or so ducklings raised yearly in America become fine table delicacies, particularly during the holiday season.

The duckling that is raised commercially receives regulated special diets and is exposed to healthy environmental conditions in order to produce a bird with sweet, tender breast meat. The scientifically bred ducklings are not often raised during the cold months because of the difficulties encountered. Spring and summer surplus is consumed during this time.

The birds are completely dressed and cleaned for the commercial market. Bound in tight, shape-conforming plastic wrap, they are quick-frozen and ready to cook after thawing is complete.

Nutritional value: Duckling is an extremely nutritious meat to serve to the family. The dark meat is rich in protein, thiamine, and riboflavin, and is a fair source of iron. A higher fat content is found in ducklings than is present in other poultry. The soft duckling fat is highly concentrated with unsaturated fatty acids.

How to select: When buying fresh duckling, remember that most of the sliceable meat comes from the breast, so select a well-developed, broad-breasted bird. A duckling is longer in appearance than a chicken and should be adequately covered with flesh. Check the skin making sure it is free from pinfeathers, breaks in skin, and bruises.

Packaged, ready-to-cook duckling is available in weights from three and one half to five pounds. Ready-to-cook wild duck is available in one to two pound weights. Check to see that the bird has been well wrapped and that there are no breaks in the package.

Allow three-fourths to one pound of duckling meat for each person. One average-size duckling will usually serve about three persons with hearty appetites.

How to store: Keep fresh duckling in a loosely covered container in the coldest part of the refrigerator. It may be kept this way between two and three days before cooking. Leftover, cooked duckling should be refrigerated immediately where it will keep well one to two days. Ducklings freeze well and can be stored in the freezer up to three months before thawing and using.

How to prepare: To develop the rich, wild duck flavor, many hunters choose to age ducks by hanging the birds by their feet in a cool, shady place for about three days. Avid duck lovers claim that aging breaks tough meat fibers, and leaving the entrails intact during aging enhances the flavor still further. If the bird has been bruised badly, the entrails should be removed before hanging the duck to age. Otherwise, there is danger that the duck will spoil.

Dressing and cleaning fresh duck requires skill and patience. Dry picking is recommended over the hot water dunking treatment as water washes away the flavor. After removing all the outer coarse guard feathers, pour melted paraffin over the soft down and pull off when dry, being careful not to tear the skin. The entrails are then drawn and the duck singed. The tedious job of removing the pinfeathers requires a great deal of patience, and a perfectionist will usually try to remove each one with a pair of tweezers.

Cut away excess fat around body openings as there is sufficient fat on the duck to self-baste the bird. Consequently, no added fat will be needed when cooking the wild duck. Sometimes the wing tips are also clipped away for added convenience.

Opinions regarding the preparation of duck before cooking also differ. The noted duck lover will simply wipe the bird and body cavity with a damp cloth assuming the cooking process will take care of any bacterial action. The novice homemaker will soak the bird for hours in water and soda solution to rid the bird of the wild flavor. Blood retains the delicate duck flavor, so personal preference dictates which method of preparation to use.

Ducks and ducklings are often marinated in wine sauces and mixtures before cooking. Unless suitable flavorings and sauces are used, marinating sometimes destroys or covers up the rich game flavor that many people expect from wild birds.

Truss the birds with skewers or twine to hold in the body juices during cooking. Pricking the skin allows the fat juices to slowly escape and baste the bird during roasting. A roasted wild duck may need to be basted occasionally.

There are three separate thoughts on the way the duckling should be cooked. One way is to fast-cook the bird in a hot oven not over 30 minutes. This usually produces a rare, pink meat with a crisp, brown crust. A second method is to allow the bird to cook in a hot oven about five to six minutes and then reduce the temperature. The third way is to cook the bird in a

---

Preparing wild duck

Because of their diets, some wild ducks have a definite fish flavor. To eliminate this flavor, place celery, carrots, or potatoes in body cavity. Simmer duck in water about 10 minutes. Discard stuffing and prepare duck for roasting as usual.

---

moderate oven till done. The bird may be brushed with a fruit glaze before done.

The famous French pressed duck (canard) or duckling (caneton) utilizes a special duck press apparatus, but this may be achieved at home by putting the meat through a food grinder using a coarse blade. Duck can also be roasted on the outdoor grill for a special company meal or for a special-occasion dinner-for-two.

Whatever way the bird is prepared, it should be served immediately. Avoid using strong, competitive flavors. Orange sauces or stuffings are good flavor accompaniments to duck and duckling. Any fruits, such as cherries or peaches, make colorful garnishes. (See also *Poultry*.)

Cranberry Duckling

    2 3- to 5-pound ready-to-cook
        domestic ducklings
        Giblets and neck
    1 10½-ounce can condensed beef
        broth
                • • •
    ¾ cup cranberry juice cocktail
    2 tablespoons butter or margarine
    2 tablespoons sugar
    2 tablespoons vinegar
    1 tablespoon cornstarch
    1 tablespoon cranberry juice
        cocktail

Follow directions for roasting domestic duck (see chart, page 824). Meanwhile, place neck and giblets in saucepan. Add beef broth and simmer, covered, for 1 hour. Strain broth; serve giblets with duck. To the strained broth add ¾ cup cranberry juice cocktail; cook till reduced to one cup. In small saucepan melt butter or margarine; blend in sugar, cook and stir till brown. Add the 2 tablespoons vinegar and the cranberry-broth mixture.

Remove ducklings from roasting pan to warm serving platter. Skim fat from meat juices; add juices to cranberry-broth mixture. Blend cornstarch with the 1 tablespoon cranberry juice cocktail; stir into sauce. Cook and stir till sauce thickens and bubbles; simmer 1 to 2 minutes. Pass sauce with duckling. Garnish the duckling with parsley and kumquats or other garnishes, if desired. Makes about 8 servings.

Wild Duck À La Orange

A succulent duck, glistening with orange glaze, spices the dinner-time meal—

    2 1- to 2-pound ready-to-cook wild
      ducks, split in halves
      lengthwise
             • • •
    1 medium onion, sliced and
      separated into rings
    2 tablespoons butter or margarine
             • • •
    2 tablespoons frozen orange juice
      concentrate, thawed
    2 tablespoons honey
    1 tablespoon lemon juice
    ½ teaspoon ground ginger
    ¼ teaspoon ground allspice

Roast duck on rack in shallow roasting pan at 400° till tender, about 1 hour. If necessary, cap with foil to prevent excess browning. Skim off fat. Last 5 to 10 minutes baste the duck with orange glaze. Makes about 4 servings.

To make orange glaze cook onion in butter till tender but not brown. Stir in thawed orange juice concentrate, honey, lemon juice, ground ginger, and ground allspice. Heat just to boiling.

Rotisserie Duck

Roast a golden duck on the barbecue grill for a change-of-pace outdoor meal—

    1 4-pound ready-to-cook domestic
      duckling
             • • •
    Salt
    2 tablespoons sugar
    Pepper

Rub inside the duckling with salt. Prick skin and truss well. Balance duckling on spit, securing with holding forks on both ends. Arrange hot coals at back and sides of firebox. Place a foil drip pan in front of coals and under the spit. (Since ducks are fat birds, a large amount of fat will cook out and drip into foil pan. It may be necessary to drain fat occasionally from the drip pan so that the fat will not become too hot and flame up.)

Attach spit, turn on motor and lower the barbecue hood. Let duck rotate over *medium* coals till done, about 2 hours. (Maintain a temperature of 300° to 325° if the grill has a heat indicator.) The last 10 minutes of roasting time sprinkle the duck with sugar and dash pepper. Continue roasting till brown. Makes 4 servings.

ROASTING CHART FOR DUCK

General Instructions: Salt inside of ready-to-cook bird. Stuff as desired. Truss bird; place, breast side up, on rack on shallow roasting pan. Roast, uncovered, till tender (refer to chart). Times may vary with age of bird; young birds are the most suitable for roasting. When necessary, place foil loosely over top of bird to prevent excess browning.

Game Bird	Ready-to-Cook Weight	Oven Temp.	Roasting Time	Amount of Serving	Special Instructions
Wild Duck	1-2 lbs.	400°	60-90 min.	1-1½ lbs.	Stuff loosely with quartered onions and apples; discard stuffing before serving. Do not brush with oil.
Domestic Duckling	3-5 lbs.	375° then 425°	1½-2 hrs. 15 min.	¾-1 lb.	Prick skin well all over to allow fat to escape. Do not rub with oil. Serve stuffing with bird.

Roast Duckling with Oranges

>   2 4- to 5-pound ready-to-cook
>   domestic ducklings
>   3 medium oranges
>   2 tablespoons sugar
>   2 teaspoons vinegar
>   2 cups canned condensed beef
>   broth
>   1½ tablespoons lemon juice
>   3 teaspoons cornstarch
>   ½ cup sweet sherry
>   ⅓ cup orange liqueur

Clean ducklings and pat dry. Rub inside of ducks with salt; skewer opening and lace shut. Prick skin well all over to allow fat to escape. Roast on a rack in shallow pan at 400°, following directions for roasting domestic duck (see chart, page 824). Spoon off fat occasionally. While ducks roast, shave peel from *2* of the oranges with vegetable parer and cut in julienne strips; squeeze the juice from *all 3* oranges. Set orange peel and juice aside until needed.

When ducks are done, place on heated platter and keep hot while making orange sauce. To prepare sauce remove drippings from roasting pan and skim off fat; set pan juices aside. Caramelize the sugar with vinegar in roasting pan; add reserved pan juices, beef broth, orange juice and peel, and lemon juice. Cook sauce rapidly to reduce by *half*. Blend cornstarch and sherry; gradually stir into sauce. Cook and stir till thickened and clear. Add orange liqueur to the sauce just before serving. Trim ducks with several orange sections, if desired. Makes 6 to 8 servings.

Roast Domestic Duck

Fruit- or celery-stuffed duck is a company treat—

Remove wing tips and first juice from one 3- to 5-pound ready-to-cook domestic duck. Sprinkle inside with salt. Stuff lightly with Orange Stuffing (see *Stuffing* for recipe), *or* celery and 1 quartered, tart apple. Prick skin all over to allow fat to escape. Do not rub with oil. Truss; place breast up on rack in shallow pan. Don't add water. Roast, uncovered, at 375° for 1½ to 2 hours. Increase temperature to 425° and cook until leg moves quite easily when tested, about 15 minutes. Makes 3 or 4 servings.

Navy Bean-Stuffed Duck

>   1 cup dry small navy beans
>   2 chicken bouillon cubes
>   ½ pound bulk pork sausage,
>   broken in bite-size pieces
>   1 medium tomato, peeled and
>   chopped
>   ½ cup finely chopped onion
>   ¼ cup finely chopped celery
>   ¼ cup snipped parsley
>   1 small clove garlic, minced
>   ½ teaspoon dried thyme leaves,
>   crushed
>   1 small bay leaf
>   ¼ cup sauterne
>   • • •
>   1 5- to 6-pound ready-to-cook
>   domestic duckling

In saucepan combine beans, 1 quart water, and chicken bouillon cubes; bring to boiling and boil gently for 2 minutes. Remove from heat; cover and let stand for 1 hour.

To the bean mixture, add sausage, tomato, onion, celery, parsley, garlic, thyme, bay leaf, and ¼ teaspoon salt. Bring to boiling; cover and simmer 1 hour. Uncover and stir in wine. Boil the mixture gently, uncovered, till the liquid is absorbed, about 30 minutes.

Salt inside of duckling; stuff lightly and truss. Roast, following directions for roasting domestic duck (see chart, page 824). Makes 4 servings.

Cantonese Duck

Season two 1- to 2-pound ready-to-cook wild ducks inside and out with salt. Place in cavity of *each* bird ½ orange, cut in wedges, and a few celery leaves. Place birds, breast side up, on rack in a shallow roasting pan. Roast, uncovered, at 400° till tender, about 1 hour. If necessary, cap with foil to prevent excess browning.

Meanwhile, prepare sauce by combining ½ cup apricot preserves, ¼ cup water, 1 tablespoon prepared mustard, 1 tablespoon soy sauce, 1 tablespoon lemon juice, and ½ teaspoon monosodium glutamate in a saucepan. Heat, stirring constantly. During the last 10 minutes of roasting, baste ducks occasionally with sauce. Remove meat from oven; discard stuffing. Serve ducks over hot cooked rice; pass remaining sauce. Makes 4 servings.

DUCK PRESS—Equipment used to press duck for particular duck dishes prepared at the table. The aluminum and stainless steel apparatus consists of a container which holds the meat and a press which forces the juices from the meat.

The duck is roasted without stuffing to a rare stage. The breast is sliced into fillets and the legs are removed. The remainder of the carcass is put through the duck press along with red wine, and the extracted juices are served as gravy or sauce with the breast and leg meat.

The French extract and use the duck blood for famous French pressed duck. It becomes a special treat to watch head-waiters in fine restaurants prepare the duck sauce with the press right at the table. A similar press technique may be achieved at home by cutting up the duck carcass and forcing it through a food chopper using the coarse blade. The extracted juices should be strained before using to obtain a better-looking, clearer gravy.

DUCK SAUCE—A Chinese sweet sauce, similar to chutney, made of fruits and served with roast duck and pork, spareribs, and egg roll. More correctly called *duk* sauce, it has a base of apricots, peaches, or plums with spices, sugar, and vinegar added.

The tangy sauce is often served in small dishes, sometimes combined with a mustard, in which the foods may be dipped.

Grandma would be envious of this hearty hot dumpling dish. Carrots, lima beans, and lamb cubes with seasoned tomato sauce and dumplings combine in Lamb Stew 'n Dumplings.

Duck sauce is found in supermarkets or specialty shops in jars and is available in several different kinds. (See also *Sauce.*)

DU JOUR *(duh zhoor', doo)* — A French term often found on menus in fine restaurants referring to the food specialty of the day, such as the soup or dessert of the day.

DULSE — A coarse, edible seaweed of the red seaweed family found along the continental and island coasts. The salty tang of dulse is acquired from the European and American North Atlantic coasts, as well as the Pacific coast, where it grows abundantly. Children of colonial America considered dulse a candy treat. Alfred W. McCann discovered from observation that healthy old fishermen who were receiving iodine from the fish that ate seaweed were free from arteriosclerosis.

At the Bay of Fundy of the Grand Manan Islands, dulsing becomes an important industry during the summer months. First, the seaweed is torn loose from the sea bottom and gathered. Then, the fresh, brownish seaweed, often transparent in the sun, is spread on huge, flat rocks to dry. After drying, dulse is packed in barrels and sacks ready for shipment. Dulse is also collected and packaged for shipping in the northern countries of Iceland, Scotland, and the Canadian Maritime Provinces.

Because dulse is grown in the sea, it is very rich in iodine. The salty, pleasing taste of dried dulse makes it desirable as a natural candy. It can be cooked like a vegetable and is popular as a relish along the coastal regions. Dulse, also known as carrageen or Irish moss, is used as a thickening agent and can be found in a great many commercial products.

DUMPLING — 1. Light, tender balls of leavened dough steamed or boiled with stews or soups. 2. Pastry-wrapped fruits, often accompanied with a sauce, served as a dessert along with the main course.

The Chinese dumpling, *chu-pao-pa*, developed thousands of years ago, was the beginning of the now universal food. These Chinese dumplings were eaten in soups or with sauces in much the same way as they are eaten today.

The Western world quickly adopted the dumpling as they heard of it from world travelers. It soon became an integral part of English and Scandinavian cookery.

There are as many types of dumplings as there are countries with traditional foods. Dumplings are ravioli in Italy, and, except for the filling, they resemble the *won ton* of China. In Germany, they are either *Kloësse, Knodel,* or *Spaetzle,* depending on the type. Dumplings are *kolodny* in Lithuania, and *Knedliky* in Czechoslovakia, *blintzes* in Slavic countries, and tamales or empanadas in countries where Spanish is spoken. Dumplings are one of the most accepted foods in the world.

In America, stewed dumplings and baked fruit dumplings are favorite menu items for many families. Plump dumplings of flour, cornmeal, cracker meal, or farina are great stew toppers. They are also excellent in soups and ragouts, or served with creamed chicken and pot roasts.

Baked fruit dumplings are a dessert specialty for any time of the year. For the mouth-watering filling, plentiful fresh fruits can be used during the summer months and convenient canned fruits in the cold, winter months.

Dip tablespoon into hot stew liquid before dropping dumplings each time. The dumplings will slide off onto meat and vegetables.

Most dumplings are grouped into one of three categories: boiled, steamed, or baked. Boiled dumplings, drop or molded, are cooked, covered or uncovered, in a simmering liquid. A slightly sweet dumpling batter is used to make drop dumplings. Some drop dumplings are cooked, uncovered, atop the simmering liquid and some in a tightly covered kettle. The liquid in which the dumplings are cooked serves as a sauce for the dumplings when served.

The molded type of boiled dumpling is often rolled and cut out of a potato dumpling dough. However, if you wish, you can shape the dough around a piece of fruit first and then drop it into the boiling water and cook it until it is done.

A steamed dumpling is made from biscuit dough. After the dough has been cut, it is most often shaped around a piece of fruit. The dumplings are then cooked over steam either in custard cups or a perforated pan. Serve steamed dumplings with a rich cream or a sauce.

Baked dumplings, apple dumplings being a good example, are made of plain pastry or a rich biscuit dough. The dough is wrapped around the fruit and placed on a baking sheet to bake. The dumpling can be poached in the oven by setting it in a shallow pan containing a thin syrup.

Beef and Dumplings

    1 beaten egg
    1 10½-ounce can condensed cream
        of celery soup
    ½ cup soft bread crumbs
    2 tablespoons dry onion soup mix
    1 pound ground beef
        • • •
    2 tablespoons shortening
    1 tablespoon all-purpose flour
    ½ teaspoon paprika
    ½ cup water
    1 3-ounce can chopped mushrooms,
        undrained (⅔ cup)
        Dumplings

Combine egg, ¼ *cup* of the soup, crumbs, and dry soup mix. Add beef; mix well. Shape into 8 meatballs. In skillet brown meatballs in hot shortening. Drain off excess fat. Blend together

remaining soup, flour, and paprika. Gradually stir in water. Add mushrooms with liquid. Pour over meatballs in *skillet*. Bring to boiling; reduce heat and simmer, covered, for 20 minutes. Pour into 1½-quart casserole. Top with Dumplings. Bake, uncovered, at 400° for 20 to 25 minutes. Makes 4 servings.

Dumplings: Combine 1 cup sifted all-purpose flour, 2 teaspoons baking powder, 1 teaspoon dry onion soup mix, and ¼ teaspoon celery salt. Combine ½ cup milk and 1 tablespoon salad oil. Stir into flour mixture till smooth. Combine 1 cup soft bread crumbs with 2 tablespoons melted butter. Divide dough into 8 portions; drop by tablespoon into buttered crumbs, turning to coat all sides. At serving time place dumplings atop the *boiling* meat mixture.

Lamb Stew 'n Dumplings

    2 pounds boneless lamb shoulder,
        cut in 1-inch cubes
    ¼ cup all-purpose flour
    1 teaspoon paprika
    ¼ teaspoon pepper
    2 tablespoons shortening
    1 8-ounce can tomato sauce
    1 clove garlic, minced
    ½ teaspoon dried thyme leaves,
        crushed
    ½ teaspoon dried marjoram leaves,
        crushed
    1 10-ounce package frozen baby
        lima beans
    6 medium carrots, cut in ½-inch
        pieces
    6 small whole onions
    ⅓ cup milk
    1 cup packaged biscuit mix

Coat lamb cubes with mixture of flour, 2 teaspoons salt, paprika, and pepper. Heat shortening; brown meat. Add 2 cups water, tomato sauce, minced garlic, thyme, and marjoram.

Cover and simmer till meat is almost tender, about 1 hour. Add frozen baby limas, carrots, and onions; cover and simmer until the lamb is very tender, about 20 minutes.

Top with 10 to 12 small Dumplings: Add milk to packaged biscuit mix. Mix well; spoon over hot bubbling stew. Cook, uncovered, over low heat 5 minutes. Cover and cook 10 minutes. Makes 6 to 8 servings.

Chicken with Raisin Dumplings

    1 5- to 6-pound ready-to-cook
         stewing chicken, cut up, *or* 2
         large broiler-fryer chickens,
         cut up
    2 sprigs parsley
    4 stalks celery with leaves
    1 carrot, sliced
    1 small onion, cut up
    2 teaspoons salt
  1/4 teaspoon pepper

        • • •

    1 cup all-purpose flour
    3 teaspoons baking powder
    1 tablespoon shortening
  1/2 cup raisins
    1 cup coarse dry bread crumbs
    1 beaten egg
  3/4 cup milk
    2 teaspoons grated onion

Place chicken pieces in Dutch oven or large kettle with enough water to cover (about 2 quarts). Add parsley sprigs, celery, sliced carrot, onion, salt, and pepper. Cover mixture; bring to boiling and cook over low heat till tender, about 2 1/2 hours.

Sift together flour, baking powder, and 1 teaspoon salt. Cut shortening into dry ingredients. Add raisins and bread crumbs. Combine egg, milk, and grated onion. Add to raisin mixture; mix just to moisten.

Drop dumpling mixture from tablespoon atop stewed chicken in boiling stock. Cover tightly (don't lift cover); simmer 20 minutes. Remove chicken and dumplings; thicken broth.

Fluffy Dumplings

    1 cup sifted all-purpose flour
    2 teaspoons baking powder
  1/2 teaspoon salt
  1/2 cup milk
    2 tablespoons salad oil

Sift flour, baking powder, and salt together in bowl. Combine milk and oil; add all at once to dry ingredients, stirring till moistened. Drop from tablespoon atop bubbling stew. Cover tightly; let mixture return to boiling. Reduce heat (don't lift cover); simmer 12 to 15 minutes. Makes about 10 dumplings.

Easy Dumplings

  2/3 cup milk
    2 cups packaged biscuit mix

Add milk to package biscuit mix all at once; stir just till mixture is moistened. Drop by rounded tablespoon atop hot, bubbling stew. Cook, uncovered, over low heat 10 minutes. Cover and cook 10 minutes longer, allowing the dumplings to rise, or till done. Makes 10 to 12 meal-perfect Easy Dumplings.

Skillet Strawberry Dumplings

    1 21-ounce can strawberry pie
         filling
 1 1/2 cups orange juice
    1 cup water
  1/4 cup sugar
    1 tablespoon butter or margarine
        Few drops red food coloring
 1 1/2 cups sifted all-purpose flour
  1/3 cup sugar
    1 tablespoon baking powder
  2/3 cup milk
    2 tablespoons salad oil
        Ground cinnamon *or* nutmeg

In electric skillet combine first 5 ingredients. Heat to boiling. Add red food coloring. In mixing bowl sift together flour, the 1/3 cup sugar, baking powder, and 1/2 teaspoon salt. Stir in milk and oil. Drop in 6 portions onto boiling fruit mixture. Sprinkle lightly with cinnamon or nutmeg. Cover; cook at 200° for 10 to 12 minutes or till dumplings are done. Serve warm with cream, if desired. Makes 6 servings.

Fruit with Dumplings

Combine one 8-ounce can fruit cocktail, 1 tablespoon sugar, 1 teaspoon butter or margarine, and 1 teaspoon lemon juice in saucepan. Bring to boil. In small bowl sift together 1/2 cup all-purpose flour, 2 tablespoons sugar, 1 teaspoon baking powder, and 1/4 teaspoon salt. Stir in 1/4 cup milk and 1 teaspoon salad oil.

Drop in 2 portions onto *boiling hot* fruit. Sprinkle lightly with ground cinnamon or ground nutmeg. Cover; cook over medium heat for 10 minutes. Serve with cream. Serves 2.

Stir up dumplings while blueberry sauce is cooking. Dovetailing, or doing two jobs at once, makes the dessert faster and easier.

Drop rounded tablespoons of dumpling batter onto the bubbling blueberry sauce. Dip spoon into hot sauce before each dumpling.

Leave the lid on and avoid peeking while the dumplings cook. Serve light and tender Blueberry Dumplings hot with cream.

Berry-filled fruit dumplings become summer fresh fruit favorites and add a warm glow to winter months using canned or dried fruits. Biscuit dough is most often used to wrap the delectable fruit and spices. Fruit dumplings are usually baked on a baking sheet but can be set in a shallow pan or allowed to poach in their own juices. Rich cream, ice cream, or sweet sauces may accompany the dumplings. (See also *Dessert*.)

Blueberry Dumplings

    1 20-ounce can frozen sweetened
          blueberries (2½ cups)
       Dash salt
    ¼ cup water
    1 tablespoon lemon juice
    1 cup sifted all-purpose flour
    2 tablespoons sugar
    2 teaspoons baking powder
    ¼ teaspoon salt
    1 tablespoon butter
    ½ cup milk

In large saucepan bring frozen, sweetened blueberries, dash salt, and water to boiling. Add lemon juice. Sift together flour, sugar, baking powder, and ¼ teaspoon salt; cut in butter till mixture resembles coarse meal. Add milk all at once, stirring till flour is moistened. Drop batter from tip of tablespoon into bubbling sauce, making 6 dumplings—don't let them overlap. Cover tightly; cook over low heat 10 minutes without uncovering. Serve hot. If desired, serve with cream. Makes 6 servings.

Basic Apple Dumplings

As good as the ones grandma used to make—

    1½ cups sugar
    1½ cups water
     ¼ teaspoon ground cinnamon
     ¼ teaspoon ground nutmeg
      8 drops red food coloring
      3 tablespoons butter or margarine
              • • •
      2 cups sifted all-purpose flour
      2 teaspoons baking powder
      1 teaspoon salt
     ⅔ cup shortening
     ½ cup milk
      6 medium, whole apples, peeled
          and cored

For syrup mix sugar, water, cinnamon, nutmeg, and red food coloring; bring to boiling. Remove from heat; add butter or margarine.

Sift together flour, baking powder, and salt; cut in shortening till mixture resembles coarse crumbs. Add milk all at once; stir just till flour is moistened. On lightly floured surface, roll to 18x12-inch rectangle.

Cut in six 6-inch squares. Place apple on each*. Sprinkle apples generously with additional sugar, cinnamon, and nutmeg; dot with butter. Moisten edges of pastry. Bring corners to center and pinch edges together.

Place 1 inch apart in *ungreased* 11x7x1½-inch baking pan. Pour syrup over dumplings; sprinkle with sugar. Bake at 375° till apples are tender, about 35 minutes. Serve warm with maple syrup, if desired. Makes 6 servings.

*Or use ½ apple, sliced, in each square.

Spice-Prune Dumplings

     ½ pound dried prunes
          (about 1½ cups)
     ½ cup sugar
     ¼ cup chopped walnuts
      2 tablespoons butter or margarine
      1 tablespoon lemon juice
     ¼ teaspoon ground cinnamon
     ½ teaspoon ground nutmeg
      2 cups biscuit mix
     ½ cup water
     ½ teaspoon ground cinnamon
     ¼ teaspoon ground nutmeg

In saucepan combine prunes with 3 cups water. Cover; bring to boiling and boil gently 20 minutes. Add sugar and cook, covered, 5 minutes more. Drain and reserve liquid (about 2 cups). Pit and chop prunes. Combine prunes with ½ cup water and cook till excess liquid is absorbed, about 2 minutes. Stir in walnuts, butter or margarine, lemon juice, ¼ teaspoon ground cinnamon, and ¼ teaspoon ground nutmeg.

Combine biscuit mix and ½ cup water; stir till dry ingredients are moistened. Turn onto floured surface and knead lightly 8 to 10 times. Roll into a 16x8-inch rectangle; cut into eight 4-inch squares. Place 2 tablespoons prune mixture in center of each square. Fold corners of dough to center and pinch edges together. Place in 12x7½x2-inch baking dish. Stir the remaining cinnamon and nutmeg into reserved prune liquid; pour over dumplings. Sprinkle dumplings with additional granulated sugar. Bake at 375° for 30 to 35 minutes. Serve warm with cream, if desired. Makes 8 servings.

Peach-Cheese Dumplings

      1 29-ounce can peach halves
    1½ cups sifted all-purpose flour
     ¾ teaspoon salt
     ½ cup shortening
     ½ cup shredded sharp process
          American cheese
          Butter
          Ground cinnamon
          Lemon Sauce

Drain peaches, reserving 1 cup syrup. Sift flour with salt; cut in shortening till size of small peas. Add cheese; mix lightly. Blend in 3 to 4 tablespoons cold water as for pastry.

Roll dough on lightly floured surface to 18x 12-inch rectangle. Cut in six 6-inch squares. Place peach half, cut side down, in center of each square. Dot with butter; dash with cinnamon. Moisten edges of pastry and fold over peach, pinching to seal. Place dumplings on *ungreased* baking sheet. Bake at 425° for 20 to 25 minutes. Makes 6 servings.

Serve with *Lemon Sauce:* In saucepan blend ¼ cup sugar, 1 tablespoon cornstarch, and dash salt; gradually add 1 cup reserved peach syrup. Cook and stir till thickened and clear. Add 1 teaspoon grated lemon peel, 1 tablespoon lemon juice, 1 tablespoon butter.

DUNGENESS CRAB *(duhn' juh nes)*—A large, reddish crab. These crabs, named for a town in Washington, live along the Pacific coast shores from Mexico to Alaska. They weigh from 1½ to 3½ pounds and are prized for their rich, tender meat.

Dungeness crabs are available on the markets in many forms—live, cooked in the shell, fresh cooked meat, frozen meat, and canned meat. The meat comes from both the body and the claws.

State laws prevent these crabs being sold in the soft-shell stage. (See also *Crab.*)

DUNLOP CHEESE—A sweet, rich, firm, white cheese that resembles Cheddar cheese. At one time Dunlop was regarded as Scotland's national cheese.

DURUM WHEAT *(door' uhm)*—A type of wheat also known as macaroni wheat. Durum is classified as a very hard wheat and is used in making pasta, such as macaroni, spaghetti, and noodles.

Durum wheat originally grew in Southwestern Asia and in the Balkan areas around the Mediterranean Sea. From there it was introduced into those sections of the world that had little rainfall. In the United States, Minnesota, Montana, and the Dakotas have become the principal areas where this wheat is raised.

For centuries, man has used this amber-colored grain to make pasta products. The characteristics that have made durum wheat desirable for pasta are its ability to become tender when cooked, yet hold its shape without a gummy or sticky texture; a nutty flavor; and a pleasing yellow color in the cooked food.

Durum wheat kernels are transformed into pasta by separating the bran and germ sections of the kernel. Then the remainder is ground into a coarse meal, called semolina. Water is mixed with semolina to make a dough. Sometimes, salt, flavoring, B vitamins, and iron are added for flavor and enrichment. This stiff mixture is then formed into one of the more than 150 different pasta shapes made for today's market. (See also *Wheat.*)

DUST—To sprinkle a dry ingredient *lightly* over food. Typical dusting ingredients are granulated sugar, confectioners' sugar, flour, and various spices. They are dusted over desserts, meats, and breads as a coating or as a garnish. The dry ingredients can be sprinkled from a spoon or sifted through a sifter or through a sieve. This latter method gives a finer, more even coating over the food.

Interesting decorations can be made by dusting sugar or spice in a design. Place a doily or stencil over the food and then dust. Carefully pick up the stencil so the design will not be disturbed.

When a heavy coating of flour or sugar is spread over the food, this is known as dredging rather than dusting.

DUTCH OVEN—A deep, heavy pan with a tight-fitting lid. Dutch ovens come in a wide range of sizes and are made of metals, such as aluminum, cast iron, and stainless steel. They may be used either in the oven or on top of the range. Electric models are also available for cooking in the kitchen, dining room, or patio.

The Dutch oven's large size and tight-fitting lid make it suitable for braising pot roasts, cooking stews, steaming foods, deep-fat frying, warming buns and rolls, and popping corn. It can also double as a saucepan when the supply of equipment is limited or an extra large saucepan is needed for preparing a large recipe. (See also *Pots and Pans.*)

DUTCH-PROCESS COCOA—A rich, dark cocoa powder treated with alkaline salt. The Dutch people in the East Indies discovered that cocoa was improved when treated with the salt. This cocoa has a darker color and less acid flavor than does regular cocoa, and has a delicate aroma. It blends well with liquids and does not separate easily. (See also *Cocoa.*)

DUXELLES *(dûk sel', duhk-, dook)*—A mixture of mushrooms, shallots, and herbs. The mushrooms and shallots are minced and cooked with the herbs in a stock until reduced to a paste or dried out.

Duxelles, usually associated with French cookery, can be used as a garnish or as a flavoring ingredient with sauces, stuffings, or meats. (See also *French Cookery.*)

E

EASTER — The annual celebration of the resurrection of Jesus Christ in the Christian religion. Easter comes in the spring of the year near the time of ancient pagan spring festivals and the Jewish Passover. Therefore, many of the traditional practices, symbols, and foods are related to those of other religions and cultures.

The English word, Easter, is derived from the name of the Anglo-Saxon goddess of spring, Eostre or Ostâra. The word for Easter in many other languages comes from the Hebrew word for Passover.

The exact date of Easter is variable, coming on a Sunday between March 22 and April 25. For those who want to figure the date for themselves, Easter comes on the first Sunday after the first full moon following March 21. These complicated calculations were arrived at centuries ago after much controversy over what calendar to use, whether the date would vary, and if Easter would always be on Sunday.

Easter has a number of traditional foods as do all holidays. Some of these foods reflect a significance of the holiday and others are inherited from ancient cultures. Breads and cakes of all sorts, meats, such as lamb and ham, and eggs are among the most vivid examples of Easter foods.

Breads: Yeast breads, rolls, buns, and coffee cakes are a significant part of the Easter celebration. Many times they are formed into symbolic shapes of rabbits, lambs, and crosses. In some countries, days of baking precede Easter Sunday and then the goods are taken to the church to be blessed before they are eaten.

Each country has its own bread that is traditionally made for Easter. The Russians bake a high, round yeast bread called *kulich.* This is served with *paskha,* a sweet cottage cheese dessert shaped like a pyramid. The Greeks make *tsoureki,* which is a braided yeast bread with brightly colored eggs arranged in the center. Other breads, familiar to Americans, are the *stollen* made in Germany and Austria, the golden bread in Ireland, the *babka* in Poland, and the *mazanetz* of Czechoslovakia.

In America one of the better-known breads is the hot cross bun. This round bun has raisins in the dough and a cross on the top made of white frosting. These are eaten during Lent, on Good Friday, and on Easter. They are traditionally broken open rather than cut open.

Breads from all over the world have been adapted to America's typical Easter menus. Large dinners at noon or in the evening usually include hot bread, buns, or rolls. Brunches, which are especially good to have after early church services, feature coffee cakes or coffee breads, sweet rolls, or buns among the holiday foods.

```
╭─────────────────────────────────╮
│         ❦ MENU ❧               │
│                                 │
│   EASTER  MORNING  BRUNCH       │
│      Chilled Tomato Juice       │
│  Canadian Bacon    Sausage Links│
│        Scrambled Eggs           │
│   Easter Nest Coffee Cake or    │
│      Spring Flower Rolls        │
│      Coffee        Tea          │
╰─────────────────────────────────╯
```

Spring Flower Rolls

    1 package active dry yeast
2¾ to 3¼ cups sifted all-purpose
      flour
              • • •
   ¾ cup milk
   ¼ cup butter or margarine
    2 tablespoons sugar
   ½ teaspoon salt
    1 slightly beaten egg
      Jams and preserves
      Butter or margarine, melted

In large mixer bowl combine yeast and *1¼ cups* flour. Heat milk, butter, sugar, and salt just till warm, stirring occasionally to melt butter. Add to dry mixture in mixing bowl; add egg. Beat at low speed with electric mixer for ½ minute, scraping sides of bowl constantly. Beat 3 minutes at high speed. By hand, stir in enough of the remaining flour to make a soft dough. Turn out on flour surface; knead till smooth and elastic, about 8 to 10 minutes. Place in lightly greased bowl, turning once to grease surface. Cover; let rise in warm place till double, about 1 hour.

Punch down. Cover; let rest 10 minutes. On lightly floured surface, roll dough to ¼-inch thickness; cut with floured 1¼-inch biscuit cutter. Grease muffin cups (about 2½ inches across); arrange 5 circles of dough, petal fashion, around sides of cup; place 1 in center.

Cover; let almost double (about 30 minutes). Lightly poke down center of each roll and fill with colorful jams and preserves.

Bake at 400° for 10 to 15 minutes. Brush with melted butter. Makes about 16 rolls.

Easter Nest Coffee Cake

    1 package active dry yeast
    3 cups sifted all-purpose flour
   ¾ cup milk
   ¼ cup sugar
   ¼ cup shortening
    1 teaspoon salt
    1 slightly beaten egg
      Shredded coconut
      Green food coloring
      Confectioners' Sugar Icing
      Candy decorations

In large mixer bowl combine yeast and *1½ cups* flour. Heat milk, sugar, shortening, and salt just till warm, stirring to melt shortening. Add to dry mixture; add egg. Beat at low speed with an electric mixer for ½ minute, scraping sides of bowl constantly. Beat 3 minutes at high speed. By hand, stir in enough of the remaining flour to make a soft dough. On floured surface, knead till smooth and elastic, 8 to 10 minutes. Place in greased bowl, turning to grease surface. Cover; let rise in warm place till double, about 1 hour. Punch down; divide in thirds. Cover; let rest 10 minutes.

Shape one-third of dough in 6 "eggs"; place close together in center of greased baking sheet. For "nest", shape remaining dough in two 26-inch ropes; twist together. Coil around "eggs"; seal ends. Cover; let rise till double (about 1 hour). Bake at 375° for 15 to 20 minutes. Cool.

Tint coconut with a few drops of food coloring. Frost coffee cake with Confectioners' Sugar Icing made by blending light cream with confectioners' sugar till of spreading consistency; sprinkle "eggs" with candy decorations, the "nest" with tinted coconut.

Meats: Various meats including turkey, both fresh and smoked pork, and lamb are traditional Easter fare. Pork has been served for centuries as a symbol of luck and lamb has religious symbolism.

Going on an Easter egg hunt

Discovering this nest of eggs delights both →
children and adults. Easter Nest Coffee Cake, made of sweet dough, is gaily frosted.

❈MENU❈

EASTER DINNER
Appetizer Relish Tray
Baked Ham with Apricots
Green Beans Amandine   Gelatin Salad
Bunny Rolls   Butter
Orange Cream Cake
Coffee   Tea

Bunny Rolls

    1 package active dry yeast
    5 to 5½ cups sifted all-purpose
      flour
 1¼ cups milk
  ½ cup shortening
  ⅓ cup sugar
    1 teaspoon salt
    2 beaten eggs
    2 tablespoons grated orange peel
  ¼ cup orange juice
              • • •
    2 cups sifted confectioners' sugar
  ¼ cup hot water
    1 teaspoon butter or margarine

In large mixer bowl combine yeast and *2¾ cups* flour. Heat milk, shortening, sugar, and salt just till warm, stirring occasionally to melt shortening. Add to dry mixture in mixing bowl; add eggs, orange peel, and orange juice. Beat at low speed with electric mixer for ½ minute, scraping sides of bowl constantly. Beat 3 minutes at high speed. By hand, stir in enough of the remaining flour to make a soft dough. Turn out on a lightly floured surface and knead till smooth and elastic, 8 or 10 minutes. Place dough in a greased bowl, turning once to grease surface. Cover and let rise in warm place till double, about 2 hours. Punch down; cover and let rest 10 minutes.

To shape: on lightly floured surface, roll dough in rectangle ½ inch thick. Cut dough in strips ½ inch wide and roll between hands to smooth into rope like strips.

For curlicue bunnies: For each bunny, use a 10-inch strip of dough for the body and a 5-inch strip for the head. On a lightly greased baking sheet, make a loose pinwheel of strip for body. Make smaller pinwheel for head and place close to body. (They'll "grow" together as dough rises.) For ears, pinch off 1½-inch strips and roll between hands till smooth and pointed at both ends. For ears: snip off both points and place next to head. Pinch off a bit of dough and roll in ball for tail.

For twist bunnies: For each bunny, use a 14-inch strip of dough. On a lightly greased baking sheet, make a figure 8 of one strip of dough. Instead of sealing ends, overlap, then spread apart to make ears. Roll small ball of dough for tail; place atop dough at bottom of figure 8.

Cover bunnies; let rise till nearly double in size, about 45 to 60 minutes. Bake at 375° for an additional 12 to 15 minutes.

For confectioners' sugar glaze: combine confectioners' sugar, hot water, and butter; beat till smooth and well blended. Brush over bunnies while warm. Makes about 30 rolls.

Orange Cream Cake

 2½ cups sifted cake flour
 1⅔ cups sugar
 3½ teaspoons baking powder
    1 teaspoon salt
    2 teaspoons grated orange peel
  ¾ cup orange juice
  ⅔ cup shortening
    3 eggs
  ⅓ cup water
  ¼ teaspoon almond extract
      Orange Cream Frosting
      Small candy Easter eggs

Into large mixer bowl sift together dry ingredients; add peel, juice, and shortening. Beat 2 minutes at medium speed with electric mixer. Add eggs, ⅓ cup water, and extract; beat 2 minutes more. Pour into greased and floured 13x9x2-inch baking pan. Bake at 350° for 40 to 45 minutes. Cool in pan. Top with frosting. Cut in squares; top with candy Easter eggs.

Orange Cream Frosting: Combine 3 cups sifted confectioners' sugar, ⅓ cup shortening, ½ teaspoon shredded orange peel, ¼ cup *hot* orange juice, 1 teaspoon lemon juice, and dash salt. If desired, add a few drops yellow food coloring. Beat with mixer at high speed till smooth. Add more confectioners' sugar, if needed.

Eggs: Eggs have long been a symbol of new life. Anyone that has seen an egg crack open and a baby chick appear can understand why this was chosen by many early cultures and carried over into our Easter tradition to depict new life.

The custom of giving eggs, dying them, and playing games with eggs are a part of Easter heritage. The early Egyptians, Persians, Greeks, Romans, and Gauls gave eggs as gifts during their spring festivals. This is still a practice with many families around the world today.

Eggs were originally painted to represent the rays of the sun or the colors of spring. Today, children delight in helping to dye eggs for Easter baskets and egg hunts. These gay eggs also make attractive centerpieces and garnishes for meat platters.

There are commercial dyes on sale to use with hard-cooked or blown eggs. For an even color, rinse the eggs in hot water and dry just before dipping in the dye. Peeled eggs can also be dyed. Use food coloring and fruit-flavored drink powder for eggs which will be colorful and edible.

Colored Easter Eggs

Garnish meat platter with colorful, peeled eggs—

Hard-cook eggs by placing eggs in saucepan and covering with cold water (at least 1 inch above egg). Rapidly bring to boiling; reduce heat to keep water just *below simmering.* Cover; cook 15 to 20 minutes. Cool at once in cold water—this helps prevent dark surface on yolk and makes peeling easier. To shell, crack shell all over, then roll between hands to loosen. Start peeling at large end where air pocket is.

To color eggs: For a variety of colors, in separate bowls dissolve 1 envelope of each of the following fruit-flavored drink powders: orange, cherry, strawberry, grape, and lemon-lime in ½ cup water. Add eggs and tint to desired color. By leaving some eggs in longer than others, you'll obtain different shades of the same hue. Drain eggs on paper toweling.

For bright yellow eggs add ¼ teaspoon yellow food coloring to ½ cup water; tint eggs, then dip briefly in solution of 1 envelope orange-drink powder in ½ cup water. For blue or green eggs use blue or green food coloring in water.

Tint peeled eggs and pipe on cream cheese. Use Colored Easter Eggs for a garnish.

To blow shell: wash egg, puncture each end with pin, enlarge hole slightly, run pin through egg to break yolk. Over a cup, blow gently in one hole. Rinse, dry, and dye shell.

Hard cook eggs; dry. Dip warm eggs into dye prepared according to package directions. Dry on rack; polish with wax or oil.

Eggs are also the focal point of Easter games. Brightly colored, hard-cooked eggs are hidden and children search for them in annual egg hunts. Rolling eggs is an English custom which Americans have adopted. President Madison initiated the egg roll on the White House lawn during his term from 1808 to 1812. This event has become an annual affair at the capitol.

The colored eggs should be returned to the refrigerator as soon as the games are finished. Used in various ways, these are good as creamed eggs or goldenrod eggs for breakfast, as a main dish for lunch, deviled, pickled, in potato salad, and in Thousand Island dressing.

❋MENU❋

AFTER THE HUNT LUNCH
Ham 'n Egg Triple Deckers
Pineapple-Cheese Salad   Corn Chips
Honey-Pecan Cake
Milk

Ham 'n Egg Triple Deckers

    2 hard-cooked eggs, shelled
1½ cups ground cooked ham
    2 tablespoons chopped green
        pepper
    1 tablespoon prepared mustard
    3 tablespoons mayonnaise
  12 slices white bread
      Butter or margarine

Chop eggs. Combine eggs, ham, green pepper, and mustard. Mix well. Stir in mayonnaise. Spread one side of each slice bread with butter or margarine. Divide *half* of the ham mixture among four slices of bread; spread evenly. Cover each with another slice bread; spread each with remaining ham mixture. Top with remaining bread slices, buttered side down.

Brush the outside of sandwiches with melted butter. Place on baking sheet; bake at 375° till brown, 15 to 20 minutes. Serves 4.

Pineapple-Cheese Salad

    1 20½-ounce can pineapple chunks
    1 16-ounce carton cream-style
        cottage cheese (2 cups)
    2 cups miniature marshmallows
½ cup pitted dates, snipped
    1 tablespoon lemon juice
      Lettuce

Drain pineapple, reserving ¼ cup syrup. Combine reserved syrup and next 4 ingredients. Mound cheese mixture on lettuce-lined plates; arrange pineapple chunks around. Top each with one whole pitted date. Serves 6 to 8.

Honey-Pecan Cake

    1 tablespoon vinegar
      Milk
    1 cup salad oil
1½ cups sugar
    3 eggs
    1 teaspoon vanilla
    2 cups sifted all-purpose flour
    3 teaspoons baking powder
½ teaspoon baking soda
    1 teaspoon ground cinnamon
¼ teaspoon ground cloves
½ cup chopped pecans
      Honey Syrup

Combine vinegar and enough milk to make 1 cup; set aside. Stir salad oil into sugar; add eggs and vanilla. Beat 1 minute at medium speed with electric mixer. Sift flour, baking powder, baking soda, cinnamon, and cloves together. Add to creamed mixture alternately with milk mixture. Beat the mixture for 1 minute more. Stir in all the pecans.

Pour into greased and floured 10-inch fluted tube pan. Bake at 350° for 40 minutes. Let stand 10 minutes. Remove from pan. Prick holes in hot cake; drizzle with Honey Syrup.

Honey Syrup: Boil ¼ cup honey, 1 tablespoon water, and 1 tablespoon lemon juice.

EAU DE VIE *(ō' duh vē')*—The French term for brandy. Sometimes the term is extended to identify the fruit used in distilling the brandy. For example, *eau de vie de cidre* is apple brandy. (See also *Brandy.*)

ÉCLAIR *(ā klâr', i klâr', ā' klâr)* — An oblong pastry shell with a sweet filling inside and a frosting or glaze over the outside. Éclairs are made from a dough much like cream puff dough. However, éclairs are piped through a pastry tube into finger shape, as well as being dropped from a spoon like the cream puff. Éclairs are served as a refreshment or dessert.

The typical éclair has a creamy filling of whipped cream, ice cream, or custard and a chocolate, vanilla, or coffee icing.

Éclairs

    ½ cup butter or margarine
    1 cup sifted all-purpose flour
    ¼ teaspoon salt
    4 eggs
      Chocolate Icing (optional)
      French Custard Filling

Melt butter in 1 cup boiling water. Add flour and salt all at once; stir vigorously. Cook and stir till mixture forms a ball that doesn't separate. Remove from heat; cool slightly. Add eggs one at a time; beat well after each.

Put dough through a pastry tube or paper cone making 4-inch strips, ¾ inch wide on a greased baking sheet. Bake at 450° for 15 minutes, then at 325° for 25 minutes. Remove from oven; split. Turn oven off; put éclairs back in to dry, about 20 minutes. Cool on rack. Frost tops, if desired. Just before serving, fill each with custard. Makes 14.

French Custard Filling: In saucepan, combine ⅔ cup sugar, 2 tablespoons all-purpose flour, 2 tablespoons cornstarch, and ½ teaspoon salt. Gradually stir in 3 cups milk. Cook and stir till mixture thickens and boils; cook and stir 2 to 3 minutes longer. Stir a little hot mixture into 2 slightly beaten egg yolks; return to hot mixture. Cook and stir just till mixture boils. Add 2 teaspoons vanilla; cool. Beat smooth. Whip 1 cup cream; fold into custard.

The grand finale

Make éclairs ahead, fill with vanilla or coffee ice cream, and freeze. At serving time, top with bold-flavored pecan sauce.

You can vary the basic éclair by flavoring with coffee, chocolate, or fruit; making the filling with a mix; or topping the éclair with a sauce. (See *Cream Puff, Dessert* for additional information.)

Coffee-Ice Cream Éclairs

Taste as good as they look—

    ½ cup butter or margarine
    1 cup boiling water
    1 cup sifted all-purpose flour
    4 eggs
    1 quart vanilla or coffee ice
        cream
            . . .
    1 cup light corn syrup
    1 tablespoon instant coffee
        powder
    3 tablespoons cornstarch
    2 tablespoons butter or margarine
    1 teaspoon vanilla
    ½ cup chopped pecans

In saucepan combine the ½ cup butter and boiling water; bring to boiling. Add flour all at once, stirring rapidly. Reduce heat. Cook and stir till mixture leaves sides of pan and gathers around spoon in smooth, compact mass. Remove from heat. Add eggs, one at a time; beat vigorously after each addition. Continue beating till mixture looks satiny and breaks off when spoon is raised.

Using about ¼ cup dough for each éclair, drop from spoon onto *ungreased* baking sheet about 2 inches apart, leaving about 6 inches between rows. With small spatula, shape each mound into a 4x1-inch rectangle, rounding sides and piling dough on top.

Bake at 400° till golden brown and puffy, about 40 minutes. Cool on rack. Cut each éclair in half lengthwise and remove webbing.

Fill bottom halves with ice cream; replace tops. Keep in freezer till serving time. Serve with sauce. Makes 10 to 12.

Coffee-Pecan Sauce: Measure corn syrup into medium saucepan. Combine 1½ cups water and coffee powder; blend in cornstarch. Stir into corn syrup in pan. Cook and stir till sauce thickens and boils. Remove from heat; add the 2 tablespoons butter and vanilla. Stir till butter melts; add pecans. Makes 2½ cups sauce.

Hurry-Up Éclairs

    ½ cup butter or margarine
    1 cup sifted all-purpose flour
    ¼ teaspoon salt
    4 eggs
    1 3- or 3¼-ounce package *regular*
        vanilla pudding mix
    1 cup whipping cream
    ½ teaspoon vanilla
        Sifted confectioners' sugar
    1 slightly beaten egg white
        Small multi-colored decorative
        candies

Melt butter in 1 cup boiling water. Add flour and salt all at once; stir vigorously. Cook and stir till mixture forms a ball that doesn't separate. Remove from heat; cool slightly. Add eggs, one at a time, beating well after each till smooth. Put through a pastry tube or paper cone making 4-inch strips, ¾ inch wide on greased cookie sheet.

Bake at 450° for 15 minutes, then at 325° for 25 minutes. Remove from oven; split. Turn oven off; put éclairs back in to dry about 20 minutes. Cool on rack.

Using only 1¾ cups milk, prepare pudding mix according to package directions; chill. Whip cream. Beat pudding smooth; fold in whipping cream and vanilla. Fill éclairs.

Add enough sifted confectioners' sugar to the egg white to make frosting of spreading consistency (about 1¼ cups). Frost tops of éclairs and sprinkle with decorative candies for confetti effect. Chill till serving time. Makes about 14 éclairs.

ÉCREVISSE *(ā kruh vēs')*—The French name for crayfish. (See also *Crayfish*.)

Slice red "cannon balls" of Edam to find milk cheese.

EDAM CHEESE (*ē′ duhm, ē′ dam*)—A mild, firm cheese usually in a round shape with a bright red covering. It has a smooth texture with no holes and a light, buttery flavor. Edam and Gouda are similar in shape and flavor. However, Edam is made partly with skim milk, while Gouda is made entirely with whole milk.

Edam was named for the town in northern Holland where it was originally made during the Middle Ages. The farmers in Edam began exporting it as early as the thirteenth century and today, it is known and exported throughout the world.

Edam has a shape and color that is the same worldwide. The characteristic red coloring was first used in the thirteenth century. At that time, the farmers agreed to distinguish their cheese by giving a reddish color to the rind. The cheese sold on modern markets still has this covering.

The form is that of a cannonball. This comparison comes from its shape and from legend. Edams, being hard, were supposedly used during a naval battle when the supply of cannonballs was exhausted.

Edam, like other cheeses, is known as a rich source of protein. It also supplies calcium and the B vitamins. A one-ounce serving contains 85 calories.

Use Edam as an appetizer or a dessert, rather than for cooking or grating. Make dips and spreads from the cheese and serve it out of the shell. Just remove the top (cut a design, if desired) and scoop out the cheese. Prepare the mixture and spoon it back into the shell. Desserts of slices of cheese with fruit, for instance oranges and grapes, are quite easy but very elegant to serve. (See also *Cheese*.)

Stuffed Edam

Bring 1 round Edam cheese to room temperature. Cut a 5- or 6-inch star pattern from heavy paper; pin to top of cheese, anchoring points. Cut around star with sharp knife. Remove star; carefully remove cheese from shell. Whip cheese with electric beater adding enough cream to make spreading consistency. Mound mixture in shell. Chill till serving time. Remove from refrigerator about 1 hour before serving. Serve with assorted crackers and apple wedges.

EDGEBONE—The aitchbone or rump bone of an animal. (See also *Meat*.)

EEL—A smooth, slender, elongated fish. Europeans and Americans consider the rich meat of eels to be quite a delicacy.

Eels, like other fish, have fins and scales. The dorsal and anal fins are long; however, there are no pelvic fins. Their minute scales are embedded in the skin. Eels are typically a green to brown color on the back and yellow on the sides.

The mysterious habits of eels have fascinated men for years. At spawning time mature eels from both America and Europe migrate to the sea around Bermuda. When spawning is completed, the eels die. In spring, the young eels, called elvers, migrate to the fresh waters where their parents lived. They live their lives in these waters, eating animal matter and hiding in mud or under rocks, until caught by fisherman or the time arrives to return to the spawning ground.

After being caught, eels are shipped to market in tank trucks which keep them alive. They are sold fresh or processed for sale by canning, pickling, or smoking.

Fresh eel is very perishable, so refrigerate and use it as soon as possible. Before cooking, remove the skin and entrails, wash, and cut into pieces. Poach, broil, marinate, fry, or bake the pieces.

Smoked eel will keep several weeks in the refrigerator. These do not have to be skinned, although skinning does make the food more attractive. Canned and pickled eel can be kept on the kitchen shelf. The supply should be rotated regularly.

Eel is served either hot or cold. Use it as an appetizer, a light lunch, snack, salad ingredient, or part of an entrée with other fish and meat. Tartar sauce, lemon juice and pepper, or mayonnaise served with eel complement the flavor.

Before cooking, eel averages 230 calories per serving and has the B vitamins and vitamin A. Smoked eel has 165 calories, but the vitamins have been lost in processing. (See also *Fish*.)

EELPOUT—Another name for the burbot, a freshwater fish related to the cod; and a small fish found in the Pacific.

EGG

From a poached breakfast egg to a late-night eggnog snack, eggs add flavor to any meal.

Even though the age-old question, "Which came first, the chicken or the egg?" is still being debated, it is a fact that the two are an inseparable pair. By definition, an egg is the hard-shelled reproductive body of an animal. Although other animal eggs are occasionally eaten, the chicken egg is the kind most commonly used in cooking.

The chicken has existed since prehistoric times and today is probably the most widely distributed food animal in the world. For centuries, the chicken egg has been an important food throughout the world. In ancient times, the scarcity of eggs made them a delicacy. For this reason, the Chinese developed a method of preserving eggs for many years in caustic lime—a procedure that still survives today. The egg does not spoil, but the inside shrinks to a dark jellylike substance.

The egg also played a part in superstitions and religions of ancient civilizations. Livia, the wife of the Roman Emperor Augustus, was advised that if she carried an egg under her breast, the sex of the chick that hatched would indicate the sex of her unborn child. Livia followed this advice. Shortly after a young cock was hatched, she gave birth to a son. This coincidence soon led other mothers-to-be to follow this uncomfortable custom.

In religion, many ancient people regarded the egg as a sacred symbol of the world and its elements. To them, each part of the egg represented a specific thing: shell (earth), white (water), yolk (fire), and air cell (air). An early Christian custom considered eggs, blessed by a local priest, to be a holy gift. Even today, gaily painted and decorated eggs are used at Easter as a symbol of the Resurrection.

Parts of the egg: The egg has three main parts—shell, white (albumen), and yolk. Each of these parts can be readily distinguished by the homemaker.

The calcium carbonate shell is a hard semipermeable membrane that makes up about 11 percent of the egg. Although in some areas one color of shell is preferred over another, the shell color is related to the hen's breed and has no effect on the egg's nutritive value or flavor.

The egg white, comprising about 58 percent of the egg, can be divided into thick and thin white. A freshly laid egg has a large amount of thick white. After the egg is laid, chemical action gradually converts the thick white to thin white.

The yolk, which comprises about a third of the egg, is the part that contains the reproductive cell. A very thin membrane separates the yolk from the white. The yolk is anchored in place by cordlike structures called the chalazae. The color of the yolk, ranging from light yellow to greenish yellow, depends on the hen's feed. A double-yolked egg occurs when two yolks drop into the hen's oviduct at the same time or very close together.

Nutritional value: Since the egg must meet the nutritional needs of the chick embryo, it is a compact package of proteins, vitamins, and minerals that can contribute much to the diet. Although the egg's size will affect its caloric value slightly, an average egg has about 75 calories.

A perfect breakfast entrée

For eggs at their best, serve Soft-Cooked Eggs. After snipping off the top with egg scissors, spoon out the warm, yellow center.

Calcium is the most abundant nutrient in the unshelled egg, but since almost all of this mineral is found in the shell, it provides little nutritionally. In addition to protein and calcium, the egg contains some sodium, phosphorus, iron, thiamine, riboflavin, vitamin A, and vitamin D.

An egg is one of the few natural foods that contain vitamin D. Although fish liver oil is the highest natural source of this vitamin, egg yolk ranks second. In the ordinary diet, eggs, milk, and butter are the major food sources of vitamin D.

Enough eggs are eaten that they make an important nutritional contribution to the American diet. One egg is recommended as an occasional protein substitute for one ounce of cooked lean meat.

How to select: Eggs can be selected according to a grading system established by the U. S. Department of Agriculture. This system applies only to eggs sold in interstate commerce, but most states also maintain these standards for intrastate sales.

The criteria used for grading eggs are: shell condition, white condition, size of air cell, yolk condition, and presence of abnormalities such as blood spots. The grade decreases as the air cell size increases, the white thins, and the yolk flattens and breaks easily after the shell is broken. Depending on their condition, eggs are classified as Grade AA (Fresh Fancy), Grade A, and Grade B.

Since fresh eggs are sold in the shell, they must be graded without breaking this shell. This is done by a process known as candling. Candling consists of using a strong light to view the air cell; the size, position, and mobility of the yolk; and the firmness and clearness of the white. Although a candle was the original source of light for this procedure, today electronic candlers are used.

To ensure quality, the break-out test is often used in combination with candling. Sample eggs from each shipment are broken out on a flat surface where quality is judged by observing the yolk and the height of the thick white. It is assumed that if the broken-out eggs are of the desired quality, then the candling operation must be grading accurately.

Although the grade of an egg is a guide to its appearance and quality, lesser grade eggs are not of a lower nutritive value. As an example, the presence of a blood spot in the egg is sufficient to lower its grade but this in no way detracts from the nutritive quality of the egg. Only the egg's appearance is affected.

Eggs are also grouped according to size. The size categories, based on minimum weight per dozen, are jumbo-30 ounces/dozen, extra large-27 ounces/dozen, large-24 ounces/dozen, medium-21 ounces/dozen, small-18 ounces/dozen, and peewee-15 ounces/dozen. Since the size and grade of an egg are not related, an egg of any size may be of any grade. Recipes usually assume the use of large or medium eggs.

All eggs on the market must have a clean shell, so, if necessary, they are washed before marketing. Since this removes the natural "bloom" or protein coating that seals the pores, the pores are resealed by spraying with a fine mist of colorless, odorless, tasteless mineral oil.

When selecting eggs, look for the label stamped on the egg carton or on the tape sealing of the carton. This gives the size and grade of the eggs and also assures you that the eggs meet USDA standards. When egg appearance or egg white volume is important, use Grade AA or Grade A eggs. These eggs contain a high proportion of thick white and, therefore, when broken do not spread out as much as eggs of a lower grade. Lower grade eggs, however, usually sell at a lower price, and as a result, are a better buy for dishes in which eggs are only one of several ingredients.

Other than shell eggs, both dried and frozen eggs are produced, primarily for use in commercial food services. Dried egg solids have at least 90 percent of the water content removed. They are available as whole egg solids, egg yolk solids, and egg white solids. These are used extensively by the manufacturers of packaged mixes, such as cake mixes.

Frozen eggs are liquid yolks, whites, or whole eggs that are thoroughly combined, then frozen. Frozen eggs should have the USDA inspection seal to assure the consumer that they are prepared from wholesome eggs under sanitary conditions.

Using frozen eggs

Thaw frozen eggs completely in the unopened carton and use them promptly. When using frozen whole eggs or egg yolks, allow for added sugar, corn syrup, or salt. Because of the possible presence of food poisoning organisms, use frozen eggs only in dishes that are cooked thoroughly.

For 1 fresh whole egg
Substitute 3 tablespoons frozen whole egg, thawed

For 1 fresh egg yolk
Substitute 4 teaspoons frozen egg yolk, thawed

For 1 fresh egg white
Substitute 2 tablespoons frozen egg white, thawed

How to store: At home, store eggs in the refrigerator in a covered container, preferably the egg carton. This decreases the absorption of odors as well as keeps the blunt end up, thus reducing the movement of the yolk. Do not wash eggs before storing as this removes the protective coating.

For best flavor and cooking quality, use eggs within one week of purchase. Although there will be some quality deterioration, eggs that have been refrigerated for several weeks are still acceptable when combined with other ingredients.

When a recipe calls for only one part of the egg, yolk or white, tightly cover and refrigerate the leftover portion. Seal egg yolks first by covering them with a layer of cold water. Egg yolks can be stored in this manner for one or two days (drain before using); leftover egg whites will keep for a maximum of seven to ten days.

If refrigerated in a sealed container, dried eggs will keep for one year. Frozen eggs should be kept solidly frozen until needed, then thawed in the refrigerator.

Eggs may be frozen at home quite easily, but it is important to use only high-quality fresh eggs. For convenience' sake, freeze eggs in serving-size quantities.

Although egg whites freeze satisfactorily without any additives, frozen whole eggs and egg yolks become lumpy when thawed. To prevent this, add one tablespoon sugar or corn syrup *or* one teaspoon salt to each cup of whole eggs and two tablespoons sugar or corn syrup *or* one teaspoon salt to each cup of egg yolks. Sweetened eggs are suitable for desserts, while salted eggs can be used in main dishes.

To freeze eggs break the eggs into a bowl, separating yolks and whites, if desired. After stirring the eggs to blend (do not beat), strain them through a medium strainer or put them through a food mill. Add sugar or salt, if required, then freeze at 0° or lower in freezer containers leaving sufficient room for expansion. Eggs can be kept frozen for 9 to 12 months.

Basic preparation

There are five basic methods of cooking eggs: scrambling, poaching, soft- or hard-cooking, baking, and frying.

Unlike eggs cooked by the other methods, scrambled eggs are beaten before cooking. How thoroughly they are beaten depends on personal taste. Perfectly scrambled eggs are tender, fluffy, moist, and have a delicate flavor. The secret to perfectly scrambled eggs is simple: do not overcook them. Adding a tablespoon of milk, cream, tomato juice, or other liquid for each egg also makes the scrambled eggs fluffier and more moist.

Basic Scrambled Eggs

Beat 6 eggs, $\frac{1}{3}$ cup milk *or* light cream, $\frac{1}{4}$ to $\frac{1}{2}$ teaspoon salt, and dash pepper with fork. (Mix slightly for eggs with streaks of yellow and white; mix well for a uniform yellow.) Heat 2 tablespoons butter, margarine, *or* bacon fat in skillet till just hot enough to make a drop of water sizzle. Pour in eggs.

Turn heat low. Don't disturb till eggs start to set, then lift and fold over with wide spatula so uncooked part goes to bottom. Avoid breaking up eggs any more than necessary.

Continue cooking till cooked throughout but still glossy and moist, 5 to 8 minutes. Remove from heat immediately. Serves 3 or 4.

Cheese Scrambled Eggs

Cream cheese adds flavor—

Prepare Basic Scrambled Eggs (see recipe, page 845) adding one 3-ounce package cream cheese with chives, cut into pieces, to the seasoned egg-milk mixture. Continue as directed in Basic Scrambled Egg recipe.

Fluffy Scrambled Eggs

Use a double boiler for this version—

Prepare Basic Scrambled Eggs (see recipe, page 845) omitting butter. Cook egg mixture in top of double boiler, stirring with spoon. Water in bottom pan should only simmer and not touch top pan. (Takes twice as long as in skillet.)

Poaching is the cooking method that consists of cooking an egg, broken from its shell, in a liquid. Water is the liquid most commonly used, although milk, cream, consommé, or soup are sometimes used to give the eggs a delicately different flavor. The shape of a poached egg is related to the quality of the egg. Since thin white spreads easily, a high-quality egg (Grade AA or A) with more thick white will give a better shaped poached egg.

If uniformly shaped eggs are desired, use an egg poacher. By the strictest definition, eggs cooked in an egg poacher are not poached since they are cooked above rather than in liquid. Nonetheless, they are still referred to as poached eggs.

Poached Eggs

Add water to a saucepan to depth of 3 to 4 inches; bring just to boiling. Stir simmering water to make a swirl, and slip egg from saucedish into middle of the swirl. (Be sure to follow the motion of the swirl with saucedish so egg goes into water in same direction.) Reduce heat to low and cook egg for 3 to 5 minutes, depending on desired doneness. Remove poached egg from water with slotted spoon. Serve immediately on hot buttered toast or English muffin, split and toasted.

One of the easiest ways to prepare eggs is to soft- or hard-cook them. They cook to perfection when the water is kept just below boiling and the cooked eggs are cooled quickly in cold running water.

The term "hard-boiled egg" is a misnomer but was once widely used. The discovery that boiling an egg makes the white tough has led to wide acceptance of the terminology "hard-cooked egg." Tough and rubbery hard-cooked eggs, often with a crumbly yolk, are the result of overcooking or cooking at too high a temperature.

For attractive hard-cooked eggs

To help prevent the harmless, greenish ring that often forms around the yolk of hard-cooked eggs, watch the cooking time carefully and cool the eggs immediately under cold running water.

Soft-Cooked or Hard-Cooked Eggs

Place eggs in saucepan and cover with cold water, at least 1 inch above eggs; rapidly bring to boiling. For *Soft-Cooked Eggs:* Cover pan tightly and remove from heat. Leave eggs in water 2 to 4 minutes, for desired doneness. For more than four eggs, don't turn off heat, but cook, covered, just *below simmering* for 4 to 6 minutes. Promptly cool in cold water.

For *Hard-Cooked Eggs:* When water boils, reduce heat at once to keep water just *below simmering.* Cover and cook eggs for 15 to 20 minutes. Cool immediately in cold water to prevent yolk darkening. To shell hard-cooked eggs, crack shell all over, then roll gently between palms of hands to loosen. Start to peel egg from large end.

The terms baked egg and shirred egg are used interchangeably. These eggs are usually baked in lightly greased individual containers such as muffin tins or custard cups, but they may also be baked on top of a casserole as is traditional with hash. For rich flavor, a little cream or milk may be poured over the unbaked eggs.

Let zesty Brunch Eggs Ranchero make a pleasant eye-opener some morning. Green chilies and tortilla rolls, that replace the usual toast, add a southwestern flavor to this dish.

Shirred (Baked) Eggs

Butter ramekins or custard cups. Break one egg into each; dash with salt and pepper. To *each*, add 1 tablespoon light cream. Set cups in shallow baking pan; pour hot water around them to depth of 1 inch. Bake at 325° till eggs are firm, about 20 minutes.

If desired, after 15 minutes of baking, top each egg with shredded sharp process American cheese. Return eggs to oven and bake till done, 5 to 10 minutes longer.

Frying is the most popular method of egg preparation. Although this method is not recommended nutritionally or from the standpoint of digestibility, thousands of Americans start out their day with an egg fried "sunny-side up" or "over easy." Careful control of the temperature of the fat is important when frying an egg. If the fat or frying pan is too hot, the egg quickly becomes overcooked. A high-quality egg (Grade AA or A) retains its shape better than a Grade B egg when fried.

Fried Eggs

Serve these "sunny-side up" or "over easy"—

In skillet melt a small amount of butter, margarine, *or* bacon fat. Break egg into saucedish; slip egg into skillet. Season with salt and pepper. When the whites are set and edges cooked, add ½ teaspoon water per egg. Cover skillet; cook eggs to desired doneness. If desired, turn egg over with wide spatula; cook briefly.

Besides the basic methods of cooking eggs, several other procedures fall under the classification of basic preparation. When whole eggs are combined with other ingredients, they are usually beaten (whipped until the whites and yolks are blended), either before or after combining them with the other ingredients.

There are various degrees of beating. Recipes usually specify beaten, slightly beaten, or well-beaten eggs. A *slightly beaten egg* is mixed with a fork only till the yolk is broken and there are streaks of white and yellow. *Well-beaten eggs* are beaten until light in color. *Well-beaten egg yolks* look like a thick, lemon-colored foam.

Eggs separate more easily when they are fresh and while they are still cold. The presence of any fat or yolk in the egg white prevents the formation of a stable foam. Therefore, if any yolk gets into the white, carefully remove all of it with the egg shell or the corner of a paper towel.

Egg whites can be whipped to two stages: the soft-peak stage and the stiffly beaten stage. The egg white is beaten to the *soft-peak stage* when the egg white peaks curl slightly. When making a meringue, the whites are beaten to this stage. Then sugar is added gradually while beating the foam to stiff peaks. *Stiffly beaten egg whites* are beaten until peaks stand up straight but are still moist and glossy. Beating past this stage may cause the foam to collapse. Egg whites are also beaten to this stage for angel cakes and soufflés.

Egg whites yield a large volume if allowed to come to room temperature before beating. Adding an acid such as cream of tartar to egg whites before beating stabilizes the beaten foam.

Dried eggs are convenient to have on hand when fresh eggs are not available. To reconstitute dried eggs, sift the egg solids, then measure. Sprinkle the egg over lukewarm water and stir to moisten. Beat until smooth. Once dried eggs have been reconstituted, they should be refrigerated and used within the hour.

In a recipe where eggs are combined with other ingredients, dried eggs need not be reconstituted. Sift with the other dry ingredients, then add the amount of reconstituting liquid to the liquid ingredients. Unless the package indicates that they were dried under rigid bacteriological control, dried eggs should be used only in dishes that are thoroughly cooked.

Uses in cooking

As a cooking ingredient, eggs have three primary functions: coagulation, leavening, and emulsification.

Although eggs coagulate (thicken to a semisoft mass) when cooked by any method, in many dishes this is their primary function. In custards, cakes, cream puffs, cream pie fillings, popovers, and breakfast eggs, the coagulation of the eggs is important in giving structural support. Eggs also bind together other ingredients in dishes such as meat loaf. When foods are dipped into egg before frying, the egg coating coagulates and browns. Eggs are sometimes used to clarify coffee or broth. As the egg thickens, it encloses small particles present in the liquid.

The amount of leavening eggs provide depends on the amount of air beaten into and retained by the eggs. Since egg white can be beaten to a much more stable foam than either egg yolk or whole egg, it is usually beaten separately for use as a leavening. The light, porous texture of food products such as angel food cakes and puffy omelets is achieved by using an egg white foam as the leavening agent.

As an egg white foam is heated, the trapped air expands and the egg coagulates, giving the foam a porous structure.

The third function of the egg in cooking is to emulsify. The classic example of this function is in mayonnaise, although egg also emulsifies cream puffs, ice cream, and hollandaise sauce ingredients. Mayonnaise is made from oil and vinegar, two substances which won't normally combine. The addition of egg yolk, however, enables the oil to stay suspended in the liquid. Egg yolk can act as an emulsifying agent because it forms a thin protein film around the oil droplets that will mix with liquids such as water or vinegar.

In addition to these three functions, eggs are used to add color and flavor to sauces, to prevent the formation of large sugar or ice crystals in candies and sherbets, and when hard-cooked, as an ingredient in or garnish for casseroles, soups, main dishes, and salads.

Using whole eggs: When talking about whole egg cookery, three dishes deserve special mention—custards, plain or French omelets, and cream puffs.

Eggs are a very important ingredient in custard since the mixture is essentially milk thickened by eggs. There are two types of custard, stirred custard and baked custard. Although both have the same ingredients, the egg in stirred custard is coagulated by cooking it on top of the range, while the egg in baked custard is coagulated by baking it in the oven.

When preparing custard, care must be taken to control the cooking temperature accurately. Overcooking results in a curdled stirred custard or a watery baked custard. Stirred custard should be cooked over low heat or over hot water in a double boiler. When baking a custard, set the cups of uncooked custard in a pan of water to equalize the temperature inside and out, thus allowing the custard to cook evenly.

Although some omelets use separated eggs, the plain or French omelet uses whole eggs. There is actually little difference between French omelets and scrambled eggs except that French omelets are stirred less. A perfect plain omelet is tender and moist, yet browned on the bottom. Specially designed omelet pans are available for use, but any shallow skillet with flared sides can be used for omelets.

Eggs perform two functions in cream puffs—emulsification and coagulation. Cream puffs have a high proportion of fat and the eggs help mix this fat with the other ingredients. As the cream puffs bake, the coagulated egg provides much of the cream puff structure.

Cherry Cream Puffs

  1 stick piecrust mix
  2 eggs
  1 21-ounce can cherry pie filling
  1 pint frozen whipped dessert
      topping, thawed
  ½ cup flaked coconut

Crumble piecrust mix into ⅔ cup boiling water; cook and stir vigorously till pastry forms ball and leaves sides of pan. Cook 1 minute over low heat, stirring constantly. Add eggs, one at a time; beat with electric mixer at low speed for 1 minute after each addition.

For *each* cream puff, drop about 3 tablespoons mixture onto greased baking sheet. Bake at 425° for 15 minutes. Reduce temperature to 350°. Continue baking till cream puffs are dry and golden brown, about 20 to 25 minutes. Remove from baking sheet; cool thoroughly.

Cut off tops; remove excess webbing. Set aside ½ *cup* of the pie filling; fold dessert topping and coconut into remaining pie filling. Using about ½ cup cherry mixture for each, fill cream puffs. Replace tops; spoon reserved pie filling over puffs. Makes 8 servings.

Tiny Cream Puffs

In saucepan combine 4 tablespoons butter or margarine and ½ cup water; heat to boiling. Add ½ cup sifted all-purpose flour and dash salt all at once; stir vigorously. Cook, stirring constantly, till mixture pulls away from sides of pan and forms a ball that doesn't separate. Remove from heat; cool slightly. Add 2 eggs, one at a time, beating vigorously after each till smooth. Drop by scant teaspoonfuls 2 inches apart on greased baking pan from toaster oven. (You can do about 1½ dozen at a time.)

Bake at 400° till golden brown, about 20 minutes. Remove from toaster oven; cool on rack. Repeat baking process with remaining dough. At serving time, cut off tops of puffs and fill with seafood or chicken salad, *or* fill with ice cream and top with chocolate sauce. Makes about 4 dozen.

Give deviled eggs a decorative appearance by squeezing the creamy egg yolk filling through a pastry tube.

After mixing the mashed egg yolk with mayonnaise and seasonings, whites can also be refilled with heaping spoonfuls of filling.

In addition to their uses in custards, plain omelets, and cream puffs, whole eggs are also used in innumerable recipes. Although they are most widely used at breakfast, whole eggs are an ingredient in so many main dishes, salads, and desserts that it is easy to include them in the menu for any meal. For brunch, try Easy Eggs À La King or Brunch Eggs Ranchero. Hot Egg Salad Deluxe is an unusual main dish for lunch and delicious Deviled Eggs are just as good for indoor meals as they are for outdoor picnics.

Deviled Eggs

Halve hard-cooked eggs lengthwise; remove yolks and mash with desired combination of seasonings, below. Refill whites.

1. For 6 eggs use ¼ cup mayonnaise, 1 teaspoon vinegar, 1 teaspoon prepared mustard, ⅛ teaspoon salt, and dash pepper.

2. For 5 eggs use 2 tablespoons mayonnaise, 2 tablespoons chopped ripe olives, 2 tablespoons vinegar, 1 teaspoon prepared mustard, and salt and pepper to taste.

3. Other combinations may include: horseradish, anchovies, parsley, chopped onions or chives, flaked seafood, chopped stuffed green olives, crisp-cooked bacon.

Spanish Eggs

A hot egg main dish—

  ½ cup chopped onion
  3 tablespoons butter or margarine
  3 tablespoons all-purpose flour
  2 teaspoons sugar
  1 28-ounce can tomatoes, undrained
  1 small bay leaf
  6 hard-cooked eggs
  ¼ cup mayonnaise
  1 teaspoon prepared mustard
  ¾ cup fine dry bread crumbs
  2 tablespoons butter, melted

Cook onion in the 3 tablespoons butter till tender. Blend in flour, sugar, ¾ teaspoon salt, and dash pepper. Add tomatoes and bay leaf. Cook and stir till thick and bubbly. Remove bay leaf. Pour into 10x6x1¾-inch baking dish.

Halve eggs lengthwise; remove yolks and mash. Mix yolks with mayonnaise, mustard, ⅛ teaspoon salt, and dash pepper; refill egg whites. Arrange in sauce. Combine crumbs and melted butter; sprinkle atop. Bake at 425° for 10 minutes. Serve over buttered noodles or toast, if desired. Serves 6.

Light-as-a-cloud gourmet dish

Be ready to accept compliments when you→ serve Fluffy Cheese Soufflé. Use a collar to let it puff above the baking dish.

Brunch Eggs Ranchero

    5 slices bacon, cut up
    1 16-ounce can tomatoes, undrained
      and cut up
    2 tablespoons chopped green
      chilies (about 2 chilies)
    1 clove garlic, minced
    4 eggs
        •   •   •
      Tortilla Rolls

In skillet cook bacon till crisp; drain off excess fat. Add tomatoes, chilies, and garlic; heat through. Divide among 4 individual bakers. Carefully slip one egg atop tomato mixture in each baker. Season lightly with salt and pepper.

Bake at 325° till eggs are set, about 20 to 25 minutes. Top each with a crisp bacon curl. Serve with Tortilla Rolls. Makes 4 servings.

Tortilla Rolls: Heat canned or frozen tortillas in boiling water according to package directions. Spread one side of each with butter. Roll up with butter inside. Place on ovenproof pan. Cover; heat at 325° for 5 to 10 minutes.

Easy Eggs À La King

In saucepan cook ½ cup chopped celery, ¼ cup chopped green pepper, and ¼ cup finely chopped onion in 2 tablespoons cooking oil till tender. Add one 10½-ounce can condensed cream of celery soup, 1 cup diced process American cheese; and ½ cup milk; heat and stir till cheese melts. Add 4 hard-cooked eggs, chopped, and 6 pimiento-stuffed green olives, sliced; heat through. Spoon over hot buttered toast. Trim with hard-cooked egg slices. Serves 4.

Hot Egg Salad Deluxe

Prepare 1½ cups finely crushed saltine cracker crumbs. Blend together *1 cup* of the crumbs; 6 hard-cooked eggs, chopped; 1 cup mayonnaise or salad dressing; 3 slices bacon, crisp-cooked and crumbled; ½ cup diced celery; 2 tablespoons diced canned pimiento; ¼ cup milk; ¼ teaspoon salt; and dash pepper. Turn into 9-inch pie plate. Blend remaining crumbs with 2 tablespoons butter or margarine, melted; sprinkle over casserole. Bake at 400° till golden, about 25 minutes. Makes 4 servings.

Using separated eggs: Although packaged in a common container, the egg yolk and egg white have widely different properties. Thus, the egg is often separated and the yolk used as an emulsifier or thickener, while the beaten egg white is used as a leavening agent. This enables the cook to prepare dishes that are very different from those using whole eggs.

Cream pie filling and hollandaise sauce, as well as mayonnaise which was discussed above, are dishes that use the egg yolk as one of their basic ingredients.

For a high, fluffy meringue, beat the room-temperature egg whites with vanilla and cream of tartar to the soft-peak stage.

While gradually adding sugar, continue beating till egg whites are stiffly beaten and sugar is all dissolved (test with fingers).

Crushed peppermint candy tops these Mint Patty Alaskas. The soft meringue covers sponge cake and peppermint ice cream.

Cream pie fillings are thickened with both egg, usually only the yolk, and starch. Since starch thickens at a higher temperature and requires a longer cooking time than egg, the starch-liquid mixture of the filling is cooked till thickened before the egg is added. If the egg were added directly to the hot starch-liquid mixture, it would coagulate immediately into small lumps. Therefore, a small amount of the hot mixture is combined with the egg, and then this mixture is stirred into the remaining portion of the hot mixture.

Hollandaise sauce, the classic accompaniment to asparagus, is made from egg yolk, butter, and lemon juice. As in mayonnaise, the egg yolk acts as an emulsifier, but in the hollandaise sauce and the mustard sauce given below it has an additional function—the egg yolk coagulates and thickens the sauce.

Cooked Mustard Sauce

In small saucepan combine 2 beaten egg yolks, ¼ cup water, 2 tablespoons prepared mustard, 2 tablespoons vinegar, 1 tablespoon sugar, and 1 teaspoon seasoned salt. Cook over low heat, stirring constantly, till mixture is thickened, about 5 minutes. Remove from heat. Blend in 1 tablespoon garlic spread. Cool mixture thoroughly. Whip ½ cup whipping cream; fold into cooled mixture. Makes 1⅓ cups.

Classic examples of the use of egg whites are meringue and angel food cake. In both of these, the egg white foam is the only leavening. Therefore, top-quality egg whites beaten to a stiff but not dry foam are vital for a satisfactory product.

Mint Patty Alaskas

Beat 2 egg whites with ¼ teaspoon cream of tartar, ¼ teaspoon vanilla, and dash salt to soft peaks. Gradually add ¼ cup sugar, beating to stiff peaks. Place 2 sponge cake dessert cups on cutting board; top *each* with a chocolate-coated peppermint ice cream patty.

Cover with meringue, spreading thicker over ice cream and thinner around cake; seal edges at bottom. Sprinkle meringue with 1 tablespoon crushed peppermint-stick candy. Bake at 500° till meringue is browned, about 2 to 3 minutes. Serve at once. Makes 2 servings.

By separating the eggs and then using both the yolks and the whites in a recipe, the cook is able to get leavening from the egg white foam as well as the whole egg's flavor and color.

A sponge cake is a foamy cake quite similar to an angel food cake, the basic difference stemming from the use of egg yolk. In a sponge cake the egg yolk adds the color and flavor. Although a sponge cake can be made using only egg yolks, both yolks and whites are used. As with an angel cake, the egg whites are the only leavening. As whenever working with an egg white foam, maximum volume is attained by quickly and carefully folding the other ingredients into the beaten egg whites.

Although the ingredients for a puffy omelet are the same as for a plain omelet, different mixing methods result in different products. When making a puffy omelet, the well-beaten egg yolks are folded into the stiffly beaten egg whites. This mixing method produces a large amount of air to make the texture light and puffy.

Sour Cream Omelet

Beat 5 egg yolks till thick and lemon-colored, about 5 minutes; beat in ½ cup dairy sour cream, and ½ teaspoon salt. Fold in 5 stiffly beaten egg whites. Melt 2 tablespoons butter or margarine in a 10-inch ovenproof skillet; pour in egg mixture, leveling gently.

Cook egg mixture over *very low* heat till lightly browned on bottom, about 8 to 10 minutes. Finish cooking at 325° till top is golden brown, 12 to 15 minutes. Loosen; slide omelet onto warm platter. Top with ½ cup dairy sour cream and fresh strawberries. To serve, break in wedges with two forks. Makes 3 to 4 servings.

A soufflé is similar to a puffy omelet except it uses a thick white sauce in combination with the egg yolks. The addition of chopped meat or fish (often leftovers) or shredded cheese turns the soufflé into an elegant main dish. If a dessert soufflé is desired, add sugar and puréed fruit or a flavoring such as chocolate or vanilla.

A soufflé should be baked in an ungreased, straight-sided baking dish to allow the soufflé to rise by clinging to the sides of the dish. As when baking a custard, set the soufflé in a pan of water to permit even cooking.

The fallen soufflé has been used so often as an example of cooking failure that many cooks are afraid to try making a soufflé. Although all soufflés shrink a certain amount as they cool, underbaking is the

An elegant brunch omelet

← Sour cream adds tangy flavor to Sour Cream Omelet. Next time, top with plump fresh blueberries instead of strawberries.

cause of their rapid collapse. To prevent this, watch the baking time and temperature carefully and serve a soufflé as soon as it comes from the oven. This is one time when the guests can wait for the food but the food will not wait for the guests.

Fluffy Cheese Soufflé

6 tablespoons butter or margarine
⅓ cup all-purpose flour
½ teaspoon salt
Dash cayenne
1½ cups milk
12 ounces sharp natural Cheddar cheese, shredded or diced
6 egg yolks
6 stiffly beaten egg whites

Melt butter; blend in flour and seasonings. Add milk all at once. Cook and stir over medium heat till thickened and bubbly. Remove from heat. Add cheese; stir till cheese melts.

Beat egg yolks till thick and lemon-colored. Slowly add cheese mixture, stirring constantly. Cool slightly. Gradually pour over beaten egg whites, folding in thoroughly. Pour into *ungreased* 2-quart soufflé dish.

Attach a "collar" to the soufflé dish for a high soufflé: Measure enough foil or waxed paper to go around casserole plus a 2- to 3-inch overlap. Fold foil in thirds, lengthwise. Lightly butter one side. Letting collar extend 2 inches above top of casserole, fasten with pins around the dish (buttered side in).

Bake at 300° till knife inserted halfway between center and edge comes out clean, about 1½ hours. Gently peel off collar and serve immediately. Makes 6 to 8 servings.

As can be seen, the egg is a versatile food that can contribute to the color, flavor, and nutritive value of any meal. In the United States, breakfast often is a tasty plate of fried eggs, a boiled or poached egg, or a scrambled egg. At lunch or brunch, an omelet, soufflé, egg sandwich, egg casserole, or eggs Benedict makes a tasty entrée. Even at company dinners, eggs can be one of the major ingredients in the angel food cake, popovers, molded aspic, or dessert soufflé.

EGG BEATER—A hand-operated rotary beater used to whip eggs as well as other liquid or semiliquid mixtures.

EGG COOKER—An electrical appliance or top-of-the-range utensil designed to poach or cook eggs in the shell.

EGGNOG—A beverage, similar in ingredients to stirred custard, made of eggs, milk, sugar, and flavoring. The name is thought to have been coined because the egg-milk mixture was served in a noggin, a small mug with an upright handle.

Eggnog, often flavored with sherry, rum, brandy, whiskey, or wine, has become a traditional Christmas drink. Because of its protein value, eggnog is served throughout the year to invalids and people with digestive problems. (See also *Beverage.*)

Guests return for seconds when the holiday beverage is Coffee Royal Eggnog. Float large dollops of whipped cream for garnish.

Instant Nog

Starts with an instant pudding mix—

    1 3¾-ounce package *instant*
          vanilla pudding mix
    ⅓ cup sugar
    1 teaspoon vanilla
    6 cups milk
    2 egg yolks
    2 stiffly beaten egg whites
       Ground nutmeg

In a large mixing bowl beat together the vanilla pudding mix, sugar, vanilla, milk, and egg yolks. Carefully fold in the stiffly beaten egg whites. Chill thoroughly. Pour into punch cups or glasses and top with a dash of nutmeg. Makes about 8 cups.

Coffee Royal Eggnog

Delicately flavored with instant coffee powder—

Combine 4 cups dairy *or* canned eggnog, well chilled; 1 pint vanilla ice cream, softened; 2 to 3 teaspoons instant coffee powder; and ½ teaspoon rum flavoring. Blend thoroughly. Pour into punch bowl or chilled cups; top with dollops of whipped cream and dash of ground nutmeg. Makes 10 to 12 servings.

Festive Freeze

    ¼ cup sugar
    2 tablespoons all-purpose flour
    ¼ teaspoon salt
    2 cups milk
    2 well-beaten egg yolks
    2 cups dairy eggnog
    1½ teaspoons vanilla
              • • •
    2 egg whites
    ¼ cup sugar

In saucepan combine the first ¼ cup sugar, flour, and salt. Gradually stir in milk. Cook, stirring constantly, till thickened. Stir small amount of hot mixture into egg yolks, return to hot mixture. Cook and stir 2 minutes more. Stir in dairy eggnog and vanilla.

Pour eggnog mixture into refrigerator tray and freeze till soft ice crystals form around edges. Turn into chilled mixing bowl and beat with electric or rotary beater till smooth and fluffy. Beat egg whites till soft peaks form; gradually add remaining sugar, beating to stiff peaks. Quickly fold meringue into eggnog mixture. Return to refrigerator tray; freeze till firm. Makes 6 to 8 servings.

Eggnog

⅓ cup sugar
2 egg yolks
4 cups milk
2 egg whites
3 tablespoons sugar
1 teaspoon vanilla
   Brandy *or* rum flavoring to
      taste
½ cup whipping cream, whipped
   Ground nutmeg

Beat the ⅓ cup sugar into egg yolks. Add ¼ teaspoon salt; stir in milk. Cook and stir over medium heat till mixture coats metal spoon; cool. Beat egg whites till foamy. Gradually add the 3 tablespoons sugar, beating to soft peaks. Add to custard and mix well. Add vanilla and flavoring. Chill 3 or 4 hours. Pour into punch bowl. Top with dollops of whipped cream; dash with nutmeg. Serves 6 to 8.

Use a sharp knife to cut homemade noodles the desired width. Make the noodles ahead, then store in plastic bag till ready to use.

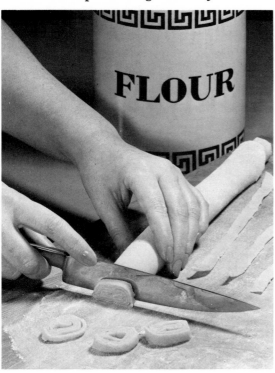

EGG NOODLE—Pasta made with whole eggs or egg yolks. After cutting in strips ranging from 1/16 of an inch to several inches wide, the noodles are dried. Noodles are about the only pasta that homemakers can make at home. (See also *Noodle*.)

Parsley-Buttered Noodles

1 beaten egg
2 tablespoons milk
½ teaspoon salt
1 cup sifted all-purpose flour
2 tablespoons butter or margarine
2 tablespoons snipped parsley

In medium bowl combine egg, milk, and salt. Add enough of the flour to make a stiff dough. Roll very thin on floured surface; let stand 20 minutes. Roll up loosely; slice into noodles ¼ inch wide. Spread out and let dry 2 hours. Place in clear plastic bag and store.

To cook, drop noodles into boiling, salted water. Cook, uncovered, for about 10 minutes. Drain. Add butter or margarine and parsley. Toss to mix well. Makes 6 servings.

EGG POACHER—A covered saucepan with an inset that has individual cups to hold eggs. Eggs dropped into the buttered cups hold their shape as they steam to the desired doneness.

EGG POACHING RING—A metal ring with handle that confines an egg to the ring's shape while it is poaching.

EGG SAUCE—Any sauce that contains egg, specifically chopped hard-cooked eggs, in a thickened cream sauce.

Creamy Egg Sauce

2 tablespoons butter or margarine
2 tablespoons all-purpose flour
1 cup milk
1 hard-cooked egg, chopped

Melt butter; blend in flour, ¼ teaspoon salt, and dash white pepper. Add milk. Cook and stir till thick and bubbly. Add egg.

Egg wedger, at left, works like scissors to cut hard-cooked egg in even wedges. Egg slicer, right, separates egg into slices.

EGG SLICER—A metal or plastic kitchen utensil with fine steel wires used to slice hard-cooked eggs. The egg is placed in the aluminum or plastic holder, and a hinged rack of evenly spaced thin wires is lowered over it, cutting the egg into even, separate wedges or slices. The sliced egg can then be used as a colorful garnish for tossed salads and vegetables or in creamed dishes.

Another utensil which works somewhat the same way, called an egg wedger, cuts a hard-cooked egg into 6 even wedges.

EGGPLANT—A purple or white pear-shaped fruit used as a vegetable. Possibly of oriental origin, the eggplant was first written about in a fifth century Chinese book. It was thought to cause insanity and so was called the "mad apple."

In the 1800s, the dark purple vegetable was used solely for table decoration and ornamentation until it was found to be safe for consumption. Today, eggplant is popular in Europe and America because of its unique eating qualities.

Also called egg fruit, aubergine, and guinea squash, the vegetable was named eggplant because the first varieties were about the size of eggs.

How eggplant is produced: Eggplant grows on a tall plant which bears woolly green leaves and purple flowers. In America, the plant is cultivated chiefly in the tropical Florida and Gulf Coast areas.

Nutritional value: Uncooked eggplant is low in calories and contains fair amounts of vitamin C, the B vitamins, and some vitamin A. However, cooked eggplant is valued for its flavor and texture rather than for its nutritional contribution.

Types of eggplant: The color of eggplant, ranging from white to yellow and violet to purple, depends on the variety. Purple eggplants are the most common variety found and used in the United States.

The shape of the vegetable varies from the familiar egg or pear-shaped form to round, oblong, and oval horticultural varieties. The long, narrow, snake eggplant and the small, smooth dwarf eggplant are examples of its diverse shapes.

How to select: Select an eggplant with a dark, shiny, smooth skin. Dark spots indicate decay, so choose one that is firm and heavy. One medium-size eggplant (about 1 pound) constitutes about four servings. Although most plentiful in August and September, eggplants are available in supermarkets throughout the year.

How to store: Store eggplants in a cool, humid place. Raw eggplant can be stored in the refrigerator for up to two weeks, while the maximum storage time for cooked eggplant is four or five days.

How to prepare: Eggplant can be peeled or the skin can be left on to hold the tender pulp together during cooking. Boiling eggplant in water removes its unique vegetable flavor, so use the French or Italian technique of baking the eggplant in skin or stewing in oil or broth. A well-cooked eggplant exhibits a crusty exterior and a moist, tender inside.

Dip eggplant slices in flour and milk mixture and deep-fat fry them. Top scalloped eggplant with cheese, mushrooms, or sour cream. Cube eggplant and combine with favorite meat chunks for kabobs.

Stuff hollowed-out eggplant with ground meat and bake. Broil thick slices of eggplant brushed with butter and seasoning and serve as a second vegetable.

How to use: Serve eggplant appetizers and hors d'oeuvres at company meals. Try a new casserole or salad with eggplant dices for the family. This versatile vegetable is delicious prepared with cheese sauces and served with favorite lamb or chicken dinners. (See also *Vegetable*.)

Pan-Fried Eggplant

Peel 1 medium eggplant (1½ pounds). Cut in half lengthwise, then cut crosswise making ½-inch slices. Combine 1 slightly beaten egg and 1 tablespoon cold water. Dip eggplant in egg mixture, then in mixture of ½ cup fine dry bread crumbs, ½ teaspoon salt, and dash pepper. Fry in hot oil till tender and brown, about 2 to 3 minutes on each side. Drain on paper toweling. Sprinkle lightly with salt. Keep warm. Makes 4 to 6 servings.

The intriguing eggplant, a distant relative of the potato, is a fruit used as a vegetable. The smooth, glossy, purple-skinned variety is popular in the United States as a table vegetable.

Eggplant-Cheese Stacks, fried seasoned stacks of eggplant and cheese slices, are served as a vegetable or main dish.

Eggplant Skillet

Sprinkle cheese over beef and eggplant dish—

    1 pound ground beef
    ¼ cup chopped onion
    ¼ cup chopped celery
    1 8-ounce can tomato sauce
        (1 cup)
    ½ cup water
    ½ to ¾ teaspoon dried oregano
        leaves, crushed
    ½ to ¾ teaspoon chili powder
    1 small eggplant, cut in ½-inch
        slices (1 pound)
    4 ounces sharp process American
        cheese, shredded (1 cup)
    Paprika
    Shredded Parmesan cheese

Cook beef, onion, and celery till meat is browned. Drain off excess fat. Stir in tomato sauce, water, oregano, and chili powder. Season eggplant slices with salt and pepper. Arrange on top of meat sauce. Cover and simmer till eggplant is tender, about 15 to 20 minutes. Top with shredded process American cheese and sprinkle with paprika. Serve with Parmesan cheese. Makes 4 or 5 servings.

Eggplant-Cheese Stacks

    1 medium eggplant (1½ pounds)
    4 or 5 slices sharp process
        American cheese
    1 slightly beaten egg
    ¼ cup milk
    1 2⅜-ounce package seasoned
        coating mix for chicken
    3 tablespoons salad oil

Peel eggplant and cut into eight or ten ½-inch slices. Cook slices, covered, in small amount of boiling water for 2 to 3 minutes; drain well. Place a slice of cheese between each 2 slices of eggplant; trim cheese to fit. Combine egg and milk. Dip both sides of eggplant stacks in egg mixture, then in coating mix. Cook in hot oil till golden brown, about 5 to 6 minutes on each side. Serves 4 or 5.

Elegant Eggplant

Peel and thinly slice 1 large eggplant (1¾ pounds). Dip into 2 well-beaten eggs, then in 1½ cups finely crushed saltine crackers (about 42 crackers). Brown eggplant slices slowly in a little hot shortening. Place *one-fourth* of the eggplant slices in bottom of 2-quart casserole; top with *one-fourth* of one 8-ounce package sliced sharp process American cheese.

Combine two 8-ounce cans tomato sauce (2 cups), ½ teaspoon Worcestershire sauce, and 1 teaspoon dried oregano leaves, crushed. Spoon *one-fourth* of the sauce (about ½ cup) over cheese. Repeat layers till all ingredients are used, ending with sauce. Cover and bake at 350° till eggplant is tender, about 50 to 60 minutes. Snip parsley over top. Serves 8.

Italian Eggplant

Peel and cut 1 medium eggplant (1½ pounds) into ½-inch slices. Dip into ½ cup butter or margarine, melted; then into mixture of ¾ cup fine dry bread crumbs and ¼ teaspoon salt. Put on greased baking sheet. Spoon one 8- or 10¾-ounce can spaghetti sauce with mushrooms atop slices. Sprinkle with 1 tablespoon dried oregano leaves, crushed; and 1 cup shredded mozzarella cheese. Bake at 450° for 10 to 12 minutes. Serves 4 or 5.

Crisp corn chips circle around the tasty eggplant and vegetable dish, Eggplant Crunch Casserole, to add texture and flavor.

Baked Eggplant

Serve eggplant for a new and different baked vegetable with a favorite meal—

　　1 medium eggplant
　½ cup salad oil
　　1 clove garlic, crushed
　　2 tablespoons snipped parsley
　　　Crushed oregano leaves
　　　Salt
　　　Freshly ground pepper
　　　　　• • •
　　2 medium tomatoes, cut in ½-inch
　　　slices
　　　Grated Parmesan cheese

Cut eggplant in half lengthwise and place in greased, shallow baking dish. Combine oil and garlic; brush *half* over cut surfaces. Sprinkle with parsley and oregano. Season with salt and pepper. Top eggplant with tomato slices; drizzle with remaining oil mixture. Sprinkle with oregano, salt, and pepper.

Bake, uncovered, at 400° till eggplant is tender, about 45 to 60 minutes. Sprinkle eggplant with additional snipped parsley before serving, if desired. Pass bowl of grated Parmesan cheese. Makes 6 servings.

Eggplant Crunch Casserole

　　1 small eggplant, peeled and
　　　cubed (1 pound)
　　　　　• • •
　　1 cup chopped celery
　½ cup chopped onion
　½ cup chopped green pepper
　¼ cup butter or margarine
　　　　　• • •
　　1 8-ounce can tomato sauce
　　4 ounces sharp process American
　　　cheese, shredded (1 cup)
　1½ cups coarsely crushed corn
　　　chips

In large skillet or saucepan cook eggplant, celery, onion, and green pepper in butter or margarine till tender, about 15 minutes. Stir in tomato sauce, cheese, and *1 cup* of the crushed corn chips. Turn into 1½-quart casserole. Bake, covered, at 350° till heated through, about 25 to 30 minutes. Before serving, wreathe casserole with the remaining ½ cup corn chips. Makes 6 to 8 servings.

Scalloped Eggplant

　　1 large eggplant, diced (4 cups)
　　　　　• • •
　⅓ cup milk
　　1 10½-ounce can condensed cream
　　　of mushroom soup
　　1 slightly beaten egg
　½ cup chopped onion
　¾ cup packaged herb-seasoned
　　　stuffing mix
　　　　　• • •
　　　Cheese Topper

Cook diced eggplant in boiling salted water till tender, 6 to 7 minutes; drain. Meanwhile, gradually stir milk into soup; blend in egg. Add drained eggplant, onion, and stuffing; toss lightly to mix. Turn into greased 10x6x1¾-inch baking dish.

For *Cheese Topper*, finely crush ½ cup packaged herb-seasoned stuffing mix; toss with 2 tablespoons melted butter or margarine. Sprinkle over casserole. Top casserole with 4 ounces sharp process American cheese, shredded (1 cup). Bake at 350° till hot, about 20 minutes. Makes 6 to 8 servings.

EGGS BENEDICT—Distinctive egg dish consisting of a toasted English muffin or bread spread with butter and topped with a ham slice and poached egg served with a hollandaise, cheese, or white sauce. This classic recipe, popular for breakfast and weekend brunches, is occasionally garnished with truffle and tomatoes or parsley.

Eggs Benedict

For each serving toast an English muffin half. Top each half with a thin slice of broiled ham and a soft-poached egg. Ladle Blender Hollandaise over the egg and sprinkle with paprika. Garnish with truffle slices and grilled tomato wedges, if desired. Serve immediately while hot.

For *Blender Hollandaise:* In blender place 3 egg yolks, 1 tablespoon lemon juice, and dash cayenne. Cover; quickly turn blender on and off. Heat ½ cup butter or margarine till melted and bubbling hot. Turn blender on high speed; slowly pour butter or margarine into egg mixture, blending till thick and fluffy, about 30 seconds. Makes about ⅔ cup sauce.

ELDERBERRY—The dark purple or red berry fruit of the elder bush, a member of the honeysuckle family. The berries, found growing in large clusters on the bushes, are used for jams, jellies, and homemade wines. Elderberries freeze well and can be dried. (See also *Berry.*)

ELECTION CAKE—A yeast-raised loaf cake flavored with fruits, spices, and liquor. Originating during the eighteenth century in Hartford, Connecticut, the highly seasoned cake was often served at town meetings. It soon became known as the Hartford Election Cake. Frugal Colonial homemakers made this cake by combining leftover bread dough with additional spices, fruits, and liquors. One of the first foods to

Classic brunch idea

Top a toasted English muffin with a ham slice and a poached egg. Spoon Blender Hollandaise over Eggs Benedict and garnish.

be associated with politics, election cake is now used as a coffee bread or dessert.

ELECTRIC PORTABLE APPLIANCE—Electric kitchen helpers that produce heat or turn motors by means of electricity to make the homemaker's work easier and faster. Some of the heating appliances available are toasters, waffle bakers, broilers, coffee makers, hot plates, corn poppers, frypans, roasters, griddles, deep-fat fryers, and rotisseries. Motor-driven portable electric appliances include appliances such as food mixers, ice crushers, can openers, juice extractors, blenders, and electric kitchen clocks and timers.

Consider family and personal needs and uses when buying a small electric appliance. Select the best size to fit family needs. Check construction and important features such as the materials it's made of, lid and feet positions, signal lights, attachments, and the Underwriters' Laboratories mark of approval.

The appliance should have a pleasing appearance, be easy to clean and store, possess an adequate guarantee, and be easily repaired and serviced by a competent serviceman. In all cases, the instruction booklet accompanying the portable electric appliance should be read very carefully and saved for future reference. (See also *Appliance*.)

ELECTRONIC COOKERY—Roasting and baking in a specialized oven which employs high frequency microwaves to cook food in a fraction of standard times. As the microwave energy penetrates, molecules within the food vibrate against each other producing the heat which does the cooking.

ELK—A large member of the deer family. The elk is hunted seasonally in such northwestern states as Colorado, Idaho, Montana, Oregon, and Washington in accordance with local game laws and animal supply. The nourishing rich meat can be prepared like beef with a slow cooking process. (See also *Game*.)

EMMENTHALER *(em' uhn tä' ler)*—The name for natural Swiss cheese developed in the Emmental Valley of Switzerland.

Many types of Swiss are made under other names. A high quality cow's milk is needed to produce Swiss, making it one of the most difficult cheeses to make. The sweet-flavored cheese is excellent for cheese dishes and toppings. (See also *Cheese*.)

EMPANADA *(em' puh nä' duh)*—A Mexican meat pie or turnover made from cheese, meat or fish, and a vegetable filling. In South America, empanadas are eaten as sandwiches and are sold on street corners. (See also *Mexican Cookery*.)

Empanadas

    1 teaspoon butter or margarine
    ¼ pound ground beef
    2 tablespoons finely chopped
        onion
    2 tablespoons chopped green
        pepper
    ½ cup finely chopped canned
        pears
    ½ cup finely chopped canned
        peaches
    ½ cup chopped tomatoes
    ⅛ to ¼ teaspoon ground cinnamon
        Crust
    1 beaten egg

Melt butter. Cook ground beef, onion, and green pepper till tender. Stir in fruits, tomatoes, cinnamon, and ¼ teaspoon salt. Cover; simmer 5 minutes. Drain. Makes 1¼ cups.

Crust: Sift together 1½ cups sifted all-purpose flour, 1 tablespoon sugar, and ¼ teaspoon salt. Cut in ½ cup shortening. Add 1 beaten egg yolk and ¼ cup milk; mix. Turn out on board and knead about 1 minute. Roll to ⅛-inch thickness. Cut in 5½-inch rounds.

Place filling on one half of dough round; moisten edge. Cover filling with remaining half of round; pinch together. Prick top. Place dough on lightly greased baking sheet. Brush tops with beaten egg. Bake at 400° for 12 to 15 minutes. Makes 5 servings.

EMULSION—A mixture of two liquid ingredients which do not dissolve into each other. One liquid is suspended in the second liquid as tiny globules.

Examples of emulsions include oil and vinegar in French salad dressing, and milk and fat in buttermilk. An oil or butter and egg yolk emulsion gives mayonnaise or hollandaise sauce its consistency.

ENCHILADA *(en' chuh lä' da, -lad' uh)* — A Mexican tortilla cooked and filled with meat and vegetables or cheese combinations and topped with spicy chili and tomato sauce or grated cheese. Baked enchiladas can be stuffed with chicken, fish, seafood, or meat with different vegetables. Enchiladas are especially popular in the Pacific Coast states and in Texas, New Orleans, Louisiana, and California. (See also *Mexican Cookery*.)

Cheese Enchiladas

Thoroughly wash 1 pound dried whole red chilies or 6 ounces (about 3⅓ cups) dried, seeded red chilies. If not already seeded, stem chilies, slit, and remove seed veins and seeds. Wash again. Cover with cold water; bring to vigorous boil. Drain and wash again. Put chilies through food chopper, then through a sieve. Stir in 1 clove garlic, crushed; ¼ teaspoon dried oregano leaves, crushed; pinch ground comino (cumin seed); and ¼ cup salad oil. To one 10½-ounce can condensed beef broth or 1¼

Fry one tortilla at a time on both sides. Use a tongs to quickly turn the tortilla, cooking it only till puffy, not browned.

cups bouillon, add water to make 2¾ cups; add to chili mixture and simmer for 20 minutes. Add salt to the chili mixture to taste.

Heat ½ cup salad oil in a skillet, and when hot, fry 8 tortillas, one at a time, on both sides. (Fry only till they puff a bit, but don't crisp or brown.) After each tortilla is fried, dip it into the hot chili mixture, then place on a platter.

Have ready 12 ounces sharp natural Cheddar cheese, shredded (3 cups); 1 medium onion, finely chopped; and ½ cup chopped pitted ripe olives. *Reserve 1 cup* of the cheese. Place a handful of cheese (about ¼ cup) on each tortilla and sprinkle with onion and olives. Roll up each tortilla and place in greased, shallow baking pan. (At this time the tortillas have become enchiladas, and they may be kept in readiness for baking at this stage.)

Half an hour before serving time, pour rest of the chili mixture over enchiladas; sprinkle with reserved 1 cup cheese. Bake at 350° for 25 minutes. Makes 8 servings. Tortillas are also available frozen or canned.

ENDIVE *(en' dīv, än' dēv)* — A salad green related to the chicory family. The early European colonists brought the sharp-flavored plants to the United States. Endive seed is planted to produce the green. Related to endive is the tightly packed Belgian or French endive. Delicately fringed and curly, endive provides a strong contrast to the broad-leaved escarole which is also a relative to endive. Besides being used as a salad green ingredient, endive is delicious prepared as a vegetable and served with a sauce. (See also *Vegetable*.)

Endive-Avocado Salad

Chill 8 French endives in ice water to crisp. Dry gently with paper toweling. Remove a few outer leaves and set aside. Cut endive stalks into large crosswise slices. In salad bowl combine endive slices; 1 avocado, halved, peeled, and sliced; and 4 scallions *or* green onions, chopped. Season to taste with salt and pepper.

Combine ¼ cup salad oil and 1 tablespoon wine vinegar; pour over endive mixture and toss lightly. Top with 2 tablespoons snipped parsley. Arrange reserved endive leaves around edge of bowl. Serves 6.